Advance praise for

A Rose Grew in Brooklyn

This is a lovely book. Full of humanity, it grants us a deeply caring and appreciative glimpse of Jewish family life in a New York now gone—people, places, relationships, events. We read and we remember; we remember and we cherish.

> LOIS SILVERSTEIN, Ph.D.
> Author, *Daughter* and *Bloodletting:*
> *A Mind at Mid-life*

Rose Fox's stories are in the best tradition of Jewish storytelling. In clear, simple language she captures the pathos, the humor, the sheer humanity of her family and their circumstance. As memoir, these stories possess a poignancy that is, at times, heartbreaking. As history, they provide us an invaluable portrait of the life of an immigrant Jewish family in the 20s and 30s. The richness and detail re-creates the people and places of her childhood in bold and honest terms. I was left wishing the stories would continue to unfold, both for my enjoyment and as an important chronicle of Jewish life.

> CHRISTA DONALDSON, Ph.D.
> Former director, Graduate Feminist
> Therapy Program, Antioch University

Reading *A Rose Grew in Brooklyn* stimulated my appreciation for how history can be personal and universal at the same time. Rose beautifully weaves her memorable stories with significant glimpses of everyone's historical legacies. These are her personal remembrances, yet I believe they will touch and stir people's hearts and souls. Rose reveals herself in language that is eloquently crafted; she is able to evoke our emotional personal memories as she writes a good story.

DAVID LEOPOLD SCHWARTZ, Ph.D.
Provost, University for
Integrative Learning

In this deeply moving personal life journey, Rose Fox does for the first generation American immigrant experience what Ansel Adams has done for granite cliff—captured and framed a set of images with breathtaking clarity, vivid contrast, and heartfelt honesty. Rose's reflections provide a powerful mirror for learning about oneself.

DR. HOWARD COHEN
Cantor, Temple Beth Hillel
Richmond, California

A Rose Grew in Brooklyn

Stories from a Jewish Girlhood

ROSE ESTHER FOX, PH.D.

Manto Press

BERKELEY, CALIFORNIA

Manto Press

1442-A Walnut Street, Suite 390
Berkeley, CA 94709

Manto was a Theban woman and an oracle
at Delphi from whose name comes the term
mantic speech, meaning prophetic words.

This book was designed and typeset
by Harrison Shaffer in 11½ point Sabon

Publisher: Rebecca Salome
Editorial: Matthew Staples, Stacey Lynn
Production: Whitewing Press

First Printing, 2002

ISBN 0-9664856-4-5
Library of Congress Control Number:
2001118072

Dedicated to the memory of Ken,
my husband, beloved partner, and best friend,
July 7, 1924–May 7, 2001,
and
To the memory of my dear son, Michael,
May 24, 1947–July 22, 1996,
and
In honor of my sweet daughter, Andrea.

9/8/08
For Danni –
Enjoy –
Rose

This poem was written to my husband in 1994, and I rededicate it to him, for it has even deeper meaning for me now that he is no longer physically at my side.

The Lost Children, 8/94

Wandering through endless time,
Alone and without direction.
The light is dim, at dusk.
The shadows fading into a darkness
that blinds the eyes.
Listening to the quiet that grows into a silent abyss.

Should she take a step?
Will she fall?
Will she come to a dead end from which there is no return?
Should she cry out though no one will hear?
And if she cries out, what if she cannot hear?

And then the fear begins to grow, and grow, and grow.
Filling the darkness and the silence until there is no
room for anything else.
The heart is pounding, the breath is strangling.

And then from nowhere, a subtle breath, a sound no louder
than a sigh.
But fills the empty darkness like the promise of sunrise.

She dares to extend her hands into the blackness.
Her breath catches in her throat.
And then, there it is.

The touch of another hand—like hers, but different.
Cool and moist, but in contact.
And the touch is sublime.

In the darkness the two draw closer.
Unable to see, they can touch.
The touch is all.
And the fingers trace the other's face.
And the arms embrace.
And the cheeks, wet with tears, touch.
And the lips smile silently.
And the little hearts begin to beat slower.
And in harmony—
Like one beat—
One breath—
One love.

And the little children are no longer alone.
And the fear now grows dimmer, and pales in the energy
of the two lost children,
Who found each other,
Whose spirit will never grow old,
Who will never forget.
And will live in their love forever.
Safe in each other's arms.
Safe in each other's eyes.
Safe in each other's hearts. *Amen!*

Contents

CONTENTS

A portfolio of photographs follows page 134.

Foreword

Reading Rose Fox's account of her experiences growing up in a Jewish immigrant family was for me like reading the pages of my own life story, only filtered through the rich understanding of an accomplished writer. Like Rose, I grew up in New York, the child of first generation immigrant parents who faced in two directions at once: eager to embrace the rhythms and opportunities of American life and determined to hold fast to the cultural traditions of their past and, of course, their Jewish identity. Rose writes with a powerful generosity of spirit and a keen sense of the paradoxical fact that sometimes the most valuable meanings in life are carried by our most painful experiences.

What is extraordinary about this memoir is not just the story Rose tells but what she brings to the telling. She brings not only a rich understanding of the immigrant experience she describes in her memoir, but a profound acceptance of it. In addition, she reconnects to the immigrant past of her parents in her own way, by deepening her personal commitment to, and knowledge of, Judaism. Rose devoted considerable energy to learning Hebrew and Yiddish. She learns from the heart, practicing every day the values of Jewish tradition we studied together.

She has been not only a dedicated student but also a teacher and guide to her fellow students and me.

Rose knows the secret of community. Her example of service has nourished the spiritual growth of our synagogue community. She has also deepened the meaning of community in her memoir. Her acceptance of the sometimes harsh realities of her personal experience and her deep engagement with the traditions of Judaism have enabled her to transform her own story into a story of the American Jewish experience. Rose Fox's memoir is an important contribution to the reclaiming of this heritage. It will help bind our community together for generations to come.

SHELLEY MICHAEL WALDENBERG
Rabbi, Temple Beth Hillel
Richmond, California

Publisher's Foreword

In your book, Rose, you pose the question: "Who would be interested in the struggles of a small, frightened Jewish girl?" After reading *A Rose Grew in Brooklyn*, I can tell you with certainty that many—and not only women—will be, upon settling into the tender, revealing, and insightful story of your childhood and your family in Brooklyn during the Great Depression.

It wasn't until my mid-thirties, later than I would have wished, that I learned one of the most powerful agents for women's emerging equality has been the willingness, indeed the compulsion, to tell our stories. To our benefit, since the 1960s, historians have readily included letters, diaries, journals, memoirs, and autobiographies in the archives we use to research, write, and, sometimes rewrite history. In scores of women's writings, we have found what was for so long missing from the textbooks— the untold story of women's participation in the history of the world.

A Rose Grew in Brooklyn, your memories of a painful childhood in Brooklyn, might not be considered primarily a history by traditional academics, but this book is just that. It tells about a girl, born in Philadelphia in the early 1920s, to a poor immigrant couple from Russia. It tells your earliest memories as an infant and a toddler in

Germantown, Philadelphia, and the rest of your childhood and school years after moving to Brownsville, New
York. It tells about your Papa Israel, coming to the Promised Land at eighteen, and your grandmother Ada, already
in her forties when the family left Russia to avoid the
growing anti-Semitism and military service for Papa and
Uncle Herschel, who was also eighteen. And it tells about
Luba, your Mama, the sixteen-year-old bride-to-be whose
impoverished struggles as a wife and mother of three would
spill over into your young life and cause so much pain.

In your introduction, you say you wrote the book to
put closure on a lifelong effort to forgive your mother
and come to terms with the very difficult conditions of
your childhood. As I read, I saw that this is what you
have done. And knowing you to be a truth-teller, I feel
the authenticity of your words. I believe the sometimes
damning statements about your mother's harsh treatment
of you and your brothers—even though there are
moments when the events you relate seem to border on
the implausible. And I believe you suffered as a Jewish
child in the midst of a mostly Gentile school. But more
than that, I trust you as a fair reporter. Your book is
deepened by your constant reflection and objective
analysis of the times and circumstances that shaped your
family's story.

A deep sadness came over me when I read about your
father's death: "When he died suddenly at the age of
forty-two, his personal belongings fit into one cardboard
box." What a stark and sorrowful picture you paint. And
you tell what your mother endured at a time in our
history when birth control and legal abortion were out of

reach for poor immigrant women. "By the time Mama was twenty-two, she had three children under the age of five. In the years that followed, she had one stillborn, several miscarriages, and at least two abortions performed on the kitchen table." I had to stop for a moment and remember not only your Mama but so many thousands of women who had to go through the same exhausting and demeaning motherhood cycle.

As your story developed, I loved the beautifully detailed memories of your childhood days—your Mama, always cleaning, usually storming through the heavy housework; Ada, your Bubbe, cooking up another storm—delicious and kosher—in the kitchen; your father's calming presence in the evenings. Your vivid recall of days in the neighborhood, and at school, where you could finally escape the chaos at home and begin to experience the education that would save your sanity and shape the rest of your life. And you tell here also the harsh truth about your teacher's open hostility and the pain of trying to fit in with Gentile classmates. Yours was the experience of so many other lonely children.

You also write in your preface: "History is not destiny." I've been fortunate to speak with you at length, so I've come to know what you mean: that our past does not have to cripple our future; that we can start each day with a fresh slate, a commitment to shape what is to come—not from merely the leftovers of the past, but out of what we have now and what we can see as possibility.

By the end of your story, I realized that *A Rose Grew in Brooklyn* is several things: a personal memoir, a history, and a firsthand ethnography of Jewish immigrant life in the eastern United States. There can never be too many of all of the above—especially by women. That is only one of the reasons I am proud to publish your book. Thank you for the courage to remember your early life and the foresight to write it down for the rest of us.

REBECCA SALOME
Publisher

A Word from the Author

For most of my adult life a nibbling at the edge of my consciousness has placed me in a paradoxical position between the desire to be known and acknowledged for my achievements and the fear of exposing the shaming poverty of my childhood, the ignorance and lack of education of my family, and my mother's physical abuse. Memories of that past could bring shudders at the threat of such exposure. The older woman I have become—educated, experienced, and strong—reframed that threat into a challenge.

My greatest concern has been that of exposing my mother—Mama—as a single-dimensioned, fierce persecutor, who cannot defend herself now because she died in 1966. As a child I was trapped in her raging care, ill equipped to understand her. Somehow, in an awareness far beyond my years, I think I wanted to forgive her, even then.

Lessons learned early in childhood get translated into necessary survival defenses. We take our cues from our caretakers. If questions, individuality, and critical thinking are forbidden, fears and prohibitions are passed from one generation to the next, as they were in my family. Anxiety, depression, and fear of change are often the legacy of such a childhood. My family's script was a predictor for limited, unfulfilled lives.

Papa was the sole support of our family of three children and three adults. He bore this burden silently and with dogged determination to keep us fed and clothed during the long years of the Depression of the thirties. He never shirked his responsibilities or asked for anything for himself. When he died suddenly at the age of forty-two, his personal belongings fit into one cardboard box. I never heard him speak a harsh word to Mama or criticize her for the punishments she meted out to me in his absence and—to a lesser degree—to my two brothers. I was his favorite, his little "maidele" (his little girl). He was my knight in shining armor. I placed our relationship on a pedestal, and I ignored the fact that he never protected me from Mama's wrath. From Papa I learned denial.

My maternal grandmother, Bubbe, as I called her, was the embodiment of nurturing, healing, and warmth. It was to her arms I would escape again and again to find refuge from Mama's anger. Any personal hopes she may have had as a young woman died when an influenza epidemic took the life of her twenty-year-old fiancé. Two arranged marriages later in life confirmed the position she had in my family—that of an indentured servant—a position she carried with a quiet grace. Resigned to her fate, she never aspired to anything more. From her I learned not to expect too much in life.

Mama was a whirlwind of frantic activity from sunrise to sundown. She was determined to keep us clean and well-behaved so that we would not bring disgrace upon her. The overwhelming responsibilities that had been placed on her young shoulders, during the years of the worst economic depression this country has known, filled her with fear and anger. Poverty demanded toughness. Tenderness and compassion were traps that threatened survival. Softness was reserved for her relationship with Papa. When he came home, Mama was transformed into a gentle, quiet-spoken woman, anticipating his every need. From her I learned not to question, to do what had to be done, and to provide for others at the expense of your own identity.

Mama died in August 1966. As a child I was too terrified even to hate her. I had suffered long years of physical and emotional torment at her ruthless hand. As an adult, however, I was able to understand her struggle. By the time Mama was twenty-two, she had three children under the age of five. In the years that followed, she had one stillborn, several miscarriages, and at least two illegal abortions performed on the kitchen table. By the time she was thirty-four, a careless doctor, unaware that she was pregnant again, gave her injections to bring on a late period. She almost hemorrhaged to death in the ambulance. Then, while she was still unconscious, he arrogantly performed a total hysterectomy. Later he boasted he had done her a favor because now she would not have to come to him with another unwanted pregnancy.

I know now that she was an unusual woman to have overcome and lived through so many hardships. Not only was she angry and fierce; she was also frightened and courageous. She was sensitive and strong. She did what she had to do in order to survive. I inherited the complexities of her strengths as well as her vulnerabilities. In the end, I could love her deeply.

What I want to pass on to my daughter, Andy, my granddaughter, Megan, and my great grandson, Tical, is the knowledge that life always provides us with options. All things are possible if we have courage. We are, after all, the creators of the value of our own lives. History is not destiny. Fear is never a good enough reason to postpone life and settle for less. Tomorrow is never promised to any of us.

Acknowledgments

Writing this is a loving task, for it finally offers me a long-awaited opportunity to thank all of the dear people who have supported me on the long journey of writing the memories of my childhood.

First and foremost, none of this would ever have been attempted without Lois Silverstein, my writing teacher and consultant. Lois also became a good friend during the devastating period after my son's sudden death in 1996 and my husband's ongoing struggle to survive cancer. Her creativity and encouragement kept me writing, and the work we did together especially during that dark time supported and strengthened me. She listened to endless rewrites, each time with a fresh ear, always respecting and supporting my efforts. Phyllis Brooks, who shared the work sessions with us, struggling to express her own family stories, patiently listened to a foreign Jewish history, transcending our cultural differences as we laughed and cried together.

Rebecca Salome, my publisher, magically appeared by virtue of my misdialing a number I had found in the yellow pages. From our first meeting, our spirits resonated with each other, uninhibited and ready to work together. Without Rebecca nothing I have written would ever have appeared on a printed page. Her knowledge, skills, and creativity in supporting and publishing women's writings have carefully and lovingly guided me through the maze of the publishing process. She lined up a team of experts who would ultimately prepare my stories for publication. At the outset she found an editor for me, whom I have yet to meet, and I nervously placed my "childhood" in the hands of a stranger, feeling exposed and vulnerable. About thirty-five pages were turned over to this nameless expert with the understanding if I were not comfortable with the editing style, Rebecca would locate another editor for me. That was not necessary. From the beginning, I was touched by the sensitive understanding and respectful handling of my personal history. I was convinced this must be a woman, a Jewish woman, who could relate to my experiences. I relaxed into the editing process. Only recently did I learn the name of my editor, Matthew Staples. Thank you, Matthew.

In 1997, still in the process of writing, self-conscious and nervous, I dared to read six of my stories, entitled "Rose Petals," to an audience at Temple Beth Hillel in Richmond, California. My husband, Ken, urged me to go public, and he composed and recorded a Yiddish potpourri as background music for this event. A composer, musician, published poet, creative therapist, and my loving soul mate, he has been at my side from the very first story I read him, always happy to put aside his own work when I would bring him another episode. I will also never forget my daughter, Andrea, tearfully hugging me at the end of the reading, never having heard these stories before. Encouraged by warm responses I received that day, I continued to write.

ACKNOWLEDGMENTS

Over the years I have received much loving support for my nostalgic pursuit from my friends and clients. Among those were Marcia Cerles, Diane Clark, Christa Donaldson, Pat Lollis, Marlena Lyons, Sandra Magen, Jett Psaris, Tharen McDavid, David Schwartz, Bill Wahman, and Rabbi Shelly Waldenberg. My thanks also to all the members of my Hebrew study group at Temple Beth Hillel, the Torah Mamas, consisting of Helen Houska, Rosemary Gerber, Maggie Jacobs, Bev Lesch, Louise Levenson, and Linda Rose, And at last, my clients: to Christina, Robin, Lisa, Lucy, Anna, Ann, Barbara, Laura, Kathy, Becky, and others, I owe much thanks for their encouragement and patience.

ROSE E. FOX

A Rose Grew in Brooklyn

Introduction

At the age of seventy-seven, most of my life is behind me. From this vantage point I can look back to the time before I had a life of my own. I can trace the changing topography of the lives of my parents and my grandmother in their struggle and determination to make a life for themselves in America. Though the obstacles and challenges that threatened my life were not the same as my family's, the fears and oppression I struggled with every day of my life mirrored theirs. This genetic tenacity has served me well through my own uncharted journey.

My grandfather (my Zada) left Russia for America with his two grown sons around 1911, leaving behind his wife, my Bubbe, with their two small children, my mother and my Uncle Harry. Many years would pass before he had saved enough money to send for them. I have only faint memories of my Zada, who died when I was about two years old. There used to be a snapshot of me sitting on his lap, playing with the gold chain on his pocket watch. Whenever I saw that picture it would stir up blurred memories of being held by a quiet, patient, smiling man.

In 1921, my Bubbe, Ada, forty-four; my Mama, Luba, fifteen; her childhood sweetheart, Israel, seventeen, who was to become my Papa; Mama's brother, Herschel

(Harry), eighteen; and his bride, Bluma, nineteen, began their arduous journey from Russia to America, the land of opportunity and freedom. They were poor Jewish peasants. The women were illiterate and had never traveled outside their small Jewish village, or *shtetl*. My uncle and Papa may have at times ventured to neighboring villages in search of employment. Such was the extent of their exposure to the outside world.

In September of 1921, Bubbe and her young wards were preparing to leave Russia, although fall was already threatening harsh winter weather. There was an urgency to leave, for Papa and my uncle were both of draft age. To wait for milder spring weather would be to risk being delivered into the hands of their anti-Semitic enemies in the Russian Army. These were the same enemies who rode through the streets of their *shtetl*, killing Jews at Christmas, Easter, or any other time their drunkenness whipped them into a sadistic frenzy. With this in mind, the family started out into the unknown.

Although their traveling documents indicate they had permission to leave Russia, I can imagine they must have been fearful of being stopped by local officials who might ignore their papers and arrest them. They traveled only at night, even though the temperature often dropped below freezing. During the warmer hours of the day, it was best to hide. Their immigration documents indicate they traveled from Geysin to Kishinev in Russia, then crossed the borders of Romania, Hungary, Poland, Yugoslavia, Czechoslovakia, Germany, France, and finally, by way of Dover, to England.

Although they must have felt relieved once they left

Russia, they came face to face with an unexpected crisis in Bucharest, Romania. Papa discovered he did not have enough money to continue the trip to America and would have to stay in Romania to work. However, before Papa was left behind, he and Mama were married. They were sixteen and eighteen. It would be one year before each was to see the other again.

The family arrived in Dover, England, at the end of October. Certificates show that they were disinfected, then quarantined for twelve days before they were allowed to board the SS *Cedric*. Once they were on the high seas, there was still no guarantee they would make it to America. They had to pass frequent medical examinations on board in order to prove they were not infected with any contagious diseases. It was not unusual for immigrants with nothing more than a common cold to be kept on board ship and sent back to Europe on the next voyage. I can only imagine the relief and joy they must have felt when they were allowed to leave the ship and when my Zada greeted them at Castle Garden, now known as New York's Ellis Island. Then they traveled on to Philadelphia where Zada lived and worked.

I was born in Germantown, North Philadelphia, on August 16, 1923, one year after Papa arrived in America. He was twenty and Mama was eighteen. Papa soon found steady employment in a factory. He was then able to purchase a small house on Dover Street in Germantown. In the Philadelphia I knew as a small child, the streets were lined with row upon row of small, attached two-story homes, each one a carbon copy of its neighbor. The streets were quiet and very, very clean. Each house had a short flight of marble steps at the entrance. Housewives would attack these steps daily with buckets of hot, soapy water and stiff brushes. They would not stop scrubbing until the steps glistened. There were large backyards facing a cobblestone alley. Most of the foot traffic was directed to the alleyways, probably to protect the shiny, white marble steps at the front of the house. I clearly remember playing with my dolls for hours in the backyard during the summer, or daydreaming as I looked out the upstairs bathroom window down into the yard, where there were a tree, some green bushes, and the long family clothesline.

I have a vague memory of one other Jewish family on our block. They lived on the corner, behind a shoe repair shop. The man spent long hours each day at his workbench with a fast-moving hammer in his hand. Our family must have stuck out like a sore thumb in this community. Our dark Semitic features were in striking contrast to those of our blonde, blue-eyed Protestant neighbors. Yet I must have played with their children, and I had at least one very close Gentile chum, Sissy, whom I adored.

Whether from fear or mistrust, Jewish people kept to themselves. I do not remember my Mama ever visiting a neighbor or any neighbors ever dropping in at our house for a chat or a cup of tea. Actually, visitors were not welcome. After all, it had not been too many years since my parents, Bubbe, and other Jews in their *shtetl* were hunted and persecuted by Gentiles, just because they were Jews.

When I started public school, I was very much in the minority. I felt alien and isolated, especially because I could speak very little English. As my family before me, I, too, was sent to a foreign land with foreign ways. I, too, did not know the language or the customs. Even my childhood Jewish name, Esther, was taken away from me and not allowed in this land of strangers, just the way arrogant immigration officers at Ellis Island arbitrarily changed foreign names that were too difficult to pronounce. Hereafter, I would answer to the name of Rose, the first name on my birth certificate. My Mama did not protest, because she felt that even in America it was not safe to challenge authority.

In school I had to submit to harsh, sometimes even cruel, treatment from strict, rigid teachers. Most teachers in those days were not sensitized to the plight of foreign children not yet socialized in American behavior. Jewish culture was often ignored, criticized, or demeaned. Only the Christian holidays were celebrated. Adding to the problem of being caught between two cultures was Mama's inclination to punish me when I brought home pictures of Santa Claus or sang a hymn I had learned that day in school.

The painful and humiliating events I experienced in school seemed to me an extension of the abuse I suffered at home. Mama often acted out her frustration by attacking me. Perhaps in doing so, she found some momentary bitter relief from her anger. The physical abuse ended about the time I was twelve, but its indelible impression lasted into adulthood. The memories of emotional domination and coercion never left. They made me into an anxious and fearful child, a depressed and inhibited adolescent, and an adult who suffered from agora-

phobia, multiple daily panic attacks, and acute psycho-
somatic symptoms.

Although our neighborhood life was lonely, there was
a network of Jewish charity and fraternal organizations,
family-arranged picnics, holiday gatherings, dances and
parties, celebrations for weddings, bar mitzvahs, and
births. Friends and neighbors from the "old country"
would suddenly show up, even though for them it meant
long rides on buses or trolley cars. Although our family
could not claim to have a rich, active social life, we could
count on at least two picnics at Strawberry Mansion Park
during the summer. Somehow attendance at the annual
Geysiner Ball was also made possible—a rare night out
for my parents.

Our family life took a turn for the worse when I was
about five years old. Before the infamous stock market
crash of 1929, the factory my father worked for went
bankrupt, and he lost his job. Unable to find work fast
enough, Papa could not pay the mortgage on our home.
The bank foreclosed. Our meager savings rapidly disappeared as he struggled to feed his growing family. Papa
went from house to house looking for repair jobs but
never found enough to take care of the family or to hold
on to our home.

We were forced to move from our modest neighborhood on Dover Street to a rented house at 2555 Stanley
Street, a poorer section of North Philadelphia. My Uncle
Harry and Aunt Bluma owned a house down the street at
2537. Their home displayed what Mama considered an
affluent lifestyle—fancy drapes at the windows, new
furniture, and household accessories. Our windows were

covered with paper blinds from the local five-and-dime store. Our furnishings were sparse but clean. Aunt Bluma's "wealth" and her superior manner caused Mama much discomfort. The two of them were enemies who ended up living in close proximity, but not by choice. However, Aunt Bluma was often the source of special treats and gifts for me because I was the first born and the only girl in the family. Unfortunately, Aunt Bluma's gifts were a reminder to Mama of how poor we were. It was not unusual for Mama to return the gifts in anger, as though Aunt Bluma were to blame for our difficulties.

In 1930 or 1931 the Depression showed no signs of releasing its stranglehold on the nation. Papa had been out of work for several years. He decided to join his brother Leo in New York City. Leo ran a small sewing machine repair business in the garment district. At last Papa had a steady job, although the salary was nominal. We moved to Brooklyn but could afford only a small, dark tenement apartment in Brownsville—a crowded Jewish ghetto.

In spite of a background of fear and panic, I hungered for knowledge and achievement. It was a lonely pursuit. Mama was illiterate. Papa could write Russian and basic English but was not up to tutoring me or supporting me through my emotional maze. Besides, early on I had learned to keep my feelings to myself. It did not seem safe in those days to approach most teachers with questions. Questions were equated with ignorance. I did not ask for help. There was no help. Nevertheless, against such odds I graduated from high school with an A average.

After many years I could no longer ignore my psycho-somatic symptoms and the daily panic attacks, which escalated in frequency and severity after the early death of my father in 1946. At the age of twenty-six, the mother of a two-year-old son, I was forced to seek help at a mental health clinic in Brooklyn, and I started my first psychotherapy treatment. It lasted eight years. In 1949 therapy had its own stigma. This added to my self-image of being flawed and different. However, I am convinced that therapy saved my life and prevented me from following in my mother's emotional footsteps of acting out rage.

Over time, therapy freed me of the most acute symptoms and I began to search for ways to pursue my interest in education. Once a week I would escape to another world, at an evening class, satisfying my hunger with the appetizing morsels waiting for me in my books. My first marriage, of seventeen years, offered me little encouragement or freedom to explore my interests. These boundaries tightened after I had my second child, a daughter. My husband believed women should stay at home, where they could be watched as they kept house and took care of the children. Nor did I receive any support from Mama or friends when I enrolled in college courses and talked about my fantasy of getting a degree. The ladies agreed with my husband and society. My place was at home. Their objections made me only more determined, as I signed up for yet another evening class in literature.

Years later, my first husband and I, with our two children, moved to California in a failed attempt to save our marriage. We divorced, and I then married a second time in 1961 to a man who was to become my soul mate. I worked for twenty years as an administrator at the University of California in Berkeley, getting closer to academia. At the age of fifty-seven I finally realized my dream of a college education and took early retirement to become a full-time student. After eight years of undergraduate and graduate education, internships and trainings, I earned a B.A., a master's degree, and a Ph.D. in psychology at the age of sixty-five and became a therapist. I know my Mama and Papa are up there smiling down on their daughter, the Doctor; and I can almost see my Bubbe glowing as she watches me from the kitchen doorway.

As the years passed and my academic goals were achieved, the need to be known and remembered became as compelling as the earlier thirst for knowledge. I never gave myself permission, however, to search and explore my past in order to spend intimate time writing about myself. Besides, in the age of computers, robots, jet planes, organ transplants, and test-tube babies, who would be interested in the struggles of a small, frightened Jewish girl raised by uneducated parents during the Great Depression?

Memories of despair, loneliness, and the confusion of a childhood sparsely sprinkled with carefree events finally found a voice when I joined Lois Silverstein's creative writing group. If it hadn't been for Lois's encouragement, I would probably never have had the courage to devote serious time to writing my memories. I shall always be grateful to her for lighting the path.

The initial pain and self-consciousness I experienced in reentering the time of my childhood seemed to change miraculously as the mute and frightened child of long ago finally was freed from her isolation of silence. As words began to come more easily, the shame I had felt all of my childhood and youth began to change into pride for that child's courage and determination.

In 1996, my stories well on their way, my life was again thrown into the deepest, darkest well of terror when my forty-nine-year-old son, Michael, died suddenly. The mystery of his death will always haunt me, as will a question I have asked myself over and over. Is there some mysterious link between my father's sudden death at forty-two, my naming my baby son after my father a year later, and my son dying suddenly at age forty-nine? There are no answers. The painful void of Michael's absence remains, but it became the source of another pursuit.

In a search for spiritual healing, I was pulled toward an old, deep longing to return to my Jewish roots. Though I speak Yiddish, I never had a Yiddish education and could not read the language. I began to study with Rivka Berlow, an older Jewish woman who had escaped the horror of the Holocaust, although others in her family did not. She had been a devoted school teacher all her adult life and had retired only recently, in her eighties. She and her husband, Moshe, lived in Israel for seventeen years, part of the Zionist pioneer movement, building a Jewish state. Thanks to Rivka's kind, loving patience I can now read Hebrew and Yiddish and have joined Temple Beth Hillel in Richmond, California. When I joined a class of twenty-five adults who wanted to study for their

Bar and Bat Mitzvahs, Rabbi Shelley Waldenberg asked me to teach Hebrew to the class. A novice myself, I was able to teach six other students. We all stood before the Torah in May 2000 and took part in the ancient ceremony.

I can look back now at my journey and better understand the switchbacks and detours taken along the way. Now I am aware of a central focal point of learning and fulfillment that kept surfacing over the years. A theme of contrasts between oppression and desire becomes more vivid, like two different-colored strands of yarn threading their way in and out of a complex tapestry. Although at times the strands go off in opposite directions, ultimately they return to twist and merge, strengthened by the effort. This seventy-seven-year-old, a composite of many threads and wounds, failures, and accomplishments, is still surprised to feel like the child I was—an outsider, an observer, wanting to be seen but too shy or proud to approach for fear of being rejected or criticized, yet never giving up. Each time the shuttle has returned to its origin, it has fixed the tapestry in a design as powerful as it is original.

I am convinced, no matter what our origins, that each of us has a link with the silent, inner world of our past. It never leaves us, and in the still of the night, or during life's traumatic events, we spontaneously regress emotionally and can become that lost, frightened child again. If we can release that inner, mute child with all of her frailties, embrace and accept her as she was never accepted before, not only can the old wounds be healed, but we can look at events with deeper understanding.

What follows then is appreciation for the vulnerable and fragile people who were our parents. They, too, started out as lonely, delicate children and became our lost and overburdened parents, raising their own vulnerable children.

I hope my personal stories, written from the heart of the child of the past, touch your heart and give you an opportunity to enter a time long gone by, an important part of the history of this country. Should you then get to look upon the faces of the children, treasure them and handle them tenderly; they are in your care for but a fleeting moment. Let them know how precious they are in a journey that continues to be fraught with land mines along the way.

Mama

Pictures of Mama at sixteen, when she arrived in America, reveal a slender, shy, dark-eyed beauty. But her shyness and beauty ended when she gave birth to me after a long, arduous labor. The stories I heard about my birth were heavy with fears and superstitions, embellished with each retelling. It has never been clear to me how my young, Jewish immigrant Mama, who spoke no English, ended up in a Catholic hospital giving birth. I must assume it was a charity hospital and also the only care available at the time.

The fact that the nurses were nuns must have terrified Mama. She probably remembered the horrors of bloody *pogroms* in Russia, perpetrated by the *goyim,* the Gentiles. Had she survived that carnage only to be slaughtered by the Catholic nuns who surrounded her? How would her prayers to her own God rise above the foreign cross that hung above her bed? I was told when I was a child that if I ever saw a nun I was to cover my mouth. If I failed to do that, all my teeth would fall out. I believed that. Now I feel that the tender care provided my mother by the nuns will always be a reminder to me of their commitment to all who called upon their charity—even prejudiced, frightened Jewish immigrants.

Putting Mama's life into perspective during that period I remind myself that when she became pregnant at seventeen, she was a very young, inexperienced woman, not much more than a girl. That changed dramatically after I was born. When she came home with me, after two weeks in the hospital, Bubbe kept her in bed for another two weeks, feeding her rich food to bring her strength back. The diet included creamy milk so that she could nurse the baby.

I can only imagine the disbelief and horror Mama felt when she was finally allowed to leave the bed, on shaky legs, and discovered she had gained about a hundred pounds, weight she would carry for the rest of her life. Family pictures of her when she was only twenty-four, and already the mother of three children, reveal an obese, matronly woman, her black hair cut short and severely plastered against her face in finger waves, her mouth expressing a faint smile for the photographer.

I have often thought her fury at me might have been an unconscious drive to punish me for what she had given up of herself in order to give birth to me, or because I was the center of attention. Papa, Bubbe, and my aunt and uncle all adored me. Mama however, had little time for reflections; by 1927 two more babies, my brothers Himey and Alec, joined the family. Simple arithmetic tells me that when I was thirteen months old, Mama, only nineteen, was already pregnant again with my brother Himey. When he was thirteen months old, I was three, and Mama, twenty-one, was pregnant again for the third time, carrying my youngest brother, Alec. Mama's experiences were not rare; the oppressive, demanding lives of women in that historical period were commonplace.

Although Papa was very loving and quiet spoken, he took for granted the entitlement of the patriarch. His control was benevolent, but it was still control. One day he hired a tutor to teach him English so that he could be more successful in this new land. Mama, visibly pregnant with me at the time, shyly drew up a chair to the table when the young man arrived. She was eager to learn English, too. She didn't want to continue being a greenhorn. Gently but firmly, Papa took her aside. He told her it was improper for her, in her condition, to be sitting at the table with a strange young man. No more needed to be said. With a blushing face, she withdrew.

It wasn't until thirty-seven years later, many years after Papa's untimely death, that she had the courage to go to school. She learned how to read and write English in order to write to me after I moved to California. Up until that time Mama was illiterate. Recently, while cleaning out a cabinet, I discovered a single page of a letter Mama wrote to my daughter, Andy, when Andy was a little girl. Mama's big, childlike scrawl and simple, loving vocabulary filled me with tears.

Papa learned English and settled down in the "golden land of opportunity." Before the stock market crash in 1929 that destroyed private dreams and hopes, hard work and ambition had rewarded Papa with an optimistic sense of security. He had a savings account and felt like a successful American capitalist. He would leave for work early every morning after first kissing all of us good-bye, a lunch box filled with a good meal prepared by Bubbe, returning at night to a hot dinner and an orderly, quiet, well-run household. Everything was as it should be. The women saw to that.

Papa never knew what transpired in his absence. The hours he was away were filled with harshness and punishments meted out by Mama. Bubbe would wring her hands and plead with Mama to spare the children. My brothers were not always spared Mama's attacks, and I, being the oldest, the only girl, and a constant reminder of her lost youth, was more often her target.

Enigma that she was, Mama showed two faces. With Papa she was the genuinely loving, adoring, attentive wife and was never out of character in his presence. She never raised her voice to him nor he to her. They spoke in whispers, their heads close together. They were a model couple, walking arm in arm on their way to Temple. Neighbors cast admiring glances at the loving couple when they strolled down the street. She never troubled him with the daily trials and tribulations of running the household and taking care of three babies. She never questioned his decisions, and I doubt if he ever consulted with her.

Their responsibilities were clearly divided into men's work and women's work, and Mama knew her place. But her character changed when Papa left the house for work. Suddenly she was whipped into a wild woman, and all of her frustration at the endless cleaning duties and responsibilities could no longer be contained. She was the day servant, cleaning, washing, buying the food, and disciplining the children. She was trapped. My Bubbe's job was to cook the meals and protect us from Mama.

The days were filled with stultifying, routinized, re- petitive chores that were never completed. Mama was constantly interrupted by the needs of her three young children. Keep in mind that those were the days before the washing machine, disposable diapers, and even refrig- erators. We did not own a car, and the physical labor entailed in daily shopping for the needs of a family of six meant numerous journeys to the market, carrying heavy parcels back to the house. This drama was repeated each day. Our icebox was small and its temperature unreliable. Perishables like meat and dairy items had to be purchased every day to prevent spoilage.

There wasn't even the modern convenience of a laun- dry tub in our cellar. Small washes were done in the kitchen sink with an aluminum washboard that bruised and lacerated Mama's hands. Harsh, strong-smelling soaps chapped and split her skin. The weekly linens and towels were first soaked in the bathtub with bleach. Mama would get on her knees and attack this load, using the same aluminum washboard. Sometimes the board would split under the sheer pressure of her determination to keep us clean. When that happened, her hands would be cut by the jagged metal, the water turning red with her blood, and she would explode with another curse.

During the freezing east coast winters, the heavy wash would be carried out to the backyard and hung on the clothesline, Mama's aching hands freezing against the wet laundry. In addition, the repetitive floor scrubbing, win- dow washing, starching, ironing, shopping, and keeping the children out of mischief would send her over the edge. There was certainly no time for reflection or for evaluating her life. She did what she had to do, because she was a woman.

Our playfulness and the perfectly normal behavior of the toddlers would add to Mama's tension, and she would scream at us, listing what penalties would befall us if we didn't quiet down. The sound of her voice alone was so terrifying that we would instantly fall silent. When her patience ran out, as it always did, she would leave the washing and scrubbing, descend upon us, screaming and striking out at whichever defenseless victim was closest. We would scurry to get out of her way, calling for Bubbe, who would always come to our rescue. Bubbe would pick up the baby, Alec, while Himey and I hid behind her. We were safe from Mama's blows for the moment, but her merciless voice was never silenced.

Mama did exercise one bit of verbal restraint. She would modify curses with a negative. But she didn't fool me. I knew she was cursing me when she screamed in Yiddish, "You should only not go to hell." "You should only not die." "A plague should only not find you." Also, she didn't fool Bubbe, who would remind her that God was listening and would punish her. She had better watch what she was saying.

Mama had one escape into fantasy from the burdens of her life. She loved to go to the movies. Several times a week she would finish her work in midafternoon and beg Bubbe to let her go to the movies. There was a new Rudolph Valentino picture she had not seen, or Mary Pickford was in a movie with Charles Farrell. Couldn't she go just this once? Our fierce mother would change and become a defenseless, pleading child, wanting just one more treat and then she would be good. How this transformation took place was a constant source of confusion for me. Was there a possibility that when she came back she would still be this pleading, compliant Mama, needing her own mother's permission to leave the house?

After minutes of Mama begging, promising, and justifying, Bubbe always gave in, with a warning that Mama was to return right after the movie was over. Mama had escaped once more, and all was quiet in the house. The baby was asleep. Himey and I would be in the kitchen with Bubbe as she prepared the evening meal, giving us delicious tidbits and warm bottles of milk to lull us into a snooze. We were grateful for the brief respite.

When Mama returned she would be less angry, but I knew this was often just a calm before the next storm. All too soon threats were again heaped upon us, as the time of Papa's return from work approached. She would threaten to tell Papa how bad and disobedient we were. She warned us that Papa would not spare us. I have no memory of Mama ever actually complaining to Papa. She did not want to burden him. Nor do I remember Papa punishing any of us, but still the threat put the fear of God into us. We didn't want Papa to know that we had misbehaved. When Papa returned at the end of the day, the house was clean, quiet, and orderly, and we were on our best behavior.

The enigma of Mama's behavior went on throughout the years of my childhood. Later I came to understand the overwhelming burdens and hardships my young immigrant Mama had to endure. Such entrapment and repression of emotional and physical needs drove many women into deep depression, anxiety, or rage. In spite of their physical or emotional condition, women were expected to fulfill all their duties, no matter how many pregnancies or responsibilities. With their bodies, their minds, and their hearts, they paid a dear price for this existence. The maternal legacy handed down from mother to daughter often created women who suffered emotional ills and psychosomatic symptoms that could not be quelled. But Mama left me another legacy as well: an image of a strong, hard-working woman. She managed to survive the poverty of the Depression. Her indomitable drive would not allow her to surrender to circumstances. Suddenly widowed at forty, with no employable skills, she found a menial, difficult job in a factory. She was determined not to be a burden to anyone.

I shed tears for the hard life that prevented her from providing me with a more peaceful and loving model during my childhood. I praise and love her for her courage during the long years we suffered together. My Mama was a survivor, and I received that legacy from her.

Papa Is a Hero

My Papa was born to poor Jewish peasants in a small Russian *shtetl* in the Ukraine in 1903. Two years later, my Mama, who was to become his childhood sweetheart and bride, was born in that same village. Though little is known of Papa's formative years, Russia's anti-Semitic history would seem to confirm that he experienced a childhood of poverty, lack of education, and bloody persecution at the hands of the Cossacks, who were given free reign to terrorize and slaughter Jews.

Children aged quickly under those extreme conditions, and at eighteen, approaching the end of his adolescence, my Papa was already a man. In 1921 he decided to leave his family and to travel with Mama and her family to America. Earlier, his older brother Leo had settled in New York. Papa was never to see his family again, and because illiteracy, ignorance, and fear were epidemic in the *shtetls*, it grew difficult and then finally became impossible to stay in touch with them—but not before Papa learned that both his sister and brother had been killed by the Germans.

The journey to America was long and arduous. Papa's maturity was challenged many times, but never more than when he had to interrupt the voyage at the Romanian border. He discovered he did not have enough money to continue. At sixteen and eighteen, my parents, the young lovers, were married, only to be parted the next day when Mama continued the trip with her family. It was a whole year before Papa would join her in America in 1922.

A posed picture of Papa as a handsome young man reveals little of his innocence and inexperience. In it he is stationed among props in a photo studio. He is dressed in borrowed, almost formal business attire, a crisp bow tie beneath his chin, and a boutonniere pinned to his lapel above a carefully displayed white handkerchief in his top pocket, with a fountain pen clipped beneath the handkerchief adding a note of confidence. An overcoat is draped casually over one of Papa's arms, and he holds gloves in the other hand. The final touch of a "young sophisticated man of the world" is a large hat balanced on the prop furniture, appearing as though it had been tossed there effortlessly.

That was the Papa I never knew. Papa did not have flair or extravagant taste. Before the 1929 market crash, he was too busy working hard and saving money so that he might someday buy a home for his growing family. During the Depression, Papa became one of the fifteen million unemployed. He was reluctant to spend money on himself, often jeopardizing his health as he struggled to take care of his family. When Papa died suddenly at the age of forty-two, he owned two pair of shoes, several shirts, some pants, a coat, and one brown pin-striped suit that he had reserved for special occasions.

Papa probably never had any illusions of achieving personal success; nor did he expect any rewards for his hard work. He was an old-world Jew who minded his own business and invested his energies in survival for himself and his family. Yet for a brief time during World War II, when Papa was all of thirty-six years old, he became a public figure.

In 1939, with Europe at war, the United States took an isolationist position and began to prepare for catastrophic possibilities. A national Civilian Defense Program was created. The call went out all across the nation for volunteers for positions as air-raid wardens. My quiet, reserved Papa answered that call. He had always listened to the radio and read the Jewish paper reports, keeping current on the progress in the struggle against Germany's powerful war machine. Here was something he could do to actively support the war against Hitler.

He came home from his first meeting wearing an official hard hat, a whistle on a chain around his neck, and a flashlight stuck on his belt. He had booklets and pamphlets that spelled out the regulations to be followed during an air-raid drill or, God forbid, an attack. Every night Papa would sit for hours, studying his manual and filling out workbooks. There was a job to be done, and he wanted to be ready for it.

At the sound of the siren, Papa would instantly jump to his feet, grab his hard hat, whistle, and flashlight, and pick up the paper bag that held his manual and citation forms. He immediately changed from the quiet Papa I knew to a man of action as he left the house to patrol the dark streets. We felt safe at home, knowing he was out there in the night making sure everyone obeyed the rules. He handed out citations to anyone who would ignore the drill or strike a match to light a cigarette during the blackout. Papa was obeyed because he was a respected officer in the Civilian Defense Program. Papa had authority.

From time to time there were meetings in our apartment, with Papa in charge. He was very serious about his duties and was soon promoted to the lofty position of block captain. This meant he would be responsible for a whole district and would supervise a team of other block air-raid wardens. This was a side of Papa I had never known.

When Papa was asked to speak at a Fourth of July celebration, I was stunned and a little nervous for him. Who would listen to him with his quiet voice and his Jewish accent? Papa never raised his voice. Papa had never spoken in public. He had, in fact, always avoided situations that would single him out for attention.

Somehow he did not allow his shyness or lack of education to stop him this time. He accepted the assignment. He slowly wrote several drafts of his speech, while sitting hunched over at the kitchen table for hours, writing on lined paper with a pencil he had sharpened with a razor blade. I would often hear him reading aloud to himself as he rehearsed his message. On July Fourth he stood before a couple of thousand people in our crowded neighborhood street, delivering a patriotic speech that inspired people to buy war bonds. I kept waiting for him to falter, stumble, and lose the attention of his audience. Yet, to my surprise, none of this happened. Silent, upturned faces were respectfully paying attention to my Papa, waiting for his next sentence.

After the speech there was loud applause, cheering, and even some whistling. People came to shake his hand and slap him on the back. Papa grinned with pride. I could finally let go of the nervous knot in my stomach. Papa had not disgraced himself. On the contrary, from that day forward he became a hero in our community. He was looked up to as a leader. At the defense meetings in our house he was treated with deference, and serious attention was paid to his instructions. The neighbors treated Mama with greater respect as well. After all, she was the wife of Sam Schwartz, the block captain of the Civilian Defense Program.

But even that success and acknowledgment did not change Papa. It did not go to his head; nor was he motivated to make a name for himself. I was proud of Papa, but I also felt a little guilty, for I had always been ashamed and self-conscious because of his accent and his lack of education. Also at sixteen I was too preoccupied with my own adolescent feelings and concerns to fully appreciate his courage and achievement. And what an achievement it was. I can still see Papa on that hot July Fourth, standing on a makeshift wooden platform with the American flag displayed at his side. He was dressed in dark pants, a white shirt, and a tie fastened carefully with a tie clip. His voice did not waiver, and his hands did not shake as he held his notes. He exuded some of the confidence and stature that he had pretended for the photographer in that earlier portrait. Papa's quiet strength, natural intelligence, and wisdom were apparent, winning the respect and attention of his neighbors. I loved Papa, my hero, even more from that day on.

AUTHOR'S NOTE

It is against the bittersweet background of my childhood that I attempt to share with you the hard lessons of life as seen through the eyes of the frightened child I was. Magical thinking and fantasy saved me from the grimness of my surroundings and went a long way to protect me from stark reality. With that in mind, I invite you to meet the Rose who grew in Brooklyn, beginning with my first memory in Philadelphia, one frosty winter morning.

The Magic Window

It is five o'clock in the morning and I am awake because my feet are so cold. I know I should have gone to bed last night wearing my soft, warm socks, but I drifted off before thought could be transformed into action. So here I lie, rubbing one icy foot against the other in an attempt to generate even a small spark of warmth. The air is cold and crisp on my face, just a little of which pokes out, barely visible above the covers I have tucked firmly under my chin and around my shoulders. The alarm won't go off for another hour and a half, so I let myself relax a bit, hoping that sleep will find me again. It is at this delicious moment, between full alertness and sleep that the beginning of a distant memory starts to find its way into my consciousness.

I am a tiny, little girl. A familiar sound has awakened me. The room is cold; it snowed during the night, and there is a soft, white mound of snowflakes heaped on the windowsill outside. I ignore the cold as I stand up in my metal crib. Holding on to the bars, I toddle toward the window. I look back over my shoulder into the dark room and can make out my parents' bed, the shape of their large bodies under the covers and the soft sound of their deep breathing. My attention is pulled back to the window as I hear again the sound that had first awakened me. There are no curtains, and the full, bright, winter moon still lights up the cloudless sky. The window shade had been lowered halfway last night as I was put to bed. I can look out and see the row houses, each one exactly like the other, with four identical marble steps leading up to the front door. The houses are all attached, and I think they must be huddling together for warmth in the frosty, winter night. The street is ghostly empty. Here and there the moonlight picks up shiny, icy patches on the paved ground. I wait quietly for what I know is about to happen. This is not the first time I have waited for this magical moment before dawn. It is not long before my patience is once again rewarded and I hear the sound of metal wheels rolling over the hard, cobblestone street. I see the horse as it enters the dim, early light. It is huge and white, and my heart leaps as it shakes its head to free its eyes from its long, silky mane. It walks with a slow, controlled gait, pulling a milk wagon behind it. It will be a while before the horse stops at my house and I can enjoy the scene that is played out every single morning. Most mornings I wake up in time and silently watch in the dark, careful not to wake my parents.

The milkman now appears in his white jacket and pants, swinging his body in and out of the slowly moving wagon that sways and creaks against his weight. The metal baskets in his hands are filled with creamy bottles of milk as he steps out of the wagon. He darts up the steps of the nearest house and exchanges his full bottles for the empty ones waiting for him outside the door. The horse knows just how to measure the rhythm of its powerful legs, taking slow steps, so that it will be near the next house when the milkman returns with his basket of empty bottles.

I love the sounds of this dance in the moonlight: the soft but distinct tone of the horse's hooves on the icy street, the creaky sounds of the wagon as the milkman jumps in and out, the clinking of empty bottles being exchanged for full ones. Every now and then this rhythm is interrupted by the horse, who paws at the ground when the milkman falls out of step and disturbs the horse's carefully measured stride. Then the milkman catches up with the wagon, first stopping to put a feed bag on the horse's great head, as a peace offering for his tardiness. He makes sure that the rope attached to the bag is placed firmly behind the horse's ears so it won't slip off. The horse becomes patient again as it begins to pick out delicious oat morsels with its tender, velvety lips, then crunches them between its broad, powerful teeth. The sway of the feed bag now joins the rhythm of the horse and wagon as they continue on their way.

My hands are icy against the metal bars of my crib, but I pay no attention for I know there is more to come. If I lean over to the left, I can still make out the back of the wagon before it disappears from sight, swallowed up in the first dim light of the dawn. For one long moment I can still hear the creaking, clanging sound, then only silence. Now I turn my head toward the right and see the gold-and-red flickering flame in the gas-lit lamppost outside the window. Dawn is barely visible in the sky, but the morning light is pushing aside the darkness of the night, and it is time for the flame to be extinguished. That is the job of the little man who carries a small triangular ladder on his back, and a metal cup with a long handle in his hand. He approaches and I hear his quick, scurrying steps as he comes into view, with his large coat collar raised high around his neck, an old battered hat on his head, and his hands partially protected from the cold by old, worn gloves, whose fingertips have long since been worn off. He has many lampposts to put to sleep before he can return to his own warm house. He is directly in front of my window now. Every step and movement is choreographed as he leans the wooden ladder expertly up against the lamppost and quickly climbs up. He opens the large glass shade that protects the flame and places the metal cup over it, at the same time using his free hand to turn off the gas. The job is done. A soft dimness spreads around him, but soon it will be penetrated by the light of the rising sun. The flame that lit up the night is gone. No matter how many times I watch him do this, I never discover where the flame goes.

Moving as quickly as when he came, the little man places the ladder on his back, grabs the cup by its long handle, and steps toward the next light down the street. He is soon out of sight. Maybe he is going to the place where the flame went.

Suddenly I become aware of the cold, and my diaper is now wet. It is time to wake Mama. I begin to cry. The bedroom door opens and Bubbe tiptoes in. She whispers loving, comforting words as she wraps me in a blanket and carries me into the kitchen where the stove has been lit. My parents are still asleep. The warmth against my face makes me drowsy. I surrender to Bubbe's loving care. I drift off into sleep just as she gently offers me a bottle of warm milk. I begin to draw on the nipple. The warm liquid coats my mouth with its sweet flavor and I settle down on my Bubbe's large, comfortable lap, my head cradled safely within her protective arms. Somewhere, off in the distance, I hear the sound of the horse's hooves again. I surrender to sleep knowing I will see the horse again tomorrow morning, through the magic window.

In the Kitchen
with Bubbe

It is Friday morning. Breakfast has been cleared away and Bubbe will be preparing tonight's *Shabbas* meal. Mama usually stays out of the kitchen. She does not cook for the family. This is Bubbe's domain. She holds all the secrets of good things to eat. Next to Sunday, when Papa is home, this is my favorite day of the week. I can spend the long hours in the kitchen with Bubbe. The *Shabbas* culinary ritual will take up most of the afternoon, and Mama is glad to have me out of the way. The baby, Alec, is in his crib. He will not stir for at least another hour. Mama puts Himey in the carriage and rushes out to buy a fresh chicken, potatoes, onions, celery, carrots, and some dill for the chicken soup. The house quiets down as soon as she leaves, but I can still hear familiar sounds from the kitchen.

The sweet smell of rising yeast in the *Shabbas challah* dough, which has already been started, greets me before I enter the kitchen. Soon its fragrance will permeate the whole house, announcing the arrival of *Shabbas*. Bubbe is standing at the table that has been covered with a clean, white cloth. She dusts the cloth generously with flour and begins to knead the shiny, white bread dough.

Her thick hands momentarily disappear as she pushes them into the mound of dough, kneading and massaging, to release little air bubbles, which snap and crackle under her expert touch. Flour dust rises up in thin clouds and more of the sweet aroma fills the room. Bubbe's hands and arms, looking like white surgical gloves, are covered with flour. This process must be repeated several times before Bubbe is satisfied. Next she will begin braiding the *challah* and then place it in the hot oven. For now, she puts the dough in a large bowl, covers it with a floured cotton towel, and sets it aside so it can rise again.

I find my place on the high kitchen stool where I can watch Bubbe as she goes about her familiar tasks. No matter how many times I witness this scene, there are always questions to ask, and Bubbe always has the answers for me. What makes the dough rise? Why does she have to knead it so many times? Why does it take so long to prepare? When can I have a piece of *challah*?

Next Bubbe begins to prepare the noodles for her tasty chicken soup. The cloud of flour increases as she begins to roll out the noodle dough to just the right thickness on the floured board. Then she reaches for her sharp knife and with deft movements cuts the dough into long strands. Each could be measured with a micrometer as testimony to her precision. Soon the back of every chair in the kitchen is draped with clean cloths and covered with noodles carefully placed to dry. As many years as I watched her, I could never understand or much less duplicate such exquisite skill. Bubbe did it as naturally as she breathed. For her it was second nature.

It is now time for the *challah* dough to receive its last

massage before it is actually braided. Bubbe cuts the dough into six equal portions and rolls each piece between her hands, creating six thick ropes. That done, she uses three of the lengths, folding them over and under each other, forming a white, braided loaf, fastening each end with a pinch from her fingers. She repeats the braiding with the remaining three ropes for a second loaf. The loaves, tapered at each end, rise to a soft, voluptuous mound in the center.

Bubbe dips a pastry brush, made from clean chicken feathers held together with string, into frothy egg yolks and gently strokes each loaf. The loaves shine under this cosmetic touch as she carefully sets them in a baking pan and places them in the hot oven. Later they will emerge with a smooth, golden crust. My mouth waters, for I can remember the flavor and the smooth inner texture of Bubbe's homemade *challah*.

There is always enough left over for the next day, when I will dip the sweet white bread into a cold glass of milk and sugar. There is nothing better than Bubbe's *challah*, unless it is her *knishes*, or *verenikas*, or *kreplach*, or cookies or cakes or—but then the list could go on forever, and even then something might be left out.

For this meal Bubbe has prepared a surprise. She is going to make potato *knishes*. I clap my hands in delight. She rolls out another batch of carefully seasoned dough. I beg her for some dough of my own and ask her to show me how to make a potato *knish*. Though there is much work to be completed before the sun sets, Bubbe is patient and gives me a small handful of dough. She tells me to roll it into a ball until she is ready to add the potato filling. As she continues to busy herself, I caress the dough in my hands, determined to make a *knish* just like Bubbe does.

As I watch, she uses a glass as a cookie cutter, to create a table full of symmetrical disks of dough. She has already prepared the mashed potatoes flavored with browned onions, chicken fat, salt and pepper, and begins to place a small mound in the center of each disk. Keeping her hands covered with flour, she skillfully seals each *knish,* securing the potatoes within the dough. The table now looks like an engineering chart with measured rows of *knishes,* each one exactly like its neighbor.

I plead with Bubbe to let me roll out my dough, so I too can make a *knish.* As she stops to help me I am disappointed. No matter how careful I have been, I have handled my dough so many times that it has lost its white sheen. My hands had been clean. Bubbe had even dusted them with flour, but the dough had not escaped the moisture of a little girl's hands. Still, Bubbe assures me as she fills my dough with the mashed potatoes and helps me seal it, that she will bake it in the oven, and that it will taste just as good as hers. Much to my surprise it does.

The intimacy of the kitchen is suddenly disturbed when Mama arrives, her voice preceding her as she warns Himey not to be noisy for fear he will awaken the baby upstairs. She herself does not make a hushed entrance, already complaining about the late hour, and how long she had to wait to get the chicken plucked, and how hard it was to carry the loaded bags all the way home. The serenity of the kitchen, the focus on the approach of the *Shabbas,* the careful attention to details and the productive abundance flowing from Bubbe's hands goes completely unnoticed. Mama's air of urgency now takes over.

Mama tries to usher me from the kitchen, warning me to keep out of the way, but Bubbe asks if I could stay long enough to wait for my potato *knish* to finish baking. Mama, preoccupied with her own chores, gives in and I reclaim my seat. Bubbe is already busying herself, opening and cleaning the chicken and sprinkling it with coarse kosher salt. Soon it will be placed in the hot boiling water and under her magical hands transformed into savory chicken soup.

Noticing that I have fallen silent at the arrival of my Mama, Bubbe tries to cheer me up by telling me stories about how my Mama, when she was a little girl, would sit with her in the kitchen, and watch the *Shabbas* meal being prepared, just as I was doing today. Somehow I can't quite imagine my large, powerful Mama ever being a little girl. Did she have a Bubbe then who was as loving and protective as mine was?

All of that is forgotten when Bubbe opens the oven door and a rush of warm, fragrant air fills the room as the *challah* and *knishes* are brought out to cool. Bubbe is right. Although my *knish* is not as round as hers, it too looks golden brown and perfectly presentable. With much restraint I wait twenty minutes for it to cool and am finally rewarded with the first bite. The potatoes are succulent, fluffy and delicious inside the dough, and I am proud of my baking results.

When Papa comes home I will tell him how I baked a *Shabbas knish,* and how good it tasted. Just like Bubbe's. Next *Shabbas* I will make two *knishes* and one will be for him. I, at the tender age of six, was already being indoctrinated into the ranks of Jewish *balaboostas* (homemakers) who took pride in their cooking and baking skills.

All the cooking was finished before sundown, leaving just enough time for Mama and Bubbe to change into their *Shabbas* dresses. My brothers and I were cleaned up and made presentable. The table was set, the candles waiting to be lit for the *Shabbas* blessing, and the fresh *challah* was covered with a special embroidered cloth, waiting for my Papa to bless it and share it with all of us. All was ready when Papa arrived. This was the one supper of the week that the whole family ate together.

The candles lit, Bubbe covered her head respectfully with a lace shawl and solemnly recited the blessing, ushering in the *Shabbas*. The moment of silence that followed was broken when Bubbe went back to her place in the kitchen. It was time to serve the meal she had so lovingly prepared for us. It was *Shabbas,* and Bubbe reigned in the kitchen. All was right with the world once again.

Mama the 'Balaboosta'

Every day of my childhood was punctuated by Mama's frenzied determination to fulfill the responsibilities of a traditional Jewish housewife (a *balaboosta*). Household chores took first priority, interrupted only by a catastrophe or crisis. Looking back, it seems that the one place in her life where Mama thought she had any control was in the rigid, self-imposed, repetitive routines she established and followed. Women's lives were hard in the twenties and thirties, filled with poverty, unexpected pregnancies, miscarriages, illegal abortions, and childbirth. By the time Mama was twenty-five she had three small children, two of them in diapers that she had to wash every day, and she was the primary caretaker for a family of six. The physical labor was back-breaking but her daily tasks were predictable, and she would attack them as though her life depended on it. The work always came first.

It was taken for granted that every Monday my Mama would strip all the beds and soak the linens in strong, hot bleach water in the bathtub. Not one to waste even a minute, she would then air out the blankets and pillows by laying them across the sills of the open windows. Mama was not alone in this fanatic commitment to cleanliness. On Mondays every tenement window in the neighborhood displayed a rainbow-colored assortment of blankets and pillows, like battle colors flying in the wind over medieval castles. Even during the coldest, iciest days of winter this job was not neglected, though the house would be freezing all day. Mama never seemed to be cold. She would be covered with sweat as she went from one frantic task to the other.

With the beds stripped, all of the coiled bedsprings were leaned up against the walls so that Mama could use a lit candle to singe every square inch of the metal in order to kill the unsuspecting bedbugs hiding there. The candle would flicker and hiss as the scorched bugs fell on the floor, to be swept away by the swift efficient strokes of Mama's broom. In spite of Mama's diligent cleaning, there was always a new crop of bed bugs waiting to be torched the next week.

Returning to the bathroom, Mama got down on her knees, and with the aid of the metal washboard she began her relentless scrubbing. Finally, the linens were soaked in a rinse of bluing solution, because no *balaboosta* worth her salt would be caught dead displaying gray or yellowed sheets and pillowcases on her clothesline for all the world to see. Next Mama assaulted our clothing with the same vigor, not stopping until the clothes for the whole family were scrubbed, bleached, and rinsed to her satisfaction. Mama had very high standards when it came to getting rid of dirt.

By now the wet clothing and linens probably weighed a couple of hundred pounds, but they still had to be lugged out to the backyard and hung on the clothesline. Bubbe would leave her cooking to help Mama, and together they hung the laundry on a rope that sagged and groaned with each added item. It was a miracle that the line did not snap more often. When that happened, it meant Mama would have to drag the muddied laundry back to the tub and begin all over again, cursing and crying all the way—another time when it was best to stay clear of Mama. If all went well up to this point, Mama and Bubbe would struggle together as they propped up the straining clothesline with a forked piece of stout wood that was pushed into the ground, raising the rope high enough to prevent the clean laundry from dragging on the dirt. Every single Monday until 1947, when we finally got our first semiautomatic washing machine, this task was repeated in the same manner. By then I was twenty-four years old.

No laborer could have worked harder than Mama on those Mondays. Even when it rained, the wash was done on time, and the cellar hung with clotheslines zigzagging across the narrow space in front of the furnace. Nor did the freezing winter weather excuse Mama from her dedication to keeping us clean. Her wet hands would become chapped and turn beet-red in the bitter cold as she hung the laundry outdoors against the bitter wind. By the time she finished, the clothes would begin to freeze and stiffen in the zero-degree weather. At times Mama would bring the frozen clothes back indoors, for they would never dry in the frigid outdoors. My brothers and I would laugh until the tears ran down our cheeks at the sight of Papa's frozen long underwear, leaning against the wall. There it would stand, like some decapitated monster as it began to defrost, finally crumbling into a wet heap on the floor. In spite of the exhausting demands of the day, even Mama and Bubbe had to laugh at this utterly comical sight. There wasn't a whole lot Mama had to laugh about, but if you could catch her off guard, before the perpetual frown on her face took over, she would relax momentarily and laugh with us. Then the grimness of the day would lessen long enough for Mama to be young and foolish and waste a few minutes. It was not the Mama I met very often.

Tuesdays were as rigorous as Mondays, because all the laundry had to be starched and ironed. We seldom had more than one or two changes of clothing or linens, so it was necessary to iron everything the next day. Mama would stand for hours at the board, ironing the linens with precise pressed folds, but first the dry laundry had to be sprinkled with a fine drizzle of water to ensure a wrinkle-free surface. Some of the clothing would be starched with a homemade mixture of potato starch and water that stuck to the iron mercilessly, often scorching the laundry no matter how careful Mama was. No wonder Mama scolded and punished when I soiled my dress, or my baby brother played with a piece of coal in the cellar. Often the linens were worn thin by constant use and Mama's powerful scrubbing. These would be given to Bubbe, who was also the seamstress for the family. Bubbe could make the neatest patches with almost invisible stitches. In time it was difficult to tell the original article from the patches.

Shopping for food was another endless and time-consuming chore. For many years we had only a small icebox. Daily trips to the local stores were mandatory, and all the groceries and perishables had to be carried home. Every morning Mama would be the first one out of bed. She didn't even take time to get dressed. She would tie up her nightgown under her faded housedress, knot her stockings above her knees, and step into her scuffed shoes. She would leave the house before sunup with two empty shopping bags, to return later with groceries, fresh-baked rolls for our breakfast, and meat or fish for dinner. Over the years, Mama's hands developed calluses in all the right places that cushioned them against the heavy loads she carried on those shopping excursions. She would walk further and further away from the neighborhood stores if she heard of a sale or a bargain, in order to save a few precious pennies.

Mama's routine was shared by hundreds of other *balaboostas*. They competed for the loaf of bread that had just come out of the oven, the slaughtered chicken that was still warm to the touch, or the biggest live fish to be killed and cleaned right then and there—assurance that the fish was absolutely fresh. All of this required elbowing through crowds of other determined housewives scouring the neighborhood for the same bargains, but Mama was a warrior and lost few of those battles.

A trip to the butcher shop was even more time consuming. Although Mama bought meat only from a kosher butcher, she did not trust him to kosher her meat, even though it was a free service he offered. She would carry the meat home first, lay it out on a board in the sink, generously sprinkle it with coarse kosher salt that purified the meat while the blood ran off the board. Then she would carefully rinse it three times with cold water, completing the koshering process. If the meat was to be used for meatloaf or hamburgers, Mama would carry it back to the butcher and watch him carefully as she instructed him to grind the meat twice, so that it would be fine enough for Bubbe's delicious recipes. Mama had to be sure that her carefully koshered meat was the same meat she would bring home, and that the butcher would not add some fat while he stole an equal amount of Mama's precious koshered meat. Those things happened if you were not vigilant all the time.

Mama did have one day of the week off from her repetitive jobs. No Jewish *balaboosta* would dare risk the wrath of God by breaking his rules of the Sabbath, the day of rest. There were no shopping trips allowed that day. All the neighborhood Jewish stores were closed. Mama, exhausted, put her work away on that day. On Saturday she would send my Papa off to work. This was long before the forty-hour week, and if you wanted to hold on to your job you had to work on Saturday, even if you were Jewish. We were all quiet as Mama went into the bedroom and lowered the blinds. Mama, completely exhausted, would sleep the rigid sleep of the martyr. Her resting period was a collapse that did not refresh. Later when I was old enough, I would take my two younger brothers to a five-cent Saturday matinee and Mama would nap until we got home. Then she would rise with a sigh and get the house ready for Papa's return. But even this precious day had to be paid for first by frantically preparing the house every Friday for the Sabbath.

On Fridays Mama's housecleaning efforts were doubled, and she had to work against the clock, for all evidence of labor had to be out of sight before sunset.

Winter Fridays were hardest of all, because the sun would set well before 5:00 P.M., shortening the time Mama had to complete her preparations. On those Fridays she would rise even earlier, rushing to the chicken market to be first in line for that fresh kosher chicken that had just been slaughtered according to kosher rules. Bubbe could then prepare the traditional Sabbath meal of gefilte fish, boiled chicken, and soup with her freshly made noodles and her own *challah*, the traditional braided bread for the Sabbath meal.

No sooner did Mama return from the market than she would frantically herd us out of her way, for she was about to thoroughly clean the house again. She washed and waxed every floor, dusted and oiled the furniture, washed the windows inside and out, and set the table for the Sabbath meal, placing the candles in the silver candlesticks to be lit at sundown for the blessing. The shiny floors would be covered with newspaper in an attempt to keep them clean a little longer. The final touch was added when Mama scrubbed the four marble steps at the entrance of our house. Once again she would get down on her hands and knees with a pail of soapy water and scrub the marble until it was milky white and sparkling. Then she would dry the steps with a cloth and buff them to a shining surface. Papa would be the first one to walk on the clean steps. He would then know the house was ready for the Sabbath. All of this was done with three small children underfoot who were scolded and chased out of the way as Mama whirled from one room to the other. She would scrub us clean, dress us, comb our hair, and warn us to sit still and stay clean until Papa arrived.

And when he did, the house was orderly and peaceful, with no sign of the frantic effort it took for Mama to be ready for the Sabbath.

Once a year Mama had to stretch herself even further as Passover approached. The entire house would have to be scoured and purged. Every single dish and utensil used during the year had to be boxed and moved to a small storage space in the cellar. As soon as the dishes, pots, and pans were removed, out would come the cockroaches that had been hiding in dark, secret places. Mama's swift broom would crush those she could reach before they scurried away. Next she would spray every shelf with a lethal dose of Black Flag insecticide, coughing and sneezing, her eyes watering until she had to stop. In those days there were no warning labels about insecticides being dangerous or harmful to humans. Only after the cupboards had been scrubbed and sprayed and lined with new shelf-paper and the kitchen walls washed would the Passover dishes be brought up from the cellar, carefully cleaned and dried and placed on the shelves. All of this had to be completed by Passover eve, the night of the first *Seder*. Bubbe would be cooking and baking, preparing the holiday dishes for days while Mama worked under tremendous pressure. Any disaster, like the icebox overflowing or the iceman coming late, would steal precious minutes from the demanding schedule of the holiday. I would stay out of Mama's way and sit in the kitchen with Bubbe, but I was always aware of the tension in the house as Mama continued to do the impossible one more time. At the end of this week-long holiday, all the Passover dishes were washed, dried, and stored away until the next year; the daily dishes would then be brought back up from the cellar, washed and dried again, and placed back on the shelves. But only after the cockroaches had been annihilated once again.

It was many years before the landlord provided a refrigerator and Mama no longer had to worry about food spoiling and could keep several days' worth of dairy and meat products in the house, reducing some of the daily shopping for food. Without any small appliances, however, the housekeeping chores went on day after day, year after year. Mama drove herself harder and harder to keep our poor house spotless. Her reward was to repeat the endless labors, day after stultifying day, cleaning and washing her youth away in the process. Mama was indeed a *balaboosta*, and she paid a bitter price.

Lies My Parents Told Me

My younger brother Himey is four years old, and Mama is getting him ready to go outdoors. A good boy, Himey submits as Mama pushes him into his clothes. His pink-and-white complexion is unusually pale today, highlighting his soft blue, soulful eyes. For some reason, Papa has taken the day off from work, and he and Mama and Himey are going off by themselves. When Papa is home he always takes me for a walk, leaving my brothers at home. Today is different. I am to be left behind. Papa tries to calm me but then becomes impatient with me when I beg to come. Gently he pushes me away, but his voice has a scolding tone as he calls for Bubbe to come and get me. I am really hurt and puzzled. Did I do something wrong? Why has Papa rejected me? Doesn't he love me any more? I try in vain to hold back the tears, embarrassed when I fail.

Bubbe does her best to quiet me, but I am inconsolable, no longer able to control myself, until I am sobbing and quite out of breath. Himey begins to cry, too, as Mama continues to bundle him against the cold weather. I hear her telling Himey that they are going for a nice ride on the trolley and then they will go to a movie. This offering does nothing to cheer him up, and the words meet my ears like a sharp knife. I have heard them before.

Those words fill me with terror. I cry louder, even kicking against Bubbe's grasp. The tightness of her grip frightens me, as if my body remembers being held down in another place, another time. Papa carries my whimpering brother out into the cold day. He disappears into the bulky winter clothing that muffles his cries.

Back in the kitchen, I refuse the warm glass of milk and cookies Bubbe offers me, and even the promise of a special treat falls on deaf ears as I continue to bewail my fate. The injustice of it all makes me angry. Finally, I am exhausted, my eyes puffy, my cheeks bright red and streaked with fingermarks where I have rubbed my hands across my eyes. Taking advantage of this lull, Bubbe carries me upstairs, whispering soft, comforting sounds, as she prepares me for a nap. I am seven and no longer nap during the day. I am not a baby any more, but I am truly worn out and protest no further, responding gratefully to Bubbe's soothing touch as she tucks me in, lowers the window blind, and quietly leaves the room. Intermittent sobs escape my lips, breaking the silence every now and then. I try to sleep but keep hearing my Mama telling Himey they are going on the trolley that will take them to a movie. Again those words fill my heart with dread. I am too tired to stay awake, but as I drift off to sleep, I remember.

I am five years old again, and Mama and Papa are taking me to a special movie. Even at five I can appreciate this is a very unusual event, so unusual that Papa has taken the day off from work. I am excited as I sit in the kitchen, having breakfast with my two little brothers. Alec is in the old high chair that used to be mine, and

Himey is at the table but has to sit on pillows so he can reach the bowl of oatmeal and glass of hot cocoa in front of him. It almost feels like a holiday. Mama and Papa are getting ready for our trip, and I can hear them talking in hushed tones. Are they planning still another surprise for me? I am so happy and impatient I do not notice that Mama is making a small bundle of some of my clothes to be taken with us to the movies. My excited thoughts are focused only on the movies. I have been there twice before, and I can remember the cartoons and the Charlie Chaplin film that made us all laugh so hard. Maybe we will see that again today. I fail to notice that Bubbe kisses me good-bye with a concerned look on her face and hugs me hard as I squirm, anxious to escape because I am going to the movies.

Once outside the house, I skip in front of my parents, frequently turning toward them with an endless amount of questions about the movies and how long it will take us to get there. The trolley is waiting for us as we round the corner and Papa carries me aboard. Ordinarily the strange smell from the trolley motor makes my stomach feel queasy, but I am much too happy to let that bother me today as I sit on Papa's lap and look out the window. When we get up to leave I am told we need only walk a short distance before we will get there. My smile is so wide it must start at one ear and end at the other as I walk between Mama and Papa, on the way to the movies.

We enter a tall, white building and walk up many marble stairs. I am greeted with a strange, unfamiliar smell. I don't remember that smell in the movies but dismiss that thought before it develops into concern. A

49

lady dressed all in white comes toward us and calls me by
name. I am caught by surprise and find refuge behind my
Papa's legs, lowering my head. All this is very strange
and nothing like the last time I went to the movies.
Where is the lady behind the window who sells the tick-
ets? Where do you get in line to wait for the door to
open?

Mama and Papa seem to know the lady in white, for
they talk to her as she writes something down on a piece
of paper. Mama hands over the package with my things,
and I am thoroughly confused. Confusion quickly turns
to stark, white fear as the lady reaches for me, pulls me
away from my Papa, and picks me up, ignoring my protests. Mama is crying now and Papa is waving good-bye,
telling me to be a good girl as the lady carries me down a
long, white hallway. My cries and screams are ignored as
she continues to carry me away, out of sight of my parents. I am terrified and helpless. The lady talks to me, but
I do not understand English. I am beginning to suspect
that I will never see Charlie Chaplin or Mama or Papa
again. My heart is beating fast and I am dizzy with panic.

I am taken to a big room with many beds, and there
are other children in some of the beds. Some are crying,
too. Others are playing with toys on the floor, ignoring
the chaos. I am still sobbing uncontrollably and pro-
testing in Yiddish as the lady places me on one of the
beds and begins to undress me. She dresses me in blue
pajamas, like the other children are wearing, and
leaves without another word. I sit on the bed, crying,
looking around, thoroughly bewildered and painfully
self-conscious. Another lady arrives, pushing a flat bed on

wheels, and picks up four of the other children. They begin to cry as she takes them away. I become totally panicked as they disappear through the doorway. Won't somebody tell me what is going to happen to me?

My terrified gaze is fixed on the doorway, and my worst fear comes true when the lady comes back for me and places me on the moving bed with three other children. She doesn't bother to quiet us. She ignores our screams and pushes the bed down a cold, dimly lit hallway. There are many doors along the way, but they are all closed. What is going on behind those doors? The lady pushes the moving bed into another room that smells strange. The lights are dim, but I can see several tables, and some of the children are being held down while another lady dressed in white is giving them enemas. I am filled with horror and the thought of being so exposed, so violated stifles me until my breath has difficulty reaching my lungs and I feel I will lose consciousness. My turn comes and my eyes are wide with fear and outrage. I must submit, but I arch my body, stiffen my muscles, and try to throw myself off the table. The lady's hands are too strong and she straps me down. She ignores my screams and mechanically forces the soapy water into my tense and frightened body. What else will be done to me before they are through with me? Does Papa know what they are doing? Will I ever see him again? Please, Papa, come and get me. I promise I will be good.

The nightmare continues as I am placed on a potty on the floor and though other children are around me on their potties, I cannot release the water that has been painfully pumped inside me. I am too ashamed. The lady scolds me and makes threatening sounds until my body explodes and I am further humiliated because I was unable to control myself. Finally, exhausted, I am taken back to the big room with the beds and the other children, and the lady gives me some cookies. I continue to sob, refusing her offering. The lights are turned out. I fall into an exhausted sleep, only to be roughly awakened by the lady. She lifts me out of my bed, places me on the moving bed, and quickly straps me down. I am crying again, and the fears that had been quieted during sleep awaken in full force and overtake me. I am wheeled into a big, cold room, with strong lights overhead that hurt my eyes. There is a man there, also dressed in white, whose face is covered with a white mask, I can see only his eyes. I have now given up any hope of being rescued, but I am screaming as one of the ladies pushes a cover on my face and the smell of the air that rushes toward me is dreadful, sickening, and stifling. I begin to hear my screams coming back to me through a long echo chamber and see terrifying swirls of black-and-white spirals coming toward me in an endless pattern that threatens to swallow me. The sound of my own voice fades. All becomes deathly silent. Time has ceased to exist. I have disappeared.

Slowly I struggle to wake up, only to fall back several times into a foggy mist. I realize I am back in my bed, which is now full of cookie crumbs. My heart begins to pound hard again as I remember the terrors. I don't understand why my voice can make no sounds and my throat is so raw and filled with pain when I try to speak. My pillow is moist with red stains and my breath smells funny. My tummy feels sick and doesn't even want to hold on to my own saliva. Nausea overtakes me and I vomit. The pain is excruciating but the sight of fresh blood leaving my mouth causes me to cry out in spite of the pain. A new lady comes running and cleans me up. This lady speaks Yiddish and explains to me that my tonsils have been removed, and because I have been such a good girl I can have all the ice cream I want. She offers me a dish of sweet vanilla ice cream, my favorite flavor. For the first time I can manage to smile through my tears and even feel a little comforted as the new lady encourages me to lick the ice cream off the spoon. Even that hurts, but it tastes so good and the cold ice cream melts and gently slides down my throat. This lady tells me my Mama and Papa will be coming tomorrow to take me home, and for the first time I allow myself to have some hope that I will leave this place alive, but I am not entirely convinced.

I doze off and on during the day, fitful naps that are interrupted by the sound of children crying. Sometimes I am awakened by my own cries. Every time I open my eyes, the horrors of the events are remembered as though they are happening all over again and I have difficulty distinguishing between the past and the present. People come and go, but it is a long, long time before Mama and Papa appear. I had given up all hope of ever seeing them again. Yet, I do not speak. I am numb from the pain and the fear and cannot meet my Papa's eyes, the eyes that I used to trust. Mama dresses me and tries to comfort me but does not ask for my forgiveness. When they take me home, my trust of my Papa is left in the hospital, replaced

by betrayal and unanswered questions. It was better not
to ask questions, for there is no way to determine whether
you will be told the truth.

I awaken from my nap, the fear still hovering over
me. Slowly, consciousness returns as I remember my baby
brother Himey being carried out on the way to the
movies. What will happen to him? Is he, too, facing tor-
turers who strap him down and hurt him? Will he ever
come back? I try to be very quiet in my bed, waiting for
Bubbe, when I hear the outside door open and the sound
of Mama's voice. I begin to tremble. I do not hear Papa
or Himey. Quietly, I climb out of bed, go to the top of
the stairs, and see my Papa placing Himey on a big pillow
on the couch. Is he asleep? His little body looks lifeless.
He doesn't move and seems to disappear in the pillow. I
creep down the stairs. My eyes open wide in terror when
I notice blood coming out of my little brother's mouth.
Will he ever open his eyes again? That same sick smell I
remembered is hovering over him and reaches me as I get
closer. I know that smell, and my stomach gurgles and
feels funny again. I put my hand over my nose to keep the
smell away. Himey continues to sleep. I can hear him
breathing now, and there are bloody bubbles leaving his
mouth with every breath, until the pillow is quite wet. I
stand there unable to move, as though turned to stone.
Mama sees me and tells me not to bother Himey—to let
him sleep. I want to ask her what happened to him, but
one look at her face is enough to freeze the words in my
mouth.

I turn away silently, the memory of being strapped
down on the table, and the man with the mask standing

over me, becoming vivid again. It is clear that they did not take Himey to the movies and that something terrible was done to him. I am too afraid to ask what happened. I cannot stop shivering, though the house is warm. I climb up on Bubbe's lap, and she rocks me silently until my pounding heart begins to calm down. I can hear Bubbe's heart beating where my head rests on her warm body, and I gratefully close my eyes. They think I am asleep. Mama, Papa, and Bubbe are talking about Himey being taken to the dentist and put to sleep so that all of his decayed baby teeth could be pulled out. So that is what happened to my baby brother. What did Himey do that all his teeth were pulled out? What did I do that my throat had been cut open? But I dare not ask. It is not safe to speak. Terrible things have happened and can happen again. Just be quiet. Don't ask questions. Wait for the nightmares to shock you into wakefulness as you listen for approaching footsteps. Maybe next time you can get away.

The Haircut

Why do I have to get a haircut today? I don't like the barber, an old Italian man who speaks little English. He smells bad. When I don't understand him he pushes my head hard until I freeze in the chair, not daring to move or raise my eyes. His shop, in front of his apartment, is cold and dimly lit. The smell of stale cigar smoke and the sweet, sickening odor of hair tonic makes my stomach want to empty itself into my throat. He really scares me.

I try to plead with Mama, though I know it will be to no avail. She shoves me out of the house. Salty tears fall on my cheeks and are soon plastered on my skin by the chilling wind. I bury my face deeper into the worn collar of my old winter coat, but it offers little warmth or protection. Mama has a locked grip on my small hand, ignoring both my tears and my dragging feet. I cannot keep up with her long, quick steps. At times she lifts me off the ground until I stumble and fall, which makes her angrier. She pushes on against the wind, and I accept that there is no turning back.

As we approach the door of the barbershop, Mama roughly wipes the traces of tears from my face, creating red streak marks across my chapped cheeks. She delivers me into the hands of the enemy. I am quiet. I know better than to protest. She pays the barber twenty-five cents for the haircut, and he lifts me carelessly and puts me down on the tall leather barber chair. This chair scares me, too; he can pump the pedal, raising it higher and higher, until I am afraid I will be pushed up against the ceiling. As uncomfortable as this is, it is very familiar to me up to this point. Then I can hardly believe my ears when I hear Mama telling the barber that she is going down the street to the butcher shop and will return in twenty minutes. She has never left me alone with this old man before. As she reaches the door she stops, turns, and warns me to sit still.

Last night I had a nightmare. I was in the barber shop and the big, dark, bad-smelling man was standing in the doorway, not allowing me to leave. Looking for a quick exit, my eyes picked up the gleaming razor resting on its side, waiting to be put to use. The thick razor strap hung from a hook, ready to sharpen the blade again. I have heard stories about this razor and I shudder, pushing them out of my mind.

I remember my dream as I sit, frozen in the barber chair. But I am not dreaming now. This is really happening, and even my scolding, rough mother is not here to protect me. I try to be very, very still, not wanting to anger the barber, as his gleaming sharp scissors cut and snip very close to my scalp. Mama has instructed him to cut my hair short so that the twenty-five cents will be well spent. Finally, he cuts my bangs above my eyebrows. I can see the sharp edges of the steel scissors moving closer and closer. My body becomes rigid with fear.

He is almost finished, and momentarily I am relieved

that I may yet survive another life-threatening visit to the barber. Then it happens. He scrutinizes me closely to determine whether a hair has dared to escape his lethal instrument. As he forces my head down to one side, my left ear is crushed against my shoulder. He goes after a wayward strand of hair across my right ear, muttering to himself as he takes aim. The left side of my neck can no longer bear the pressure. I move my head in an attempt to free myself at the same moment that the blades of the scissors meet with a sharp, hissing sound. The strand of hair is gone but so is a slice of my right ear lobe. I am terrified as the pain spreads over and through my ear, but I can't even make a sound. This is worse than my nightmare. The barber lets out a hoarse groan. His eyes are filled with anger and fear. He leaps into action and begins to apply a dirty towel to my ear. So obedient am I that I do not move or dare to cry. I am stunned into painful, passive silence. I remember the razor on the shelf behind me. I wonder what will happen next.

Any minute now my Mama will come back. There is no assurance that she will defend me. The horror of being scolded and punished by her in front of my attacker makes me feel dizzy. Yet I yearn for her return. Quietly I submit to the application of the caustic styptic pencil the barber applies to my ear. It bubbles, hisses, and burns, but the bleeding finally stops. He continues to mutter in Italian. Momentarily I am thankful that Mama has not returned to witness this massacre. Finally the barber lifts me from the chair, turns away, and dismisses me as he busies himself destroying the evidence of his attack. He keeps his head down. He does not look at me. Somehow I find the energy to pull my hat over my ears, hiding the dirty deed.

I stand at the door, the minutes barely passing, waiting for Mama. I am aware, though I am only six, that the barber and I must have a secret. I will not tell. Was it my fault? My ear is beginning to throb and pulse against the rough fabric of my hat, but I must stay calm. Will Mama remember to come back for me? My stomach knots in fear and anxiety. But I will not cry.

The door opens and Mama is there. I go to her with a smile, glad to see her, and acting as though nothing has happened. She is late, and in her haste she does not stop to examine my haircut. She is preoccupied with the urgency of getting home in time to prepare supper for Papa, who will soon be home from work. I say nothing, allowing myself to be dragged all the way home, keeping my hat carefully pulled over my ears. Maybe I will be able to distract Mama, and she will never find out that the barber sliced off the tip of my ear. Maybe she won't notice. Maybe I will escape this time.

My First Day in School

The first day of school was fast approaching. I was excited but began to wake up at night, worrying. What if I didn't like being in school, away from home all morning? Would the teacher let me go home? Where would Mama be when I was away? Perhaps being a big girl was not going to be as much fun as I thought. Last year I watched Sissy, my very best friend, leaving for school every day. I envied her and longed to go, too. I loved Sissy and missed her when she was away. I was only four then and was left behind. I was bigger now. I was five. Himey was only three and Alec barely a year old. They were still babies and would be left at home with Bubbe while I went off to school. When it finally came time for Mama to register me for kindergarten, I began to have second thoughts about being a big girl.

At the school building, three blocks from my house, there was much activity and excitement. Long lines of Mamas, and more children than I had ever seen in one place before, were standing in front of three desks. A lady at each desk was busily writing as each Mama answered questions. Some children were crying, clinging to their Mamas. Others were playing tag, running down the hallway, ignoring their Mamas' calls entirely. There were also children who were painfully shy, avoiding eye contact with anyone. I was one of these. I envied the freedom of the running children but dared not join them. I was too afraid that if I got separated from Mama I might never find her again. I held on to her in silence, waiting for my turn. I knew Mama was getting impatient as she jerked me closer to her and warned me not to wander off. She pursed her lips and shifted her weight from one foot to the other. She was getting cross, but I did not know why. I was, after all, being such a good girl, holding on to her hand or her dress, never leaving her side.

At last our turn came. Mama spoke in short, hesitant sentences to the lady at the desk. She had remembered to bring my birth certificate, and the lady seemed pleased. I stood close to Mama, the desk reaching to just below my nose. I glanced at the lady's face as she wrote. She seemed to have trouble understanding Mama's Russian-Jewish accent and soon became impatient. Her pencil raced angrily across the registration form. I disappeared behind Mama where I felt safer.

This scene was very confusing because I spoke only Yiddish and the lady at the desk was so impatient, speaking English very rapidly. I was not aware that I would become even more perplexed. Though I had always been called Esther—my middle name and my Yiddish name, I had been registered under Rose, the first name on my birth certificate. Neither the lady nor Mama had taken the time to explain that to me. Finally, the questions stopped, and Mama was asked to sign the form. In embarrassment Mama had to admit she could not write. The lady rolled her eyes, as she showed Mama where to place an X.

We had been gone for hours. I was tired and hungry. My legs would not carry me fast enough to keep up with Mama's big steps as we headed for home. Why was she in such a hurry? I did not know she had to rush back to nurse my baby brother. Her milk was beginning to leak out of her breasts, causing a stain that spread across the front of her faded house dress, adding embarrassment to her anger. Every now and then she scolded me for lagging behind. Though we were both out of breath she ordered me to walk faster and faster.

During the days that followed this daunting experience, my fears about going to school increased, but there was no one I could turn to for help. I couldn't talk to Mama. She had been so angry when I was registered at school. Papa praised me for being so grown up and I wanted him to be proud of me, so I smiled and never told him how scared I was. Bubbe had no answers for me. I was, after all, the first child in our family who would attend public school in America. The process was as mysterious to Bubbe and my parents as it was to me. I began to have difficulty eating as the first day of school approached. Bubbe tried to comfort me with a slice of her warm, fresh, homemade bread. Even that mouth-watering treat did not tempt my waning appetite.

I wanted to crawl away and forget about ever going to school, but there was no place to hide. In preparation for the big event, Aunt Bluma had made a new, red silk dress for me. Papa even found the money to buy me a new pair of shoes for the occasion. My new outfit did little to calm my fears. The day before school, anxiety changed to panic. I began to cry and could not stop. Only when Mama promised me she would not leave me alone in the schoolroom did my sobbing subside.

With a pounding heart, I held on to Mama's hand as we walked to school. The level of my nervousness increased as the distance to the school building decreased. We turned the corner, and there it was, a menacing, gray, stone structure with open doorways, like a monster with a huge, gaping mouth, ready to swallow me up. There were hundreds of children of all ages streaming into the building without any apparent concern for the fate that awaited them. Inside the noise was deafening. Everyone was talking. I held on tighter to Mama's hand. Loud, shrill bells began to ring, echoing down the long corridor and stabbing my eardrums. Mama quickened her step, pulling me with her. Finally we arrived at the kindergarten room. Inside the room bedlam had erupted. Mothers lost control of excited children. The cacophony caused by many foreign languages spoken at once added to the confusion. The two teachers in the room were having difficulty being heard as they attempted to establish order. Their patience was stretched further when the twenty children in the room realized they were about to be separated from their mothers. It didn't seem possible that the noise level could increase, but it did. Even children who had been laughing and playing minutes ago, were affected by other crying children. They, too, began to wail and cling to their mothers. I was terrified.

One of the teachers released a sharp blast from a whistle. It sliced right through the cries and sobs, and the noise stopped. She ordered all mothers out of the room at once. I clung to Mama, reminding her she had promised not to leave. After much effort, Mama finally convinced me that although she had to leave the room, she would stand outside the door where I could see her through the window. I did not take my eyes off her as she left. The door closed with a sickening sound, but she stationed herself in full view in the window, just as she had promised. I felt flushed and hot and kept turning my eyes toward the door. Mama was there every time. Relieved, I began to play with a doll and blanket I had been given. I held them close to my quivering body, continuing to cast quick glances at the door. Mama was still there. She had not left me. Within the hour I felt secure enough to make a new friend and play house. I even forgot to look for Mama.

The teachers were smiling now as they talked to the calmer, playful children. I was not so afraid as I turned to smile again at Mama in the doorway. To my horror she had disappeared. I broke out in a sweat. My breath refused to reach any further than my throat. I let out a piercing scream. "Mama, Mama, where are you? You promised not to leave me." I became hysterical. The sound of my screams threatened several other children who began to cry, disturbing the earlier tranquility. I escaped past the teacher, pushing the door open, searching for Mama. She was nowhere in sight. My cries echoed through the empty hallway until a teacher caught up with me. She carried me back to the room though I kicked and screamed. She called me Rose, but I did not know she was talking to me. My name was Esther. She may have been trying to comfort me, but I could not understand the unfamiliar sounds of English that were spoken so rapidly and without a Yiddish accent. I was a terrified foreigner in an alien land, and there were no translators. Embarrassment joined my panic, slowing down my tears but not the terror that continued to fill my heart. Why had Mama left me? She always told me I was a bad girl. Maybe she had at last found a way to get rid of me. I would never go home again. Papa would never carry me up to bed at night. The warm, comforting times I spent with Bubbe in the kitchen watching her cook were over. I slowly began to accept my fate. I sat on the teacher's lap, exhausted, curled up in a small ball, holding on to her for dear life.

There was no way to measure time that morning. When the room filled with the sound of an alarm bell, I thought it might be announcing some new torture. In fact, it signified the end of the first morning of school. Children lined up. Mothers began to arrive and claim their children. I knew no one was coming for me and would not release my grip on the teacher. I was the last child in the room when I heard Mama's excited voice talking to the other teacher. I immediately rushed toward her, finding new energy in my desperation. I clung to Mama and pleaded with her to take me home.

As the teacher and Mama talked, I began to understand the meaning of some of their words. Mama explained she could not wait for me at school all morning because she had to hurry home to nurse my baby brother Alec. They talked for several minutes. To my relief it was becoming clear that I did not have to return to kindergarten the next day. I was not a big girl after all and was not ready for school. I blushed with shame, but inside I was relieved and slowly began to relax.

I clung to Mama all the way home. Risking her anger, I asked why she had left me. Impatiently Mama explained in Yiddish that she could not leave my baby brother for a whole morning. That did little to console me because her voice was angry again. Once more I began to cry, "Please, Mama, I don't want to go back there. I'll be good. I don't understand what they are saying. The teacher didn't even know my name." To my surprise and relief Mama told me I didn't have to go back to school until next year, when I turned six years old. I would go to the first grade then. Slowly, I dared to believe her. Somehow a miracle had saved me.

Later I felt ashamed because I was the only five-year-old on the block who was not going to school that year. I pretended I didn't care, playing with my doll alone or sitting with Bubbe in the kitchen. I was safe. Even Mama's anger was not as frightening as the nightmare of that one day in kindergarten. I was happy to wait to be a big girl for another year.

Hair

The joy I woke up with this morning disappears abruptly when Mama grabs me as I prepare to leave for school. I am dressed in my white middy blouse, which Bubbe has ironed for me. Today is auditorium day, and all the girls wear white middy blouses and the boys wear white shirts. Caught up in the joyful expectation of being with my favorite teacher, Miss March, whom I like more than anyone except Papa and Bubbe, I had blissfully forgotten that I could not leave before Mama combed my hair into the long finger curls I hate. So eager was I to get to school that I had gulped down my cocoa and oatmeal, grabbed my book and pencil, and was on my way to freedom when Mama stopped me.

I have to stand close to Mama, obedient and unprotesting as she begins to drag the comb with the broken teeth through my curly hair. The jagged edges of the comb catch as Mama drags it across my scalp. I hate those finger curls, not only because Mama hurts me, but because they make me look like a baby. After all, I am seven now and would like to wear my hair away from my face, held back with a pretty ribbon, like my friend Evelyn. Mama will not hear of it. Adding to my discomfort, all the time that Mama is pulling my hair she is muttering and complaining, and she tugs harder when I squirm to get away. She yanks my head and threatens to slap me if I move one more time. I try to stifle my tears, but they run down my cheeks, and the lump in my throat begins to swell. I force myself to stand still for long, torturous minutes. Mama becomes more impatient and angry as she goes after every hair with a vengeance each time I move or whimper. At Mama's merciless determination to tame my hair, it seems to become alive with stubborn resistance, taking on a life and will of its own. The tangles become more tangled and the curls refuse to obey.

Finally, my hair has been pulled and stretched, and all the knots and tangles have been smoothed out. Mama begins to part my hair in sections preparing for the hated long curls. She dips the comb into a glass of cold water and moistens each carefully measured section of hair, wrapping it around the comb in a spiral. Immediately my curls come alive. When the comb comes to the end of a section of hair, a long bouncy curl has been created. While all of this painful attention is being paid to me, I must remind myself not to move. I dare not raise my head to look up at the mirror to see how much longer this torture will last. The clicking of the comb as it dips into the glass of water and its release at the end of each completed curl is my only measure of time. To move would only extend the agony; for I would receive a slap for daring to disobey her. Mama does not stop until my head is covered with these corkscrews. The torture finally ends but I am not yet free to go. I must continue to stand still for inspection so Mama can scrutinize her handiwork. Only when she is satisfied that she has done a good job does she release me with the usual warnings to stay clean and come right home after school. Mama always wins. I am no match for her.

With a heavy heart I start out for school. (I did not know then that the feeling inside me was depression.) My breath comes in deep sighs. As I turn the corner I realize Mama can no longer see me from the house. The weight in my chest begins to lighten, and I consider shaking my head real hard, releasing all the tight curls. Do I dare? Why not? By the time I come home from school the curls are usually loosened anyway. What if I just shake my head and run my fingers through my hair? Surely, Mama would not find out. Or would she?

The bubbly feeling has grown into a rare streak of daring and independence. I feel positively mischievous and rebellious as I shake my head in every direction and run my fingers through my hair until the curls are gone. My step becomes quicker and lighter. I am anxious to see Miss March. When I get to my classroom, however, Miss March is not there. She is sick today, and a large, angry-looking woman has taken her place. The joy inside me dies, depression takes over. This teacher, Miss Murdock, announces that before we go to the auditorium, everyone's hair must be examined for lice. The class lets out a groan to which Miss Murdock responds with a threat to keep us all after school if we do not behave. Immediately silence returns as we line up, waiting for the executioner to examine our hair. There are thirty children in the room so this process is not to be hurried. Miss Murdock, with pinched nostrils and eyeglasses slipping down to the end of her nose, looks at the first child. The two pencils in her hand she uses like weapons or spears that she pushes through the child's hair. After several minutes of jabbing and poking, the child is released with a clean bill of health. "Next," Mrs. Murdock booms. It is my friend Julius's turn and he bows his head in silence in front of the teacher as she repeats the inspection, parting his hair with her pencils, and lets out a cry for all to hear. "You have lice. What a filthy, disgusting boy you are. Take this note and go home to your mother and tell her not to send you back to school until she has given you a good scrubbing and the lice are gone." Humiliated, Julius slinks out of the door on his way home while the next child presents herself.

After an interminable half-hour, my stomach is nervous and upset, and I am in a state of high anxiety. My turn comes. I console myself that I will pass because I took a bath last night. My hair was washed and Bubbe had used a fine comb to search for and remove any lice. She had found none. But no sooner does Miss Murdock part my hair with her pencils than she lets out her blood-curdling scream, covering me with her bad breath. She calls out my name for all the world to hear and gives me one of those letters to take home to Mama. There must be a mistake. My head has not itched for weeks and Bubbe had assured me last night that my scalp was clean. I am shocked and horrified, though I am not the only child to be treated in this brutal manner. Miss Murdock must be wrong. She pushes me aside before I can even open my mouth to protest, then pounces on the next innocent victim. It didn't occur to me until years later that perhaps Miss Murdock was more than a little responsible for infecting the whole class. She used the same set of pencils on all the children, transferring lice from one child to the next.

I trudge home with a heavy and fearful heart. I know that Mama will somehow find reason to punish me. Adding to my distress, I must read the note for Mama, because she cannot read. She lets out a scream that would put Miss Murdock's bellow to shame. The hair on the back of my neck stands up in fear. She yanks me toward her and begins to search my head for the offending intruders. Once again I am subjected to her touch, which now is much more forceful because she is angry. She begins to think out loud again. Mama does that a lot. "God, what do you want from me? Don't I have enough to do today? Why have you humiliated and cursed me this day?" I stand there, my head turned to one side, ready to dodge the blow that any minute will come down on me.

Mercifully, Bubbe comes out of the kitchen with a jar in her hand and tells Mama to send me to the corner paint store to get some kerosene so she can wash my hair with the evil-smelling chemical guaranteed to kill the lice. Bubbe hands me the jar and gives me five cents as Mama shouts at me not to stop along the way, not to lose the money, not to break the jar, and to come right back home. Soon, I am out of earshot and for the moment have escaped. At the paint store the old man adds to my shame by teasing me when I ask for the kerosene and wanting to know how many lice I have. I am crushed again but lack the energy to deny his accusations. Besides, you are not supposed to talk back to grown-ups. I know better than that. I am a good girl.

My head hangs lower and lower as I get closer to home, the lethal remedy held tightly in my arms. Bubbe is waiting for me at the door and tells me that she will wash my hair, so I relax. Bubbe will be gentle and won't hurt me the way Mama does. I bend over the kitchen sink, an old towel over my eyes. Bubbe first washes my hair with a bar of laundry soap and rinses it thoroughly. Then she applies a final rinse of pure kerosene over my whole scalp. Making sure my hair is completely soaked, Bubbe dries my head with a large towel. All the time she is talking to me in loving, soothing tones, telling me what a good girl I am and that I will be able to go back to school tomorrow and that it wasn't my fault. After the fumigation, Bubbe carefully and gently combs out all the snarls. She then braids my hair so firmly that my scalp pulls my eyelids upward into elongated almond shapes. Thoroughly scoured, I am now free and do not have to go back to school until tomorrow.

That night, my hair held in place by the braids, it is a while before I can fall asleep. It has been quite a day. I dream of waking up in the morning and being allowed to go to school with my hair hanging loosely around my shoulders. It is a very pleasing dream. I can feel the wind blowing and the delicious touch of my hair against the skin on my neck and cheeks. I run and skip on the way to school in my dream, my hair trailing behind me in the breeze.

Morning comes quickly, and I do not remember the assaults of yesterday until I see my face in the bathroom mirror. There are the braids from the night before. Not a hair is out of place. I remember the dream, and then a broad smile spreads across my face. The dream will come true, for every time my hair is washed with kerosene and braided, it sets into a crinkly, wavy pattern when the braids are released. It cannot be curled. In addition, the kerosene creates a shiny, squeaky-clean texture to my hair, and it glistens in the sun. Bubbe releases the braids and easily combs my hair. There isn't a knot or a tangle anywhere. It cascades around my shoulders just like in the dream, crinkly waves from the top of my scalp to my shoulders. Bubbe has even found a ribbon and ties it around my head into a pretty bow.

The touch of my hair against my skin sends shivers of delight down my spine with each shake of my head when I walk. Mama manages to scold me one more time, but it doesn't affect me at all. I don't even hear her and I am not afraid. I am free, my hair is free, and I won't be sent home from school. Maybe Miss March will be waiting for me, and I will be her special girl today.

The Charity Shoes

I am barely seven years old and do not yet understand the way of grown-ups. I am confused by Mama's orders, but I know better than to not follow them. She teaches me her lessons with a harsh hand. She tells me to hide our poverty, as though we had done something wrong and should be ashamed. She tells me not to take food from my Aunt Bluma, though my stomach rumbles with hunger pains. Mama would say we are proud and do not take charity. "We must hide from the self-righteous eyes of the generous," she says. Why then does she now tell me to stand up in front of my class and tell the teacher that Papa is too poor to buy shoes for me? I wish I did not have to go to school today.

I enter the classroom, my heart pounding, my chest filled with dread and also feelings for which I have no names. I stand up when the teacher calls for the children whose parents cannot afford to buy them new shoes. I remember Mama's orders. My head is low. I do not know why I am feeling ashamed. I dare to lift my eyes. I notice that I am not standing alone. But I still feel exposed in front of all my classmates.

The teacher walks toward us with pinched nostrils and judging eyes, obviously trying to keep her distance from the poor children. There is no escape now. With a horror I have not known before, I listen as the teacher begins to interrogate the first child in line. "What is your name? Where do you live? How many children are in your family? Is your father working? Do you have another pair of shoes at home?" Is it Papa's fault that he cannot buy me new shoes? Did he do something wrong? Did I do something wrong? I feel alone in my terror as the teacher comes closer to the end of the line where I stand. Can I pass her test?

I can't believe this is happening to me. It was only this morning that my Aunt Bluma brought me a lovely red silk dress she had made for me to wear to school that day. I had felt so special and festive, wrapped in the cool luxury of the fabric against my skin. Even my torn, scuffed shoes did not destroy the joy of wearing the new dress. Nor did Mama's anger stop me from feeling happy when I saw the frown on her face. I knew she was angry. She did not approve of Aunt Bluma's gift. Before she could speak, I walked out the door, the red silk brushing against my bare legs as I escaped.

The sound of the teacher's voice brings me back to stark reality. It is my turn. When she calls out my name, I answer with a dry mouth and a trembling voice. I look across the classroom for a moment, hoping to find support, only to see two girls whispering to each other and pointing at me. I lower my head and mumble when the teacher demands answers to her humiliating questions. She gets impatient. She is merciless as she continues to destroy what little pride I may have had. Finally she points to my beautiful dress, which only this morning had made me so happy. "What are you doing on this line in your silk dress? You are dressed better than anyone in the room. This line is only for the poor who have no shoes. Who do you think you are?" My voice froze in my throat. What does the teacher want to hear? How will I find the right words to convince her I really need new shoes? I dare not go home empty-handed and face Mama.

Shamelessly, I plead with my persecutor, describing how my parents struggle when they cannot feed three hungry children. She stops her battering questions in disgust, tired of her attack. She has done her job well, but I don't know if she will let me have any shoes. My head is spinning. My beautiful dress now feels hot and searing. It must be wrong to wear a pretty red silk dress to school or else why did it make the teacher so angry?

I am suddenly aware of the tall charity lady coming toward me. She holds a large pair of shoes in her hands. She tells me to put them on, for they are mine. They are black, ugly, old-lady oxfords with thick, stacked heels. I feel ashamed as I fumble with them. They are too big and ill fitting and do not support my seven-year-old feet. They trip me when I try to walk. Soon my knees are scratched and bloody. The children laugh at me. But there is no place to hide and no way to retrieve my old, torn comfortable shoes. They have been taken by the charity lady —evidence of her job well done.

I slink against buildings on the way home until I am out of sight of the taunting faces and jeering voices of my classmates. I try to walk carefully but keep twisting my ankles and falling off the high heels. My pretty red dress becomes a problem because it won't let me be invisible. I cannot hide from disapproving and questioning eyes.

Home at last. It is silent as I open the door, but I know I must soon face another inquisitor—Mama. I expect to be attacked by the explosion of her angry curses. I know she will make me wear the shoes no matter how many times I fall. To my surprise, Mama bursts into tears at the sight of me standing there, bound to the torn linoleum kitchen floor by those monstrous shoes, my knees bruised, my new dress torn. Momentarily she appears to be as vulnerable as I feel. Carefully, she takes the shoes off my sore feet and tells me I will never have to ask for charity again, nor do I have to wear the shoes. I am relieved and filled with unfamiliar feelings of gratitude and compassion for Mama. Only now, years later, do I understand Mama's suffering, forced upon her by the circumstances of poverty. Fears and desperation created an anger in her that locked us into its unrelenting grasp. On this day, Mama had looked at me and for the first time recognized my pain. She tells me I do not have to return to school tomorrow. Maybe by the time I get back to school everything will be forgotten, and no one will point at me again. Today I didn't have to be afraid of Mama. We understood each other, and she protected me. In that brief moment, I prayed the anger would never return.

Passover Wine

It is dark and cold this morning when I wake to the sound of Bubbe stoking the fire in the old furnace in the cellar. The air in the room is so frigid, my breath is a frosty vapor. Last week Papa earned enough money to pay for a load of coal to ward off the cold. The house will be warm today.

I stay under the covers in my long winter underwear, keeping warm until the moment Mama insists it is time to get up. Suddenly I realize today is Saturday. I can postpone that moment when my bare feet first come in contact with the icy floor. Some winter mornings my brothers and I run squealing down to the cellar. We stand close to the furnace, holding our hands out to the sound of the crackling fire. We dress next to its warmth. For now, I slide down deeper under the covers, waiting for the first hot breath of the furnace to reach the pipes in my room.

From my warm cocoon I listen for the kitchen sounds that announce Bubbe's breakfast preparations, but it is strangely silent. I sit straight up in bed, remembering that this Saturday is different. This is the morning Bubbe will be in the cellar, repeating the annual ritual of skimming the fermented grapes off the Passover wine that she had put up weeks ago. Determined to get to the cellar before my two younger brothers, I ignore the cold room. I race down the steps in the stillness of the dim light.

I can just make out the coal piled in the corner. The big black furnace is already displaying red flickering flames through the grating in the door. There are the crocks of wine, neatly lined up at a safe distance from the heat. Bubbe is bending over, removing the lid of the crock nearest her. The sight of her familiar figure reminds me that Bubbe is the source of good smells, good things to eat, and soft protective arms. Sensing my presence, she turns, making a space for me to stand closer to the heat.

This year I am finally taller than the huge crocks and can look down into the sweet bubbly mixture inside. For the first time Bubbe asks me to help her. She gives me a large slotted spoon and shows me how to dip it into the darkness of the aromatic wine, remove the fermented grapes, and put them aside in a large bowl. As she demonstrates, I marvel at her ability to scoop up the grapes, waiting just long enough for the wine to drain through the slots in the spoon, never spilling a drop.

I relish this quiet private time with Bubbe, knowing that when my noisy brothers arrive, the spell of this moment will be destroyed by their teasing, laughing voices. Mama will surely be close behind, with her warnings and threats. I follow Bubbe's instructions carefully and try to imitate her movements, but my small hands cannot hold the big spoon steady. Bubbe does not scold when the deep, red, liquid trickles onto my hands. Soon the wine leaves a trail of dark red rivulets on the floor around my bare feet. In an effort to control the juice dripping off my hands, I lick the wine from my fingers. It tastes warm and sweet, and the warmth seems to last inside my mouth for long minutes. It tastes so good that I place a grape in my mouth and swallow it.

Soon I feel aglow and happy, forgetting all concerns about my brothers, Mama, or the mess I am making. The warmer I feel, the more grapes I want to eat. The more grapes I eat, the less steady my hands become and the more wine trails down my arms onto the floor. Now my eyes won't focus, and I giggle when the wine crock seems to move, as though this is some new game of tag, when I aim the spoon toward it.

I have been very quiet until now, but feeling the effect of the wine I begin to chatter freely. This is unusual. I am shy and do not like to call attention to myself. Now that doesn't seem to matter, and my laughter is soon joined by a squeaky hiccup. At the sound of my voice, Bubbe turns to me, but she cannot understand my slurred speech. She sees my long white underwear, now streaked with deep red blotches, like blood. My feet, too, are smeared with the wine I have spilled on the floor. My hands are discolored, and my mouth is like a painted, grinning pomegranate. Even my teeth are red.

Bubbe is amused when she realizes I am quite drunk. Through my happy daze I see her expression change from surprise to concern. She knows that if Mama finds out what happened, Bubbe will surely feel the brunt of her tongue, and I will be severely punished. Quickly she picks me up, transferring some of the red stains from my underwear to her clean white apron. My slow-motion experience is galvanized into action as Bubbe fills the laundry tub with hot water, undresses me, and eases me into the bath. I feel dizzy and have some difficulty keeping my head from disappearing under the water. Bubbe keeps a watchful eye on me. She washes both me and my underwear with strong-smelling laundry soap. The water turns red as the wine is washed away. No matter, for I am blissfully warm and relaxed.

Soon I am glowing outside as well as inside. My voice sounds strange in my ears, far away and full of echoes. My giggles seem to disappear into the water, changing into bubbles. My eyelids just won't stay open as Bubbe sweeps me into a towel that smells sweet from drying outside in the spring wind. She holds me against her body, dries me efficiently, dresses me in clean underwear, and carries me up to bed. I am back in my warm, safe cocoon again.

I can barely hear Bubbe's voice as she whispers to me not to worry. She will tell Mama I woke up with a fever and need to stay in bed today. This would not be hard to believe, for my face is warm, my cheeks are flushed, and drops of perspiration glisten on my forehead. My soggy brain tries to hold on to the meaning of her words, and although they make no sense at all, I feel safe. I always feel safe with Bubbe. I drift off into a deep and delicious sleep, dreaming about the first time I got to make Passover wine with Bubbe.

Graham Crackers and Milk

Providing three meals for a family of six during the bleak Depression years was a daily challenge for Mama. Even so, we were never sent off to school without a hot breakfast. Food had to be conserved at every opportunity, so cocoa, for instance, was always prepared with half water and half milk. Mama and Bubbe were determined to stretch every penny to make ends meet. In spite of Mama's and Bubbe's best efforts, the threat of hunger or even starvation was never far away. Many days I would run home from school at lunchtime, expecting a tasty dish to quiet my growling, hungry stomach. More often than not I was disappointed. Instead I would be met by Mama with orders to go to the corner delicatessen to buy three thin slices of baloney—lunch for myself and my two brothers. Although my stomach protested, I would run all the way to the store. Finally, my reward was one-third of this purchase between two thin slices of white bread. The aroma of the baloney continued to taunt me long after I had wolfed it down. But, this lunch was more filling than those that consisted of reheated breakfast oatmeal.

I learned very early that money was scarce and not to ask for anything my parents could not afford. I scolded my brothers when they begged for a dime to buy a balsawood airplane kit. I knew my parents didn't have the money. It hurt me to see the despondent expression on Mama's or Papa's face when our smallest requests could not be granted. Papa would look dejected and guilty. His eyes became sad behind their half-closed lids, as though he was ashamed of not being able to provide us with simple pleasures. Mama, on the other hand, would react with a scolding that everyone in the whole neighborhood could hear. On rare occasions, however, Mama's screaming mouth was not quick enough to provide a barrier against more tender feelings. Then I would see that same expression of guilt and shame in her eyes. She had to be firm in order to survive the severity of daily life, her anger offering her a sense of control over the responsibilities harshened by the poverty. Under those austere circumstances, I became resigned to the spoken and unspoken fears that shared our cramped home. Those fears were like uninvited guests who stayed for years. There was little relief from the rigid routines and reminders of scarcity.

When I was old enough to brave the initial terror of separation, I escaped to school. I loved its books and stories that opened up a rich fantasy world. There was no escape, however, from the fear and shame of poverty that followed me to school every day. Though most of the children were as poor as I was, it did not stop them from taunting me because my shoes were scuffed and torn or because hand-me-down clothing didn't quite cover my fast-growing arms and legs. I learned to keep to myself, and I became more isolated. Clearly I didn't belong, and my heart felt old and troubled.

The joy of going to school in the morning would often begin to fade around 10:00 o'clock, the time of the first recess. Weather permitting, we would dutifully file out of the classroom into the schoolyard. After ten minutes, a shrill whistle announced the end of freedom. Silently we lined up again and marched back to our desks, automatically assuming the expected demeanor, sitting in silence, our hands clasped in front of us. The teacher stood in front of the blackboard until all fidgeting had ceased. Only then would she ask, "Who has brought five cents for milk and graham crackers today?" Immediately the hands of the blessed and fortunate went up. Convinced that I was the only one whose hand was not raised, I would look around stealthily, trying not to call attention to myself. Never mind that others would go without milk and graham crackers that morning; I was convinced that the brand of poverty was on my forehead for all to see. The teacher called on worthier children to come forward with their money. They returned to their seats with their precious prize. In a matter of minutes, the classroom was filled with the sweet fragrance of graham crackers and sound of milk being sipped or slurped, filling my ears. I would tell myself I didn't like graham crackers anyway. Maybe the milk was even sour today. But my mouth watered, and my eyes filled with tears that had to be held back. I tensed my body and held my breath until I regained my composure, while the sounds of my rumbling stomach seemed to fill the room to betray me. To cry in public and be pitied was the ultimate humiliation. Being cast aside or overlooked was punishment enough. Tears would only invite more bullying from heartless classmates who were always on the search for victims.

At the end of this privileged respite, all evidence of my torture was collected and disposed of. By then my palms were moist, and I was light-headed and dizzy from lack of oxygen. The silent taunting was over for that day, but it was repeated daily for years. In all that time Mama was seldom able to surprise me with a nickel or five pennies before I left for school; nor did I ever ask her for the money. On those rare days when a nickel was pressed into my hand, my heart would start racing with anticipation for the delicacy that awaited me. By the time I got to school, my palm would bear an exact imprint of the coin where I had gripped it fiercely. On those mornings my hand would be the first one raised when the teacher asked for evidence of solvency. Now I was one of the entitled. I didn't even notice the silence of despondent children who had to watch while this time I sipped the milk. I nibbled at the sweet graham crackers, hoping to make them last. This required a lot of skill, for whatever was not eaten during the ten-minute break was collected and discarded. You were not allowed to keep the crackers. Sometimes I would try to escape the teacher's piercing eyes and hide the remaining sweet morsels in my desk. If I was successful in this daring defiance, I could eat the crackers slowly on the way home at lunchtime. Then I would hold the cracker in my mouth, sucking on it like candy, until it melted. But if the teacher discovered my crime, I would have to stand in front of the class in silence for as long as an hour, while she scolded, threatened, and embarrassed me. Once again I would clench my hands and hold my breath, filled with anxiety and shame.

Fortunately, the blessing of a child's short-term memory helped to cloud and erase the imprints of these experiences. Being called upon in class to read a favorite story and doing it flawlessly contented me far more than any recess treat. My stomach would relax and a smile would take the place of clenched teeth when the teacher acknowledged my recital with "Well done!" No one could take that away from me. Over the years I hoarded such memories, creating a boundless treasure chest to which I often returned for more nourishment than graham crackers and milk ever could supply.

The Christmas Stocking

At age seven I expected to have more friends in school because I could speak English. I would no longer have to worry about being rejected by the other children who always seemed to be having so much fun. Mama didn't want me to play with them, because they were not Jewish. I could not afford to disobey Mama, but I did want to be like the laughing children. Why was it wrong for Jewish children to have fun in school? I never got an answer to that question. I became timid, shy, and lonelier as time went on. School was so different from home. I had to learn how to keep the two separate and remember what was expected of me in these opposite worlds. At home we did not speak English, only Yiddish. In school I was not allowed to speak Yiddish, only English. Sometimes I got mixed up in school, and the teacher did not like that. Early attempts to get Mama to help with my homework only separated my two worlds further. Mama could not read. I was too shy to ask the teacher for help for fear she would call me stupid. I learned not to tell Mama what went on in school because it often upset her. So I kept secrets but felt guilty.

In my Jewish neighborhood there were also Italian families, Polish families, and even an Irish family. Mama would remind me I was not to go to their homes, and those children were never allowed to come to my home. Sometimes I forgot. Mama would come looking for me if I was out of sight for too long, calling my name until I appeared. If she had interrupted an innocent game with a non-Jewish friend, or saw me coming out of her house, Mama would scold me, grab my ear, and pull me all the way home. My ear would hurt, but the embarrassment was far greater than the pain. In school, however, I would talk to these children and play with them during recess. I wanted them to like me. I wanted to be one of them.

One day I came home from school innocently singing a Thanksgiving hymn I had learned. Mama became very angry. Didn't I know that was a Christian song and Christians would try to convert me and take me to church? Terrified and puzzled, I said nothing. I did not understand Mama's fears, and anything I said would only have made matters worse. I remembered not to sing that song again. But there came a time one Christmas when my longing to be accepted into the magic circle of the celebrations became so strong that even Mama's threats were pushed aside and I dared to defy her secretly.

One cold and snowy December day, I came home from school and saw Bubbe grating potatoes for her delicious Chanukah potato *latkes* (pancakes). The menorah glistened on the dining room table. Special candles were lit each night of this joyous, eight-day holiday. My brothers and I would receive small gifts each day. Happy songs would be sung, games would be played, and we would also be given Chanukah *gelt* (money) for our very own, perhaps only four or five shiny pennies, but that was more than we got any other time. What fun. But in school there had been no mention of Chanukah. Once again I was puzzled. When I asked Bubbe about this she merely shrugged her shoulders and said it had always been that way. Her serious expression implied that she was not telling me everything.

At school the holiday activities increased as the Christmas season approached. Every day we drew pictures of Christmas trees, though I had never seen one, trimmed with colored balls and silvery strands of tinsel. The teacher read the story of the birth of Jesus and Bethlehem to us. Most of us were Jewish children of immigrant families and did not grasp the meanings of these stories. When the teacher called on me with questions about Jesus, I was mute—even when I knew the answer. I remembered Mama's warnings about the threat of conversion to Christianity and said nothing. The teacher looked at me disapprovingly and put a mark next to my name. I would blush and hang my head.

The Italian children in the class got caught up in the excitement of Christmas. They talked about special church services and prayers that sounded foreign and ominous to my ears. Their boasting about grand presents, family gatherings, and celebrations seemed to overshadow the Chanukah rituals. The teacher was not Jewish. She had formed alliances with the Italian children that clearly did not include the rest of us. I felt excluded. That familiar feeling of being left out overcame me.

As Christmas approached and the days disappeared in the early winter darkness, I began to wonder why I could not be part of this celebration after all. The teacher had told us Jesus—whoever he was—loved all children. Maybe he also loved Jewish children. The mystery of the holiday intensified when stories of Santa Claus were added, and pictures on the wall displayed a happy, jolly, bearded man in a beautiful red-and-white suit with a sack of presents on his shoulder. He did not look evil or threatening. I learned about Santa's arrival Christmas evening, and his trip down the chimney. As the children slept he silently deposited presents under the Christmas tree, to be discovered the next morning. I was fascinated and wondered how he got down the chimney. My fantasy was disturbed when I remembered we did not have a chimney, only a big, black, iron furnace in the cellar. How would Santa find me? Even as I formulated that thought I feared that Santa might not want to find me. Jewish children didn't have a Santa Claus. Besides, Mama would never permit him inside our house. He was a Christian.

In spite of my fears and doubts, a small thread of hope emerged when I learned that Santa filled up your stocking if you hung it on the mantelpiece on Christmas Eve. The first spark of a plan began to emerge. If I hung up my stocking, might I find a present from Santa on Christmas morning? With that thought I immediately felt guilty, for having broken the bond of my Jewish heritage, and fearful, for if Mama found out I certainly would be punished first by her and then by God. I remembered how angry Mama was when I proudly brought home my drawing of a decorated Christmas tree that had earned me a gold star from the teacher. I did not know why it made Mama so angry when the teacher had been so pleased.

This inner struggle tortured me every day and every night as I prepared for bed. I continued to imagine my empty stocking tied to the foot of my bed and waking to a surprise of presents—proof that Santa Claus loved Jewish children after all. But even in the fantasy that happy thought was soon destroyed by the arrival of Mama, who would discover my heathen behavior and beat me as she cried to the heavens, asking God what she had done to deserve such a child. Still the threat of such punishment didn't quell the plans I continued to formulate in my head. I was unable to control my evil thoughts, and they alternated between panic and defiance. When Christmas Eve finally did come, I realized that it was now or never.

I put off sleep as long as I could without raising suspicion, then went up to my room quietly and prepared for bed. I undressed, glad to be wearing my long underwear, which also served as pajamas, for the room was very cold. Quickly I jumped into bed and wrapped myself in the blankets, determined to stay awake until everyone else was asleep, for the deed had to be done under the cover of darkness, in absolute silence. I listened for the sound of footsteps on the stairs and for the last signs that the day had come to an end and all activity had ceased. My brothers were tucked in, Bubbe had gone to her bed, and soon even the sounds of Mama and Papa talking in their room ceased. If I listened hard enough I could make out the soft sounds of Papa's snoring. This was the moment.

I jumped out of bed, shivering when the icy night air chilled my body. I put the cold out of my mind. Stealthily

I tiptoed to the foot of the bed, the bright moonlight streaming through the window lighting my way. I found my long, white cotton stocking where I had placed it near the foot of my bed and attached it to the bedpost with some string I had saved for this moment. Making it secure, I stepped back and examined my handiwork, satisfied that the knot was tight enough to hold any packages Santa would leave during the night. By now I had convinced myself that the only reason Santa had never brought me a present was that I had never hung up my stocking. He knew there would be no place to deposit a gift, and so he had never made a stop at my house. Tonight would be different.

Trembling, I jumped back into bed, not knowing whether I shivered from the cold or the fear of being discovered by Mama. In spite of this apprehension, and my determination to stay awake and witness Santa's arrival, sleep soon quieted my thoughts. I drifted off into the silence of the night. In my dream, sounds on the roof announced Santa's arrival, but my body was leaden. I could not move. My eyes were sealed shut and remained so until the first faint rays of daylight entered my chilly room.

I awoke with a start, disappointed that I had slept through the night and missed seeing Santa Claus. The sound of my heart racing filled my ears as I leapt out of bed and approached the stocking. My hopes were high. I was convinced that Santa Claus had left a special gift for me while I slept. These hopes began to waver when, in the dim light, I discovered my limp stocking hanging where I had left it last night. Still I drew closer. Maybe the package was too big, and Santa had to place it on the floor, or under the bed, or someplace else in the room. I searched, first carefully then frantically. Finally I had to accept the inevitable; Santa had not come to my house after all. Perhaps he didn't think I deserved a present. Had I been a bad girl? Could he not find the house because we had no chimney?

My heart was broken and my hopes were crumbled. I was grateful there was no school that day because it was Christmas. I would not have to listen to the children laughing as they told of all the presents that had been stuffed into their stockings while they slept. I could no longer hold back the tears. Only after Mama called me a third time did I dry my face, dress, and slowly go downstairs to the kitchen.

My faith shattered, I never again asked questions about Christmas or hung my stocking up on Christmas Eve. I learned to accept the fact that I was different because I was Jewish, and that Jewish children were not allowed to enjoy the festivities of Christmas. They were not wanted. I felt ashamed. It was a painful, familiar feeling, and a long, long time passed before I could erase the disappointment of that Christmas day when my stocking hung empty from my bedpost.

Mrs. Marenchick
the Boarder

After months of searching desperately for work every day, only to return home at night with empty pockets, Papa realized he had to take extreme measures if the family were to survive. I knew we were in the middle of a new crisis when Papa, Mama, and Bubbe held one of their rare conferences. I could hear them speaking Russian in the kitchen late at night. I knew something serious had happened or was about to happen. Russian was the grown-ups' private language. This, however, was one time a secret could not be kept from the children, because Papa had decided to rent my room to a boarder to provide more money for food. Though this was not an uncommon practice in our poor neighborhood, it was a sign of defeat to take a stranger into your home. Mama knew it would be impossible to keep this humiliating development from Aunt Bluma's prying eyes, because it was her husband, Uncle Harry, who had first put the idea into Papa's head. Earlier he had approached Papa, encouraging him to consider renting a room to a young sewing machine operator who worked in his factory.

The tension in the house was extreme during the struggle surrounding this distasteful solution. Uncle

Harry kept pressing Papa for an answer, warning him that time was running out, and this window of opportunity would disappear if he hesitated too long. So it was with heavy hearts and yet another surrender in the battle against poverty that Mama, Papa, and Bubbe agreed to take in Mrs. Marenchick as a boarder. For the sum of five dollars a week—a fortune in those days—she was to have my room and would be provided with clean linens and breakfast and dinner. As a result, Mama and Bubbe would sink to the lowest level in the hierarchy of the Jewish ghetto because they would be cleaning up after a boarder. They would be no better than servants, an inferior position reserved for destitute, ignorant girls of ill repute.

A great frenzy of cleaning, scouring, and moving of furniture preceded the arrival of the boarder. Mama's reputation as a *balaboosta*, an impeccable housekeeper, was at stake. Mama applied herself to the distasteful tasks. The house reeked of harsh laundry soap and bleach for days. We would be clean, but it would no longer be possible for us to keep our family affairs private. There would always be a witness who might spread rumors or gossip to enemies, real or imaginary. We would have to be on guard constantly so as not to reveal family problems or secrets that could now have a direct line to Aunt Bluma.

My curiosity about the frantic activities was often squelched by Mama's angry words or by the sight of Papa's hunched shoulders that seemed to have collapsed under the weight of this latest disaster. Even Bubbe refused to answer my questions. Bubbe tried to comfort

Mama, attempting to minimize the impact of their down-fall, but Mama cried angry, bitter tears.

In spite of Mama's and Bubbe's best efforts, they were anxious for fear Mrs. Marenchick might not be satisfied with the lodgings. The only thing that was more shaming than taking in a boarder was being rejected by one. This suspenseful situation was put to a bitter test on the Sunday Uncle Harry brought Mrs. Marenchick to the house to inspect the room. At the last minute Papa was spared this disgrace. He was called to a neighbor's house to fix the plumbing. Mama was left to settle the deal. We were warned once more to be quiet and not to get in the way when Mrs. Marenchick came, to convince her that we were well-behaved children.

Mama's determination to meet the prospective boarder with an air of superiority was shattered when she opened the door and came face to face with Aunt Bluma. She had not been invited, but that never stopped her. There my aunt stood, blocking the doorway with her ample body, arms folded across her well-fed bosom. Her lipsticked cupid-bow lips wore a false smile that didn't fool Mama for a minute. Mama knew there was no way to avoid Aunt Bluma's prying eyes this time, and she was not going to add to her predicament by arguing with her while Uncle Harry and the young woman stood watch-ing. Mama stepped aside.

Mrs. Marenchick, the embodiment of a threatening stranger, was a small, thin person, whose face was almost completely hidden by a large felt hat with a veil. She wore a dark suit that buttoned at her tapered waist. She wore white gloves and carried a shiny handbag. Her shoes were not new, but they were clean and polished. A faint scent of Coty's face powder and perfumed soap floated from her as she quietly greeted us. She smelled good. It was hard to remember why this young woman had been the cause of so much frenzy and suspicion. I was immediately fascinated by her. I liked Mrs. Marenchick from the start.

I looked at Mama as she began to take this demure, unwanted person up the stairs. Mama's complexion was dark. Her face looked angry though her voice was controlled. Across the room, I could almost feel the heat from Mama's body as she tried in vain to direct Aunt Bluma away from the center of this activity. At this she failed. Aunt Bluma thoroughly enjoyed Mama's difficulty. She ignored Uncle Harry's suggestion to stay downstairs and visit with Bubbe. In fact, she was the first one up the stairs, leading the way to the bedroom that was for rent.

Mrs. Marenchick was pleased with the room. She paid five dollars rent for the first week. At that point she became part of our household. I didn't even mind having to again share a room with Bubbe, as I did when I was a baby. I was totally captivated by this slender stranger. In time we learned she was a widow, her young husband having died in the influenza epidemic. Mrs. Marenchick had no one to depend on. She was the first of her family to leave Russia and had to take a job in a factory to support herself. It was there she met Uncle Harry. This sad tale did little to ingratiate her with Mama, who resented Mrs. Marenchick from the outset, as though she was the cause of her problems instead of the solution. Also Mama was aware of Uncle Harry's admiring glances in Mrs.

Marenchick's direction and suspected that Uncle Harry and Mrs. Marenchick were more than just co-workers. Mama kept these feelings to herself, but she was immediately suspicious of this young widow who worked in a factory with so many men.

In time the house settled down to a schedule that accommodated Mrs. Marenchick. All meals were eaten in the kitchen. Usually the children were fed first, with Mama and Bubbe standing by to serve and clear the table. They never sat down during mealtime and ate whatever we left over on our plates. Papa's dinnertime was unpredictable, because he would stay out as long as possible, hoping to pick up an odd job before the day was over. He often ate last and alone. Because Mrs. Marenchick had a regular job, she would sometimes arrive early enough to have dinner with the children. When that happened, Mama was visibly annoyed, but those were my favorite times. If I could not sit next to Mrs. Marenchick, I sat facing her, where I could watch how carefully she used the silverware, cutting her food and placing small bites into her delicate little mouth. I had never seen anyone with such dainty manners. Mama, however, felt Mrs. Marenchick was putting on airs—one more reason for Mama not to like her. Did she think she was better than we were? My little brothers, too young to understand the new meal protocol, often complained when a choice morsel was served to Mrs. Marenchick. Mama and Bubbe had decided to make this sacrifice in order to hold on to our unwelcome housemate. Mrs. Marenchick only made matters worse when she offered to share her plate with the boys. It made Mama very angry.

After some timid attempts to be friendly, Mrs. Marenchick sensed that Mama did not intend to welcome her. In time she seemed to be as eager to stay out of Mama's way as Mama was to avoid her presence. However, my bashful approaches toward Mrs. Marenchick were finally rewarded. For three magical mornings I sat on the bed and watched her pat sweet-smelling face powder on her smooth, white skin, her delicate hands coaxing her curls into a neat bun held in place with a mother-of-pearl clip. She had an attractive way of standing back in the far corner of the small room so she could get a full view of herself in the bureau mirror. It was like a sweet little dance, almost as sweet as the cookie or candy she had for me each morning. I was in love.

My attachment to Mrs. Marenchick did not go unnoticed by Mama. She warned me not to bother the boarder. I was smitten and became daring enough to disobey Mama. One morning Mama was in the hallway and through the open doorway saw me gazing up at Mrs. Marenchick. To my horror, she stomped into the room and humiliated me by slapping my face. Mama ordered me not to disturb the boarder and to leave the room and never come back. Horrified, Mrs. Marenchick assured Mama that she not only didn't mind my visits but that she enjoyed having me around. I was never permitted to spend any more private time with my sweet friend after that. There were times, however, when I met Mrs. Marenchick's eyes and relished the warm, silent messages she sent me.

Mrs. Marenchick did not stay with us very long, though I am sure every day was an interminable reminder to Mama of how low she herself had fallen. Mama acted out this unjust but self-inflicted sentence with a begrudging attitude. She continued to reject this sweet young woman who was struggling to support herself under her own difficult circumstances. To Mama, Mrs. Marenchick was a cause for shame and humiliation. Another source of resentment and disappointment was the hard fact that the five dollars rent she received did little to lessen our economic tensions. The work and effort Mama and Bubbe had taken on far outweighed the expected advantages.

Mrs. Marenchick was not asked to leave, but Mama continued to treat her as an intruder. One day Mrs. Marenchick came to Mama and said she was leaving at the end of the week. Mama was relieved. Mrs. Marenchick had found a room with kitchen privileges that was closer to the factory. A friend would move in with her to help pay for the larger quarters. Our good-byes were brief. Mama saw to that. But there was a moment when Mrs. Marenchick looked at me directly, speaking to me with her eyes. We exchanged a brief, loving glance. I knew I would miss her sweet fragrance and gentle manner. I would gladly have continued to give up my room if Mrs. Marenchick had stayed, but I never saw her again. Mama and Bubbe wasted no time ridding the house of any trace of the boarder. Furniture was rearranged and I was moved back into my own room that very day.

That night Uncle Harry stopped by to find out why Mrs. Marenchick had left. I could not believe the things I heard Mama tell him. She said Mrs. Marenchick was dirty, loud, disrespectful, and interfered when Mama disciplined the children and that she could not be satisfied no matter how Mama went out of her way to please her. She complained about everything. She was a real "fancy lady" and nothing was to her liking. Mama just out-and-out lied. I knew the truth. I missed Mrs. Marenchick and felt guilty that I didn't have enough courage to defend my friend against Mama.

I missed Mrs. Marenchick for a very long time. I would think of her often before I fell asleep, in the dark silence of my room, pretending she was still there. In fact, in spite of Mama's strong laundry soap scrubbings, her sweet scent lingered long after she had gone and it greeted me when I opened up my dresser drawers. But in time the fragrance grew faint until it, too, was nowhere to be found. Even Mrs. Marenchick's face became dim in my memory. She had offered me an image of a young woman who was entirely different from Mama. Perhaps I thought it might be possible one day for me to be like Mrs. Marenchick, using silverware to delicately cut my food with graceful hands and powdering my face with Coty face powder. I never fully forgot Mrs. Marenchick.

Uncle Harry's 'Heldzle'

My Bubbe had a well-earned reputation of being a first-class Jewish culinary wizard. As a very small child, I loved sitting in the kitchen, watching her perform her magic. No matter how closely I watched, so swift and expert were her experienced hands that delicacies would flow from her work-worn fingers without disclosing their secrets. She could make something out of nothing and create a gourmet dish that would bring a rush of saliva to your mouth as soon as you walked into the house and smelled the kitchen aroma. Those were the days before weight concerns and health-consciousness ran our lives. No mercy was shown with regard to calories or cholesterol. Most Jewish dishes had a generous portion of rendered chicken fat—the Jewish housewife's flavorful staple. One such dish was stuffed chicken neck, or *heldzle*, which was prepared for the traditional Friday night meal. Before we go any further, I feel it is mandatory that a description of this delicacy be given. The archaic recipe has long since disappeared.

First, a kosher-slaughtered chicken, still warm to the touch, would be brought home from the market; that way you were sure it was absolutely fresh. If money was no object that week, the luxury of paying five cents to the chicken-plucker would eliminate the tedious, dirty task of separating the chicken from its feathers. To dispense with the fine hairs left on the chicken after it had been "undressed," Bubbe would singe the chicken over an open flame on the stove. The odor of scorched skin permeating the kitchen was a small price to pay, because the flame would also dispose of any lice that might have escaped the chicken plucker. The smooth, clean chicken was then scrutinized for any wayward pinfeathers. Bubbe made short work of them as she applied the tip of her sharp knife to the base of each offender, until it surrendered its hold on the carcass.

Bubbe was then ready to create a *heldzle*. First she would decapitate the chicken, then run her sharp knife completely around its body, several inches below the wings. Careful not to puncture or tear the skin, she would tug and pull, periodically slipping her knife beneath it to facilitate the process. In a matter of minutes, the chicken would surrender the skin on the upper half of its body, like a resistant child refusing to get undressed. Bubbe always won this contest. The opening at the neck was then sewn with strong, white thread, completely sealing that end. The larger opening in the skin, which had encircled the middle of the chicken, was stuffed with seasoned flour, grated carrots, and onions and was generously punctuated with small pieces of raw chicken fat. That opening would then be sewn, creating an eerie headless object.

Everyone loved Bubbe's stuffed *heldzle,* but Uncle Harry loved it more than anyone else and usually got first call. A story told often about Bubbe's stuffed *heldzle* never failed to bring peals of laughter, no matter how many times we heard it.

On a particular early Friday morning, before I had to be separated from the ritual of the *Shabbas* meal preparation and dragged to school, I positioned myself in the high chair, the best seat in the house, to watch my Bubbe as she performed her sorcery on the chicken. My young heart was saddened when I learned that this *heldzle* was for Uncle Harry. But even that did not totally dampen my spirits as I watched the drama with round eyes and bated breath. This chicken was a particularly plump stewing hen and surrendered a large portion of itself to my Bubbe's swift knife. She had already prepared the stuffing, which now waited to fill the *heldzle*. Now this was no small feat for to fill it too sparingly meant that the *heldzle* would be limp and lumpy. To stuff it too full might cause it to burst, spilling its contents and ruining the soup. The stuffing also had to be blended with just the right ingredients so that it would be neither too firm nor too runny as it simmered. No one could do it better than my Bubbe. Her hands would soon be covered with flour and smell of seasonings. Bubbe never took her eyes off of the task at hand, but she would keep up an endless patter of talk and always had time to answer my questions. She never missed a stroke.

The *heldzle* safely stuffed and sealed—the wings providing a precarious balance—would be eased into the large pot of chicken soup. Quickly it rose to the surface, like a headless swimmer basking in the warmth of the broth. There it would silently simmer and stew, the melting fat in the flour releasing its juicy flavor. At the right moment, Bubbe would retrieve the *heldzle,* giving it enough time to cool down. This day it was to be Uncle Harry's lunch. It was left to drain on a kitchen towel, but no period of time could render it completely fatless. Bubbe carefully wrapped the *heldzle* in a double brown paper bag and gave it to Uncle Harry to take to work that day.

Uncle Harry was a cutter in the garment industry in Philadelphia and worked in a tall building that had an elevator. With the promise of the cooked *heldzle* held in the thick paper bags, he waited in the crowded lobby for the elevator to arrive. Unbeknownst to him, the fatty drippings of his lunch had long since soaked through the bags. He was, therefore, unaware as he rushed to the open elevator, that the *heldzle* was no longer contained in its wrapping and had slipped out, landing on the marble floor outside the elevator. There it rested, perched on its wings like two extended arms, its headless body erect as if posturing for battle, like some evil alien out of the Dark Ages. Too late Uncle Harry realized his devastating loss and was helpless to retrieve the *heldzle,* for he had been pushed to the back of the elevator by the many bodies being carried to their jobs. Just before the elevator door closed he heard the collective laughter, as well as the scream of at least one woman who was confronted with this threatening, headless beast.

Risking the wrath of his boss for being late, Uncle Harry left the elevator as soon as it stopped, pushed his way through the crowd, and headed down many flights of stairs in the hope of salvaging his lunch. When he finally arrived, sweating and out of breath, he discovered

just where he had lost his *heldzle*. There was a circle of
people, three deep, talking and laughing and stopping
traffic in all directions. With some effort he pushed his
way through. There was his lunch, sitting on its wings in
silence, in a spreading ring of chicken fat. No one had
dared to touch it. Nearby, within the circle, was a poor
unsuspecting woman who had fainted dead away and
was lying on the cold marble floor, practically unnoticed.

Now a more self-conscious fellow would have quickly
turned away from this scene and feigned innocence,
denying ownership, but not Uncle Harry. He loved a
good story and a joke better than anyone else. He let out
a roar of laughter and, barely able to catch his breath, he
began to explain to the gathered crowd what had transpired here. By now the lobby was rocking with shrieks
and laughter as the witnesses repeated his words to those
around them. As a result, waves of laughter ebbed and
flowed for quite a while after the words came out of
Uncle Harry's mouth. He was in his element, the jester
holding court to an appreciative audience.

So long had this event halted all activity in this usually bustling work center that messengers had been sent
from the shops to determine why people weren't at their
assigned posts. Only threats of penalties and firings interrupted this three-ring circus. A fainter soul might have
resented being the object of everyone's laughter, but not
Uncle Harry. With some flair and expertise, he retrieved
the *heldzle*, wrapped it in his clean handkerchief and
transported it to his workbench, where carefully
placed it on a shelf well within sight, for fear it might
attempt to strut out of the factory. He was determined to

have his lunch, no matter what. But for the rest of the, day friends, acquaintances, and strangers would come up to him with a pat on his back, stimulating another burst of laughter. The story was retold over and over again, until the boss came screaming out of his cubicle and threatened to fire the lot of them.

That night Uncle Harry repeated the escape of the *heldzle* to the family, and the mirth and fun knew no limits until we were all holding our sides with pain, unable to draw another breath, tears rolling down our cheeks. No mention was ever made of the lady who fainted on the cold marble floor. I wondered what happened to her each time the story was told, and especially on Fridays when Bubbe would make *heldzle*.

Aunt Bluma's Charity

Mama, Papa, and Bubbe came from proud Russian peasant stock. Appearance was everything and had to be upheld at all costs, no matter how poor we were. They held their heads high because they accepted help from no one during the years of the Depression. If help was offered or forced upon us, it was not received gracefully, much less gratefully. Unsolicited acts of charity angered Mama and humiliated Papa. Their pride was forced upon us hungry children, as we held on to growling stomachs, reminding us of a shame we did not understand.

In Philadelphia we lived in a small rented row house at 2555 Stanley Street. Uncle Harry and Aunt Bluma lived down the street at 2537. Although we were neighbors, our families were divided by extreme economic differences. My Papa was a laborer and often out of work. Uncle Harry, on the other hand, held an enviable position as a cutter in the garment district. Because the production of the factory, its reputation, and its profits were dependent upon the skills of the cutters, Uncle Harry enjoyed steady employment. As visible evidence of his success, Uncle Harry always had a Chevrolet with a rumble seat, and on rare occasions he would treat us to a ride in this luxurious vehicle. It had leather seats, little crystal vases with artificial flowers placed next to porthole windows on either side of the back seat, and lots of chrome trimming. Often I would watch from half-drawn shades as Uncle Harry and Aunt Bluma drove down the street. I craned my neck until they were out of sight. Whenever Mama caught me in such clandestine behavior, she would furiously drag me away by my ear and lower the blind.

Of course, Aunt Bluma thoroughly enjoyed her position of wealth and superiority. She often attempted to force charity upon us: dried up boxes of cocoa or sugar, sticky dried fruit or other staples, which were stale or no longer of good enough quality for her to use. She did not fool Mama with her false generosity. When Mama saw Aunt Bluma coming down the street with one of her packages, she would quickly draw the blinds, lock the door, and order us to be quiet. I knew better than to disobey Mama at such times. I understood even then Mama did not want to be trapped in her own home, defeated by Aunt Bluma's charity. Not easily daunted, Aunt Bluma would huff and puff on her fat ankles, balancing the package of her latest benevolence, as she attacked our front door with her fleshy fist. She was usually met with silence, which only encouraged her to attack with greater purpose, calling to Mama and Bubbe to open the door. She knew we were in the house. We did not stir. More determined than ever, Aunt Bluma would place her offering on the steps and approach the house from the rear, battering the back door. Her voice would get louder and louder. The more frustrated she became, the more she demanded to be let in the house.

In spite of Aunt Bluma's determination, Mama succeeded more often than not in keeping her from forceful entry. There were times, however, when she was caught by surprise. Then she had to swallow the bitter pill, gagging and stuttering the insincere words of gratitude that she forced from her lips. For the three of us hungry children, this feud was totally confusing and unreasonable. It seemed grossly unfair that we would have to do without cocoa because Mama could not accept Aunt Bluma's gift. One such event stands out in my memory even today, decades later.

Mama must have gone out to do whatever little grocery shopping she could afford or, more likely, to plead with the butcher to give her credit one more time. As usual we were left in Bubbe's care with the familiar warnings not to get into any kind of mischief. I sat outside on the front steps, watching my brothers play a stupid, endless game of tag. They saw Aunt Bluma first, coming down the street with a large shopping bag. Forgetting Mama's warning, both of them immediately ran toward her in anticipation of a treat. I was horrified, knowing full well this was one of Aunt Bluma's relentless charity missions. Mama would be very angry. I called to my brothers who couldn't possibly hear me above their loud laughter and greetings. I ran to Bubbe to warn her of the impending invasion. I pleaded with her to lock the doors. It was too late.

Bubbe was totally powerless in the face of this ambush. She tried to calm me, then went to the front door to greet Aunt Bluma and attempt to block her entrance. Aunt Bluma arrived flushed with victory, as my brothers escorted her into our little house, left unguarded by

Mama. I kept an eye out for Mama, hoping we could at least escape what seemed like an inevitable confrontation between two mortal enemies. Still oblivious to the danger, my brothers attacked the shopping bag. Out poured its treasures—old boxes of cocoa and sugar, crumbled crackers, an open box of oatmeal, a sticky jar of honey, and some spearmint gum. Aunt Bluma endowed chewing gum with mysterious healing and nutritional qualities. She was never without a stick of it in her mouth.

Aunt Bluma brushed Bubbe aside as she opened cupboards and closet doors, sniffing at our poverty. All the time she was openly criticizing Mama and Papa for not providing food for the children. The tension increased as I darted back and forth to the front door, looking for Mama, hoping to warn her of Aunt Bluma's assault. Aunt Bluma in the meantime became bolder by the minute. She was about to go upstairs to the bedrooms to continue her inspection when I saw Mama coming up the street, struggling with two bags of groceries.

I let out a cry for all to hear, stopping Aunt Bluma in her tracks. Even my brothers quieted down as Bubbe went to the front door to warn Mama that Aunt Bluma had managed to enter our house before anyone could stop her. Mama's face turned beet red, sending shudders down my spine, for I knew what that look meant. Her anger was sure to explode, and there would be hell to pay. Someone would be blamed for this vile intrusion. I hid behind Bubbe, attempting to escape Mama's wrath. This time Mama was not looking for me. Her fierce attention was aimed at Aunt Bluma, who balked when she saw Mama's rage.

Mama was faced with two equally objectionable choices: to bodily throw Aunt Bluma out of the house, thereby severing relations with her only brother, or to feign gratitude for her enemy's generosity. She chose the latter. Skillfully she led Aunt Bluma out the front door, attempting to thank Aunt Bluma through clenched teeth. Caught totally off guard, Aunt Bluma was soon outside, the empty shopping bag in her hand where Mama had placed it, her mouth open, breathing heavily. However, she regained her superior posture quickly. She straightened her back and shoulders as she walked to her house. She could not wait to tell Uncle Harry how his ungrateful sister had thrown her out when she brought cocoa for the hungry children.

In the meantime, Mama lost no time in attacking Bubbe, blaming her for allowing this humiliation. She screamed accusations, drowning out the feeble attempts Bubbe made to explain or defend herself. Afraid that I would be attacked also, I had moved away from Bubbe, attempting to hide behind the kitchen table. My brothers had long since left the room, no longer interested in the drama.

It seemed like an eternity before Mama's temper was spent. Then she gathered up the dried cocoa and sugar; the sticky honey, which had made a mess all over the table; and the oatmeal, crackers, and chewing gum and threw them out. Having purged the house of this attempted hostile takeover, she sank down on the kitchen floor and cried. She appealed to God not to punish her any further than she had already been punished and asked for strength to bear this latest disgrace. She even let

Bubbe comfort her. The two women vowed never to let their guard down. They must be ever vigilant against Aunt Bluma's attacks of charity and never, never let her in the house again, under any circumstances. I had not ever seen Mama so defeated. I was relieved when the storm was over, but I could not help but feel disappointed, for there would be no hot cocoa for breakfast. I did not dare look at Mama, fearing she would read my thoughts.

In time Mama regained her composure. The tension that had been so palpable disappeared as though it had joined the rejected charity in the garbage can. Then and only then were my brothers and I instructed one more time to never, ever greet Aunt Bluma or let her come into the house when Mama was not there. I took in the full impact of those instructions. Silently I vowed to be even more cautious and take more responsibility for keeping my brothers out of such mischief. As terrifying as this event had been, I had somehow escaped Mama's wrath. Perhaps I was spared by the tears of helplessness that washed over Mama after her rage had been spent.

I had never seen Mama cry like that before. The sight of those tears confused me. How could Mama be omnipotent and helpless at the same time? It was a question that plagued me for many years. Also, why was it wrong to accept charity when we were so hungry?

The Geysiner Ball

Carefree events were scarce in our home, considering the economic austerity of the 1920s and 30s. The somber drudgery of our daily existence was interrupted only by annual holiday events and rituals, when we were allowed to be relaxed and playful. Only one other time during the year did Mama and Papa dress up and leave the house, as if they were going to attend services at the Temple. This was not for any religious service, however. This outing heralded the Geysiner Ball, an annual dance and get-together for all the immigrants who had come from Geysin, the area in Russia where my parents had been raised and where my father's family still lived. Not only was it an occasion for old friends to meet, dance to live Russian music, drink homemade wines, and nosh on Jewish treats, but it was a nostalgic spectacle where the displaced people from Russia could reconnect with relatives and friends from their homeland. Gossip was exchanged; births, deaths and weddings were reported, as well as information about the arrivals and departures of an endless flow of humanity from Eastern Europe to America. It was also an opportunity to display new riches, if only for the evening—riches that often belied the hardships these greenhorns endured every day.

Somehow, no matter how poor we were, Papa always

found a way to provide Mama with a new dress for the ball. His wife was not going to wear last year's dress. Here every man was a rich man in America, his wife or sweetheart decked out in a colorful evening gown, no matter that old patent leather shoes squeaked and pinched with every step, so that calluses and bunions were inflamed by the end of the evening. Mama, too, had her reasons for being so extravagant. She had her pride and did not want to advertise our desperate poverty. Besides, she had to compete with Aunt Bluma, who would not only be decked out in a new gown, but would be wearing jewelry and even perfume.

Long before I was old enough to understand what all the excitement was about, I would get caught up in the preparations and all the tumult as the date of the ball approached, longing to go with Mama and Papa as they walked down the front steps, arm in arm. Mama would carefully press Papa's only suit, placing a cloth between the worn, shiny fabric and the hot iron. She would wash and starch his white shirt and watch as he changed from hard-working Papa to her well-dressed, handsome escort to the Geysiner Ball.

Mama would be in a long dress, her hair painstakingly arranged in flat, tight waves above her ears. She would walk stiffly in the hard, patent leather shoes that pressed on every nerve of her poor, tired feet. But the night of the ball she could be a Cinderella, transformed from her humble position to that of a princess. Later I would see the dress hanging from a hook in the one clothes closet we had for the whole family, where it joined other dresses from other years, shapeless, dis-

carded, limp markers of dances long since past and forgotten. When I was about seven, I begged and begged
Mama to let me go to the ball, for surely I was old
enough. Finally, worn down by my tears and pleading,
Mama consented. My heart expanded with excitement,
and it was all I could do to allow myself to sleep at night
as the days slowly approached this magical event. Mama
even let me accept the silk dress Aunt Bluma made for
me for the occasion. Aunt Bluma was a skillful seamstress. Her embroidery and smocking could transform
any simple pattern into a festive party dress. At least I
would not be an additional financial burden on Papa; he
would not have been able to afford a new dress for me,
too. When I tried on the dress, however, and squeezed
into my old patent leather shoes left over from Passover,
my heart sank because the shoes were badly scuffed, as if
to sadistically remind me how poor we were. Everyone
would know I was an imposter no matter how pretty my
dress was and how hard I could try to hide my torn
shoes. Those old shoes took the joy out of my new dress
until Bubbe came to the rescue. She applied black polish
to the scuffed areas and then gave the shoes a professional shine with Vaseline, which made the patent
leather sparkle and come to life once more. My happiness
was complete.

As the date of the ball approached, Mama's mood
changed. She became happy and spent at least an hour of
every day dancing with me and even taught me some new
steps. In short order I considered myself an accomplished
dancer and in turn attempted to teach my little brothers
some of the steps, leading them around and around the

room to the music played on the Victrola, lifting them off the floor when they stumbled so as not to miss a beat.

Mama and Bubbe laughed and clapped their hands, and I did not stop until I was thoroughly dizzy and out of breath, collapsing with my brothers into a giggling heap on the floor. In spite of such carefree hours, however, I was always on the lookout for a scowl or a sharp word from Mama, fearing she would find some reason to change her mind and not allow me to go to the ball.

I did everything I could to please Mama, even eating all the food on my plate though my small stomach rebelled. I stood perfectly still every day when Mama pulled my hair as she curled it around her fingers. I didn't protest when she made me wear a jacket, though the weather was mild. I watched my baby brother for hours, in the hopes she would find no reason not to let me go. Miracle of miracles, she did not change her mind.

Finally, the day of the ball arrived. Bubbe put the boys to bed early so that she could bathe and dress me for my first ball. After I was sparkling clean and smelled of talcum powder, Bubbe slipped the beautiful red, silk embroidered dress over my head, carefully settling it on my bony shoulders so that the folds of the dress would hang evenly. Then she gently curled my freshly washed hair. Aunt Bluma had also made a big red ribbon for my hair, and Bubbe tied it into place. There was even a pair of white silky socks to go with the polished patent leather shoes.

Bubbe stood me up on a chair so I could see myself in the dresser mirror. There I was, my cheeks pink, my mouth grinning with happiness, and my eyes not believing the lovely child I saw looking back at me from the mirror. I was ready to leave that moment but had to continue being on my best behavior. Mama was still getting dressed.

I tried not to get in her way but couldn't help peeking at her as she struggled, pushing her ample body into a laced corset and attaching wrinkled rayon hose to the garters. Visibly perspiring and out of breath, she had to pull the new gown over her head without disturbing her carefully combed hair. She winced as she forced her feet into her tight shoes, walking gingerly to avoid the pain.

The last touch to Mama's costume was Bubbe's pearls, adding an air of wealth and substance. Finally, we were ready. Papa, starched, ironed, and smelling of sweet after-shave lotion; Mama combed, powdered, and decked out in a new ball gown; and myself, feeling like a fairy-tale princess. Even the long ride to the ballroom on the smelly street car did not lessen the magic of this joyous event. We were quite a sight in our festive glory, escapees from the drabness of home.

It was a short walk from the street car to the hall. We were soon joined by other people who were laughing, talking, and shouting greetings to one another on the way to the Geysiner Ball. I was happily sandwiched between Mama and Papa, holding on to their hands so as not to get separated in the crowd. I had never seen so many people in one place. There were other children there, already running, laughing, and teasing each other, but I hung back, holding on to Papa's hand.

Papa led me over to a long table that was covered with mounds of food. He began to feed me delicious treats. Proudly he introduced me to people and bragged about what a good dancer I was. I hung my head in shyness, but my heart was beating with excitement, impatient for the music to begin. I had never seen or heard live music. The whole evening was filled with one magical surprise after the other, until I felt quite light-headed.

After what seemed like an endless time, the musicians were in place and the first waltz was played. I sat alone, not daring to make eye contact with anyone as Mama and Papa joined the other dancers on the floor. In spite of her weight, Mama was immediately transformed into a light-stepping dancer and looked so very graceful on Papa's arm as he twirled her around the room. Not once did they bump into any of the other dancers on the crowded dance floor. I kept time with the music by tapping my feet and imagining that I was dancing. I wanted to go out there so desperately, but my bashfulness held me back, until Papa came to get me.

Mama was happily engaged, chatting with an old friend as Papa led me across the floor. I placed my left hand as close to his shoulder as I could reach—he was very tall—and my small right hand disappeared into his strong grasp. Gracefully and skillfully I followed him around the floor. Gone was my shyness and lack of confidence. I was dancing with my Papa, and all the world was watching me. My red silk dress whirled around my legs and my shiny black shoes gleamed with each step I took. I never stumbled once, and noticed Mama smiling at us as we danced by.

If only the music would go on forever and this feeling of joy and freedom would never end. It did, of course, and not a moment too soon, for I had begun to feel tired and the late hour made my head feel heavy and limp. I did not protest when Mama and Papa said it was time to leave. I waited until we were out of sight of the hall before I would let Papa pick me up and carry me. I didn't have to be a big girl any more. I was a tired, sleepy, little girl, resting my head on my Papa's shoulder, his rough jacket against my cheek, my body rocking gently with his gait as I slept.

I did not remember being undressed or being put to bed as I snuggled under the covers and began to dream even before my eyes shut. In the dream I was once again dancing to the Russian waltz, but this time I was quite grown, tall, slender and dressed in an elegant flowing gown that trailed behind me as I was held in the embrace of a tall, young prince who had eyes only for me. This time I did not get tired or sleepy. This time the dance went on forever.

Papa Sells Produce

The Depression years were difficult for all of us, but they took a double toll on Papa because he was the sole support of his five dependents. Papa was a gentle, soft-spoken man who carried his burdens without complaint, but he could not always hide the defeated slope of his shoulders on those days when he returned home to his hungry family empty handed. He could and would do anything to feed us. He was a plumber, a mechanic, a carpenter, a painter—a real jack-of-all-trades. No job was too small or too difficult. No matter how dismal the future looked, he would leave the house every day before sunrise with a heavy bag of tools on his shoulder and filled with hope. Maybe today would be his lucky day.

I always knew when Papa had been successful. On those days he would walk up the street and enter the house through the front door. His step was light and he would whistle softly to himself. On days when he found no work, his step was as heavy as the tools he carried. His head was down, his back hunched, and he was too ashamed to walk down the street. On such days he would take the alley route, delaying the moment when he would have to meet the expectancy and then disappointment in our eyes. When that happened, Papa, Mama, and Bubbe would exchange a silent glance. We dared hope that this day he had earned some money and Mama could go shopping and even buy a chicken. Somehow, despite the almost daily grim scenario, Papa always faced the next day with a plan, or some scheme that might put food on the table.

One summer day Papa and Uncle Jake, Mama's half brother, decided to rent a horse and wagon and peddle produce to the neighborhood housewives. Uncle Jake was not creative enough to have planned such an enterprise. He was a powerless and beaten man with six children and an invalid wife, Tessie, with a sharp tongue. The whole thing was my Papa's idea, and out of kindness he included Uncle Jake in his plan.

Neither Papa nor Uncle Jake had ever sold produce or driven a horse and wagon. But desperate times called for desperate measures. I'll never know how they worked out the logistics of this enterprise, for while I had seen many horses pulling wagons when I was growing up, I had never seen any stables. Where would they find a horse and wagon? The only produce I had seen was at the small greengrocer down the street. Where the produce came from, I had no idea.

After days of planning, organizing, and somehow scraping together the few dollars it would take to launch this venture, Papa and Uncle Jake went off early one morning, before sunrise, while everyone was still asleep. Later, when my brothers and I were playing outdoors in front of the house, I saw a horse and wagon slowly making its way up the street. This was not an uncommon sight, so I paid little attention to it until I recognized Papa's low whistle. There he was, holding the reins, sitting high up on the wagon, already stocked with produce. Uncle Jake sat beside him and they were laughing and joking and calling out to Mama and Bubbe, who both came running out of the house. I had not seen such merriment in a long, long time. My brothers and I quickly became caught up in this celebratory scene. Papa reached down, pulled me up onto his lap, and gave me the reins. The excitement was almost more than I could take in and totally obliterated the hungry feeling in my stomach.

The horse was a pretty sorry specimen and looked like a Depression horse: swaybacked, just enough skin to hold its bones together, its head lowered in total resignation to the heavy day's work ahead of him. Even when Papa put a feed bag on his head, the horse began to eat with slow, sad, chewing sounds, as if he thought it might be his last meal.

Papa and Uncle Jake had stopped by so Mama could tell them how much to charge for their merchandise. She was the shopper for the family and had knowledge of such things. While this collaboration was going on, a small crowd of neighborhood children had gathered. I could see their envious expressions as they looked at me holding the reins on the wagon, making clucking sounds with my tongue, pretending to guide the indifferent horse. I felt very smug and superior. The horse was not impressed, however, and never even turned his head. He just kept on stamping his hooves and swishing his tail to brush off the annoying stream of flies that had begun to circle over his head and attack his hindquarters. He just kept on chewing.

The warm summer morning promised a hot afternoon,

and the new business partners were eager to get started on their campaign. Mama gave them one last piece of advice, directing them to the other side of town and a better neighborhood that might increase the possibility of their success. I was handed down from the wagon to Bubbe's waiting arms. I began to cry. I was starting to feel part of this adventure and had thought I would be accompanying Papa and Uncle Jake. I had even begun to compose a script in my head, one that took me to far-away places, sitting on my Papa's lap like a princess in a caravan.

With much propriety and authority, Papa removed the feed bag from the horse's head, gave me a kiss, and dried my tears. He swung himself up onto the wagon again, promising to return with an empty wagon and full pockets at the end of the day. I was so impressed with his agility that I stopped crying and watched open-mouthed as he pulled back on the reins. I was convinced Papa really could do anything he set his mind to, even drive a horse and wagon to places no one had ever seen before.

The horse, which up until now had been unresponsive, suddenly came alive and began to turn around, pulling the wagon, my Papa and Uncle Jake up the street. Soon they were out of sight. I wondered how long it would be before they returned. In an attempt to maintain my exalted position in the eyes of the neighborhood kids, I turned toward them and told them the next time my Papa had promised to take me with him, and I would be directing the horse.

The summer sun continued its journey across the cloudless sky and soon the warmth changed to heat.

Someone opened up the fire hydrant in front of our house. My brothers and I pleaded with Mama to allow us to cool off in the spraying water. Mama gave in easily this time. It was too hot to argue. No one could afford bathing suits, so we stripped down to our underwear. We joined the other children, running in and out of the water, laughing and squealing with delight at this rare and refreshing treat. The hours passed and in the delight of the children, the horse and wagon were forgotten.

It was four o'clock in the afternoon. Papa had been gone for hours. Suppertime was approaching and Bubbe was using the last meager ingredients in the house for a pot of soup. The soup would be thin and meatless that night, but Bubbe could make anything taste good, and the smells in the kitchen taunted my appetite. I heard Mama and Bubbe planning meals for the next few days. The fact that Papa was not back yet suggested that he was busily selling produce. At that point my brother Himey came running into the house, announcing Papa's return. Joyously, we all ran out to greet him. Mama instantly sized up the situation when she saw Papa and the wagon. She stopped us dead in our tracks. This was no time for laughter or celebration. Papa and Uncle Jake looked as dejected and depressed as the horse. They had been gone all day, but the wagon was still stocked with fruit and vegetables, now wilted and picked over. Papa was not smiling or whistling, and Uncle Jake was not joking as they wearily climbed down from the wagon. Uncle Jake put the feed bag on the horse once more, but the exhausted animal tossed his head and threw it to the ground. The horse was hot, worn out, and just wanted to be set free. He lowered his head and began to fall asleep. He would wait. He was used to waiting.

Slowly the story was told—how many miles they had covered, how the housewives quickly found fault with the quality of the produce, pinching and squeezing the tomatoes until they were soft and bruised, and picking through the grapes and peaches, making a mess of the orderly display Papa and Uncle Jake had arranged. Many would bargain, and leave if they did not get a deal on such worn and weary produce. After hours of such discouraging attempts, Papa and Uncle Jake decided to make their way home—hot, exhausted, and defeated.

I was mortified, afraid that now the neighborhood kids would tease me about how my Papa couldn't do everything after all. Why, he couldn't even sell produce! My sinking feeling doubled when I looked into my Papa's sad eyes. I could see his defeat, and my heart went out to him. But I was also ashamed—ashamed of being hungry, ashamed of having hopes dashed, and ashamed of being poor. I was afraid it would always be like this. The grown-ups all went into the house. My brothers and I followed in silence.

Bubbe, always the optimist, accepted her thwarted expectations and began to gather the wilted bounty from the wagon. The whole time she talked out loud to herself, planning rich vegetable soup and fruit compote swimming in clear juices, *kreplach* filled with mashed potatoes, cherry *knishes,* and plum jam. The list seemed endless. My mood lifted and my fantasies revived.

Considering the volume of produce on the wagon, it became apparent to Bubbe that we would not be able to consume everything. This produce had long since passed its bloom. We had only a small icebox, and today there had been no money to buy the usual five-cent block of ice. But Bubbe refused to be daunted. She selected the best of the lot and told us to tell the neighbors they could help themselves to whatever was left on the wagon. Once again I felt like a proud princess as I delivered the message to the neighbors, my brothers and I running from house to house. Women and children came out of their houses with pots and sacks, quickly emptying the wagon. I felt restored.

Meanwhile, at home Mama and Bubbe were busy washing, cleaning, peeling, chopping, and slicing. Huge pots of water were boiling on the stove. This is where my Bubbe reigned with complete authority. She was not just a boarder in her daughter's house. She was a source of great knowledge and skill. Bubbe could turn a lowly beet into savory borscht and wrinkled plums into delicious jams to delight us for many days to come.

Even Papa and Uncle Jake cheered up and began to see the bright side of things and the humor of their dilemma. They started swapping stories of their day's journey as they dined on the soup, filled with a medley of vegetables that could melt all negative feelings. When bellies were full, Papa and Uncle Jake prepared to take the horse and wagon back to the stable. Uncle Jake carried a large sack of produce for his family, and Bubbe had given him a pot of cold borscht for their dinner. Maybe Aunt Tessie would sweeten up if she had something good to eat and the children were not hungry.

It had been a long, hot day, but at least we were not

hungry anymore and there was enough food for several days. Papa would be back soon, probably ready with another plan for tomorrow. But something told me he might not risk being a produce merchant again. I fell asleep that night riding a big, white horse with a thick, flowing mane and bright eyes that glistened in the sunshine. In my dream I heard my Papa's soft whistle calling me home, and I smiled, as any princess would.

Bubbe's Pearls

My Bubbe was poor all her life. From the day she was born in 1877, in a small Russian Jewish *shtetl,* to the day she died at age 72 in Brooklyn, she scarcely ever had more than one or two changes of clothing. When Bubbe smuggled herself and her family out of Russia one cold November night in 1921, there was little time to gather their meager belongings, thus simplifying decisions of what to take and what to leave behind. It was safer to travel light. You never knew when military search parties would be on the prowl for illegal Jewish immigrants. You had to be ready to run, crawl, climb, or dig your way into a hillside for shelter—anywhere to hide from the murderous Red Army soldiers. Punishment was swift and they took no prisoners.

There were two priceless possessions Bubbe would not leave behind: her strand of pearls and her two silver candlesticks that held the *Shabbas* candles every Friday night. Both had been given to her when she married my grandfather, my Zada, designating her a proper wife and *balaboosta.* She could not leave Russia without these treasures.

The candlesticks were placed deep in the pockets of her worn winter coat, the pearls wrapped in a soft cloth and hidden under her clothing. Throughout the hardships of the long passage to America, Bubbe was never separated from the pearls or the candlesticks. They were her status symbols. When Bubbe wore her pearls as she lit the candles and repeated the ancient, sacred words of the *Shabbas* benediction, she was no longer a poor, humble peasant woman. In the eyes of God she was a woman of stature, to be respected and honored.

Bubbe was only forty-two when she arrived in America, but looked much older. Her prematurely gray hair was pulled back in a dignified, tight bun. She was painfully conscious of her gray hair. When she discovered a hair-coloring lotion at the local drugstore, she applied it secretly. It was the only cosmetic I ever knew her to use. She must have saved her pennies for weeks, exchanging the precious coins for another bottle of this magic potion. Such frivolous expenditures had little priority compared to the need to fill the hungry bellies of the family or pay the rent on time. Those were the days when heartless landlords ordered the sheriff to throw families out on the street, without warning, even in the dead of winter, if the rent was late. This was a common occurrence during the Depression years, and I will never know how we escaped that humiliation.

No matter how strapped for money, Bubbe washed and starched her limited wardrobe, ironing it to perfection. She was always neat and clean. Although her apron had been patched and mended many times, it was always spotless in spite of her hours in the kitchen every single day. After all, she was a *balaboosta*, a wise and accomplished homemaker, even in the new land and even though she had no home of her own.

As a child, knowing little of Bubbe's poignant history, I sensed the importance of the pearls and the candlesticks. With the *Shabbas* meal simmering on the stove, the table set, and the candles in place, Bubbe would wash herself, comb her hair into the tight, decorous bun, and put on her dark *Shabbas* dress. She would retrieve the pearls from their resting place in the drawer where they were wrapped in a small piece of fine fabric. They were the last touch she applied to her *Shabbas* outfit. Only then was she elevated to a proper woman of means.

Despite Bubbe's heedful care, the strand would break at times, the pearls falling and scattering in all directions. Bubbe would let out a horrified cry as she tried to catch the beads in her thick, work-worn hands before they rolled out of sight. Inevitably, some pearls were lost forever even though the whole family crawled on the floor, scrambling to find them. If this happened on a Friday night, the search would be delayed because the candles must be lit before darkness ushered in the day of rest, and all activity ceased.

On such occasions Bubbe would be inconsolable. Her head would ache and she would apply a wet compress to her throbbing temples, refusing to eat or to be comforted. She would take to her bed, appealing to God with rhetorical questions. What had she done to deserve such a fate? What if the pearls could not be found? What if she never owned a strand of pearls again? She would have to hang her head in shame on Friday nights. Perhaps she could sew a dress with a high collar, covering the bareness of her throat. But the pearls were irreplaceable, marked with years of joyous events as well as painful sacrifices. They carried Bubbe's history. Even if the pearls could be replaced, it would never be the same for her.

Somehow over the years, enough of the pearls were salvaged after each disaster to save my Bubbe from her worst fears. She never did sink so low as to be a *balaboosta* without pearls. Bubbe was an expert at restringing her necklace. As she got older, however, her eyesight began to fail, and there was no money to fit her with eyeglasses. It became my task, as the oldest grand-child and the only girl, to assist Bubbe whenever she pre-pared to restring her pearls. I did not complain. These were treasured times for me, private female times with my Bubbe, away from the noise and boisterous games of my brothers, and away from Mama's verbal and physical attacks. Bubbe whispered her private thoughts to me and we shared many secrets while exchanging knowing glances.

Sitting close to Bubbe, I watched as she cautiously opened the fabric cloth sack that held a scramble of loose beads that threatened to drop to the floor as soon as they were released from the tight package. Bubbe lined the pearls up in a dish. Then I was called upon to thread the needle and hand her one pearl at a time, so Bubbe could add each to the new strand. She would squint and hunch over. I could hear her deep breaths of concentration with each pass of the needle. Only when she had successfully added a pearl to the strand did she let out a sigh of relief, straighten her back for a moment, and rub her tired eyes. That was a sign for me to pick up the next bead in line, to transfer it from my small hand to her large, stiff fin-gers. That in itself was a challenge. Often, in spite of my best efforts, one more pearl escaped. Instantly, I catapulted into furious action, determined that my Bubbe would not lose another single pearl.

When such a catastrophe occurred, I could not bear to see the pain in her eyes. But it quickly turned to relief when I found the bead and handed it to her. There were times, unfortunately, when a pearl would disappear. I would search and search, creeping under the kitchen furniture, close to tears. At the sight of my anxious face, Bubbe would resign herself to one more loss and find the strength to comfort me, though she herself was inconsolable. What couldn't be helped had to be accepted. When all the pearls were strung, Bubbe would have to meet one more challenge—that of attaching the fine silver clasp to the strand—to lock the pearls in place. This required even greater dexterity. Finally, the pearls were delicately rewrapped, ready for the next *Shabbas*.

Stringing the pearls was a very serious task, requiring intense focus. It was the one time Bubbe did not talk to me or tell stories. Nor did I distract her with an endless stream of questions. Every ounce of our energy and concentration had to be invested in this solemn undertaking. Only upon its completion would she turn her smiling gaze on me, praise me for my assistance. Often, I would be rewarded with a treat she had especially saved for me. Relaxed again, she would repeat the stories about the pearls. How happy and proud she had been when they were given to her on her wedding day, how she had always worn them every Friday night since then, how she had smuggled them out of Russia. One day they would be given to my mother and in turn they would be passed on to me. Actually they never were. Over the years, all the pearls finally rolled out of reach and were lost. But the happiness I felt each time I helped Bubbe string her pearls transformed the pain and loneliness of my childhood. Those hours created a timeless space that was our very own, as precious as the pearls.

Photographs

Passport certificate, 1921, *(left to right)*
Aunt Bluma, Bubbe, and Mama.

Passport certificate, 1921, Uncle Harry.

Transmigrant certificate, medical examination card, and inspection card *(opposite),* on White Star Line, 1921.

Contract Ticket No. *73863*

INSPECTION CARD.
(Immigrants and Steerage Passengers.)

Port of Departure, LIVERPOOL,   Date of Departure,

Name of Ship "CEDRIC."   Nov. 12th 1921

Name of Immigrant *London Gidea*

Last Residence *Russia*

Inspected and passed at

	Passed at Quarantine, port of	Passed by Immigration Bureau,
	U.S. port of	
	5	NOV 22 1921
	(Date.)	(Date.)

(The following to be filled in by ship's surgeon or agent prior to or after embarkation.)

Ship's list or manifest, ... No. on ship's list or manifest, ... 27

Berth No.	Steamship Inspection	1st day	2	3	4	5	6	7	8	9	10	11	12	13	14	To be punched by ship's surgeon at daily inspection

---

Keep this Card to avoid detention at Quarantine and on Railroads in the United States.

Behåll detta kort for att förekomma dröjsmal vid Karantän-stationen och på Jernvägarna i Förenta Staterna.

Diese Karte muss aufbewahrt werden, um Aufenthalt an der Quarantäne, sowie auf den Eisenbahnen der Vereinigten Staaten zu vermeiden.

Cette carte doit être conservée pour éviter une détention à la Quarantaine, ainsi que sur les chemins de fer des États-Unis.

Deze kaart moet bewaard worden, ten einde oponthoud aan de Quarantijn, alsook op de ijzeren wegen der Vereenigde Staten te vermijden.

Tento listek musite uschovati, nechcete-li ukarantény (zastavení ohledně zjistěni zdravi) neb na dráze ve spojenych státech zdrženi byti.

Tuto kartócku treba trimať u sebe aby sa predéslo zderzo-vánu v karantene aj na železnici ve Spojenych Státoch.

VACCINATED.
(SIGNATURE OF STAMP).

Zada *(seated)*, who came to America several years earlier,
with his two sons, Uncle Jake *(r)* and Uncle Tsein *(l)*.

Papa became a citizen of the United States on February 29, 1932. He also changed his name from Israel to Samuel.

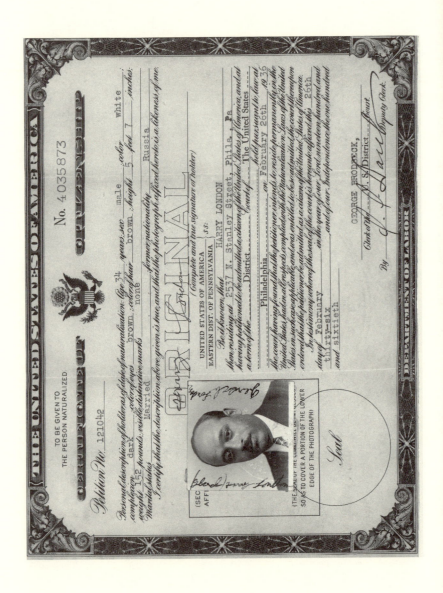

Uncle Harry became a citizen on February 26, 1936,
and changed his name from Gersch to Harry.

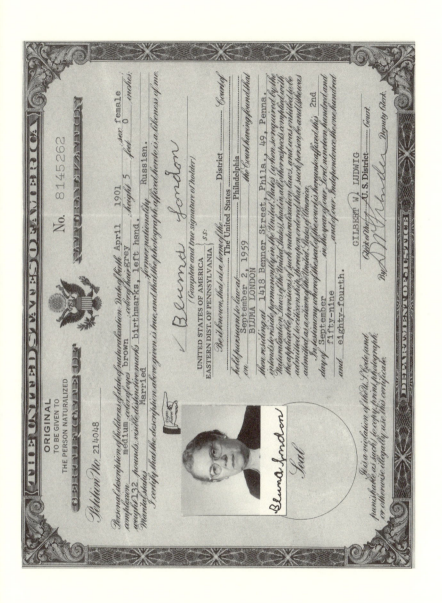

Aunt Bluma became a citizen of the United States
on September 2, 1959.

Papa, newly arrived in America, probably 1922.

Two of Papa's brothers who remained in Russia, dated 1927. They were both killed by the Germans during World War II.

Uncle Leo, Papa's older brother, who came to America earlier. His wife, Aunt Nina, stands behind him.

Mama *(l)*, about seventeen years old, and Bubbe
(seated), about 44. Uncle Jake is on the right.

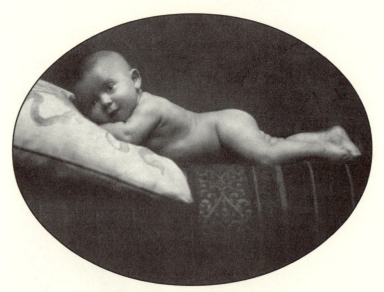

Esther (Rose) at age nine months.

Esther, probably
one and a half
years old, 1924.

Uncle Harry and Aunt Bluma, probably during their
first year in America, 1922.

My cousin Charlotte, about age five. Uncle Harry's and
Aunt Bluma's second adopted child, Charlotte died at age
seven due to complications during illness with measles.

Uncle Harry, cousin Charlotte, and Aunt Bluma. Charlotte wears
one of Aunt Bluma's handmade silk dresses, which she smocked
and embroidered. Taken during the beginning of the Depression
years, though Aunt Bluma wears jewelry and a watch.

Picture taken 1928, Papa on left, Mama on right, each resting
arms on Bubbe's shoulders. Bubbe holds my baby brother Alec,
who is a year old. Esther on the right, probably wearing one of
Aunt Bluma's handmade, smocked silk dresses, is five years
old, and brother Himey, on the left, is three.

Esther with the hated long curls, about seven years old, holding brother Himey's hand. He is about five years old.

Esther, about twelve years old, dressed in a gypsy costume that Mama made for a school play.

Brother Himey's Bar Mitzvah picture. He is thirteen but does not yet wear long pants. Little brother Alec, on the left, is eleven, also dressed in knickers. Their jackets fit poorly, but the proper handkerchief is tucked in their pockets. Rose, fifteen, wears a maroon dress with suede shoes. All three look seriously into the camera.

Rose, age eighteen, graduates from Thomas Jefferson High School in Brooklyn, New York, the same month Pearl Harbor is attacked.

Brother Himey graduates high school in 1943.

Mama, who had been illiterate, learned how to write English in 1962, after I left Brooklyn for California. The letter is to my daughter, Andrea, who would have been ten years old at the time.

The New Victrola

It is hard to remember my childhood without remembering the abject poverty of the Depression years. When the stock market crashed in 1929, it was like a tidal wave, slamming over the walls of security, destroying dreams and plans, leaving a wake of destruction that disordered the lives of a nation for years to come. My Papa's dreams and plans were added to that casualty list. He lost his factory job on the assembly line. Then the bank locked its doors against desperate depositors who panicked for their hard-earned money. Papa was unable to pay the mortgage and the bank took our house. No work, no money, and no options; real poverty raised its ruthless hand, grasping us all and threatening never to let go.

There was a time, before I was six, when we were secure and not hungry. There was money for holiday celebrations, even for small luxuries every now and then. Papa had a savings account into which he made weekly deposits, proudly displaying the bankbook to Mama every payday. He was hardworking and ambitious and took pride in being the breadwinner. My parents and Bubbe had been in this country less than eight years and already the American dream was becoming a reality for them. Every night after work, Papa spent long hours studying to become a proper American citizen. He was no longer a greenhorn and had stopped believing the streets were paved with gold. A future free from persecution and hunger was becoming more than a promise now. There was no hunger in America. We were all safe and secure. Life was good. You could dare to be happy and allow yourself to have a few luxuries. Well, at least one.

One day a truck stopped in front of our house. Two men balancing a large wooden cabinet between them struggled up the steps. My brothers were too small to know what was in that cabinet, but I knew it was a Victrola. I had heard the music that came out of a magic box when I visited Uncle Harry and Aunt Bluma. They had had a Victrola for a long time. Aunt Bluma, always prideful, boasted of this expensive possession, frequently announcing that Uncle Harry had paid cash for it. They did not have to put it on the installment plan as some people did. And now there stood our very own Victrola in the middle of our living room. The cabinet was made from shiny-grained, solid oak, supported by four gracefully carved legs ending in the shape of claws. The lower half opened to reveal a storage space containing a box of records. Above the box was the speaker through which the miracle of music would escape and fill the room as soon as Papa came home.

It was one of the longest days of my life, and I frequently pressed my face against the window, hoping to be the first one to announce Papa's arrival, until Mama scolded me for leaving my fingerprints on her clean window pane. But the Victrola was patient and just stood there. I plagued Mama with questions. I was so impatient that it felt as though I were in pain. "What time is it?" "When will Papa come home?" "When will the music come out?" "Are we really going to keep the Victrola?" Mama's own excitement got the better of her, and for once she was not brusque or angry. She smiled and even joked with Bubbe and hummed as she went about her chores that day, repeatedly cautioning us to keep out of the living room and not to touch the Victrola. My baby brother, Alec, only a year old, began to cry, overwhelmed by the unusual excitement. He had to be picked up and quieted, while my brother Himey hid behind Bubbe. Bubbe, who was always in the kitchen this time of the day to prepare the evening meal, had left her post at the stove to admire the new arrival and keep my brothers out of the way. Supper would be late.

At last Papa came home. I rushed to him before he had a chance to close the door behind him and badgered him with all the questions Mama could not answer. Papa beamed, picked me up, and with pride began to tell us about the Victrola. It was the very latest model manufactured by the Majestic Victrola Company. Papa continued to hold me as he lifted the dome-shaped lid. I caught my breath. The living room was immediately transformed into a fairy land. I looked down into the cabinet and saw the turntable and the silver cup that held a supply of shiny Victrola needles. Next to the turntable rested the silver metal S-shaped arm with a head and a small opening, into which you inserted one of the needles held with a screw that had to be hand tightened. I was so excited I forgot to breathe, and only when I began to feel light-headed did I finally take a full breath.

I protested as Papa handed me to Bubbe so he could be free to operate the Victrola. A passionate discussion ensued as the three adults put their heads together to make a serious decision as to which record would be played first. The consultation seemed interminable to me, but I knew this was no time to interrupt—it was important business and a historical moment. For the first time there would be music in our house. From now on we would not have to go to Uncle Harry's to hear the Russian melodies or the Yiddish ballads or the comedic antics of Eddie Cantor and Al Jolson.

After much deliberation, it was decided we would listen to Al Jolson singing "Sonny Boy," a very popular Yiddish tearjerker. Papa meticulously placed the record on the turntable, cranked up the Victrola, being careful not to overwind, and released a small lever on the side of the turntable. Surely Papa had powers even I was not aware of, for at his touch, the turntable began to spin. Now the most delicate step. Papa had to swing the arm above the moving record, check the screw that held the needle, making sure it was in place, and ever so slowly lower the head and place it on the moving disk. Immediately the room was filled with the sad lament of the ballad. "Friends may forsake me. Let them all forsake me. I'll still have you, Sonny Boy. You're sent from Heaven and I know your worth. You've made a heaven for me right here on earth."

Jolson sang in heart-wrenching Yiddish, and in a matter of minutes there wasn't a dry eye in the house. The tears were soon forgotten, however, for on the other side of the record was a comic rendition of "Mi Ken Laibin,

Nor Mi Lust Nisht." "You Can Live, But They Won't Let You." Jolson laughed, teased, and joked his way through the song, ending with a lively whistling rendition of the final chorus, totally changing the earlier sadness to joy and laughter.

Caught up in the lightheartedness of the evening, Papa played a Russian waltz, and I watched in awe as he and Mama danced to the haunting, swaying melody. My eyes were opened wide in disbelief as my parents whirled around the floor. My Mama, not slender or graceful as she went about the drudgery of her endless chores, was transformed into a light-stepping dancer. She followed my Papa's lead, her feet scarcely touching the floor. Her heavy body was flowing with the rhythm of the music, and she seemed light as a feather in her faded housedress and scuffed shoes. Even my Bubbe got caught up in the carefree atmosphere and, to my delight, began to spin me around on the floor. My younger brothers, taking advantage of the playful spirit, began to stamp their feet and clap their hands. It was a virtual dancing party, and a good time was had by all.

Even after the stock market crash, we managed to hold on to the Victrola, although records that became worn or were broken could not be replaced. In time, Mama learned how to operate this complex machine, and there were afternoons when she would allow herself to put aside drudgery and worries and listen to the music. One such afternoon when I was about seven years old, I returned from school and heard the sound of a Russian waltz as I opened the door. Mama was standing in front of the Victrola as if in a daydream, listening to the haunting melody. I had never seen my Mama in such a private moment. I hoped she would not be angry with me for interrupting her. To my relief, she did not attack me as soon as I came into the house. Instead she turned to me in a relaxed manner and put her arms out, inviting me to dance with her. "Mama," I pleaded, "I can't dance. I don't know how." She said, "Come, I will show you how." This was a side of my Mama I had never known, and at first I did not trust her invitation. But the request transcended all the scoldings. The music was so inviting. I put aside my fears and I went to her. She told me to take my shoes off and stand on her feet, as she supported me with a hand behind my back. I gingerly placed my right hand in hers. The unfamiliar closeness automatically alerted me to put my guard up and I could feel my small muscles tensing at her touch. The familiar scent of her closeness added to the emotion that began to fill me, a terror that I knew only too well. Yet when the haunting Russian waltz began to fill the room, I allowed myself to let out my breath and dared hope that it was safe to be so close to Mama. Then another miracle took place. I felt myself being carried on Mama's feet to the rhythm of the waltz. For that moment I forgot to be afraid of Mama. We became as one body, held in the embrace of the music and the rhythm we shared. I closed my eyes, allowing myself to experience the unexperienced. I was being held by my Mama, but not in a life-threatening struggle at the mercy of her fierce, unspent anger. I was being held by her in a loving embrace made possible by the music and the moment of the dance, a transcending moment that carried us both into a fantasy. I leaned into her. At that instant I became a part of her body, part of her blood again as I had been in time before I had breath of my own. The momentary bond was all that mattered, and I could relax long enough to have it for my very own. For reasons beyond my understanding, I knew that my Mama was also feeling what I felt, that she could allow herself to stay with me a little longer, putting aside her burdens. She became as a carefree girl again. Time seemed endless as we danced and moved to the music.

Even before the record ended, I had already committed the waltz steps to memory, begging Mama to allow me to try my newly acquired talent. We danced again but this time as equals, my feet on the floor, expertly following my Mama's lead. Mama even praised me for catching on so fast. I felt so proud and happy. Out of the corner of my eye I caught sight of my Bubbe watching from the kitchen doorway, in silence, not wanting to interrupt this rare and precious scene.

The Victrola lasted for many years, providing joy and comfort to the family during the dark days of the Depression. It was one of the last reminders of happier, carefree days. There would be afternoons when fears and anger were put aside, and Mama and I would dance together again. During the dance we were as one, in harmony, in rhythm, escaping from the brutal existence of poverty. Each time I was blessedly released from the fear of Mama. I could love her. The music and the dance made it safe. Mama and I were free. We could forget our troubles. We were dancing.

The Picnic

Sundays were the only days my Papa didn't have to work. That made the day special and different, but during the summer months, Sunday might also include a picnic in Strawberry Mansion Park in Philadelphia. When the time came for the first picnic of the season, our excitement and anticipation could not be contained. Would Sunday never come? Mama's impatience sometimes joined ours, but she silenced us with a shout, a glare, or a well-placed slap if all else failed. I might be silenced, but that did not stop me from remembering picnics of the past as holiday respites from the repetitive daily routines. I would fall asleep each night dreaming about the Sunday picnic, still days away. I remembered the freedom of the open green space, the feel of the cool grass against my bare legs as I rolled down a hill, the sound of birds, and singing just for the joy of it, a sound, I might add, that was totally absent from the treeless street where I lived. More than anything, I remembered the spontaneous laughter of playing children everywhere, children finally released from the crowded enclosures of their living quarters and allowed to be children in the open space of the park. The adults would visit with each other. They were all immigrants from Russia, and picnics offered them a rare opportunity to reconnect after the long winter months. Gossip was exchanged: who had died, who was ill, who was newly arrived from the old country, who was pregnant again, whose husband had deserted the family, and every now and then news of a family who could not adjust to life in America and had gone back to Russia. There were new babies, and brides and grooms starting out on their lives together. They would share their joys as well as their hard-luck stories.

Before such a holiday could take place, much had to be done. Mama, Papa, and Bubbe would begin to make plans for the excursion. Mama had to shop for food on Friday, because the stores were closed Saturdays. Saturday was a day of rest for our Jewish Orthodox family, so all of the work had to be done Friday before sunset or very early Sunday morning. The park was several miles from the house and because we did not have a car, the first obstacle was transportation—how to move a family with three small children and all of the picnic paraphernalia from here to there. Those were the days before plastics, Saran Wrap, or aluminum foil were invented; they would have gone a long way to lighten the load. All the food had to be carried in heavy pots, pans, and jars. There were no paper plates, so dishes had to be added to this hefty cargo. Changes of clothing for the children and diapers for my baby brother were also carried. These preparations were in addition to the already full workload that Mama and Bubbe had to contend with every day. In spite of that, they must have looked forward to the picnic as a welcome change of scenery.

The arrival of the first warm spring day after freezing winter temperatures usually resulted in an exodus of tenants from the densely populated neighborhoods into the wide open spaces of the park. Papa had a very important role in the picnic arrangements. It was his responsibility to stake out a table in the park for the family. There were never enough picnic tables to accommodate everyone, so Papa would leave at sunrise on Sunday morning, catch a trolley, and hope to arrive early enough to find a table for us. The competition was fierce. Belligerent fellows often ended up attacking each other, pushing and shoving. My Papa was not one of those, but no matter how early he arrived, some tables would already have been taken. Men would be sitting on wooden benches, demonstrating ownership by their presence, daring anyone to challenge them. Soon, however, they began joking with each other to pass the time. The camaraderie would take on a quieter note as men settled in for the long, boring hours before their families arrived. Papa would take advantage of the tranquility of the outdoors, stretch out on top of the hard table, place the Yiddish newspaper on his face, and enjoy a quiet, peaceful, uninterrupted nap.

Meanwhile on the home front the scene was anything but tranquil. In the midst of the frantic activity caused by three impatient children, Bubbe stayed in the kitchen preparing the picnic food, always of the same menu, no matter how many picnics we could cram in during one summer: cold, well-seasoned hamburgers; crusty, fresh rolls that Mama had bought at the bakery that morning; potatoes boiled in their skins; Bubbe's pickled herring; a variety of her best baked goods; some fruit; milk for the children; and hot tea for the adults. In the meantime Mama frantically dressed us and tried to keep us clean and out of mischief until we were ready to leave. In spite of all her threats and punishments, she often failed at that task. Even Mama could not always contain our collective exuberance. As she furiously went about organizing what would soon be the picnic caravan, she always had an ear cocked in our direction, ready to pounce on whomever was making the most noise. Tension increased as time ticked away. It was imperative that we get to the park early enough to take full advantage of this holiday. To this was added the urgency of not wanting to make Papa wait too long. He could not leave his post for any reason. Our table might be grabbed by squatters.

At the front of our picnic caravan was a little red metal wagon. In it we placed my little brother Alec. He was too small to walk the long distance to the park. He was also too small to appreciate the luxury of getting a ride in the wagon while the rest of us had to walk. He would squirm and complain and create problems as Mama and Bubbe began to pack the picnic food and bundles all around him. In spite of his protests, he would finally be surrounded by aromatic containers holding the mouth-watering picnic meal and supplies for the Sunday event. There he stayed, surrounded by the cargo, which was held in place with an intricate arrangement of rope or string.

Alec was a baby who loved to eat and he had a knack for getting into jars and sacks, defying what should have been the limitations of his fat little fingers. No matter how often Mama scolded him or slapped his pudgy, dimpled, baby hands, he was undaunted. Tears might still be moist on his cheeks, but in a matter of minutes he would have poked a hole in a paper bag or managed to dip into the pot of hamburgers and would be smacking his lips and licking his fingers again. It was predictable that Himey and I would begin to beg for food. We were hungry, too. At times we would win out, and the procession would come to a halt while Mama, scolding all the time, tried to extricate some nosh or snack for us without toppling the carefully loaded wagon. Alec would hold up his arms, crying and wanting to be freed from his restraints. Mama, furious, would warn us of dire circumstances if this happened one more time. But of course it did, for it was a long, hot walk to the park.

The wagon was alternately pulled by Mama and Bubbe, often threatening to dump its load every time it went over a bump or a curb. Sometimes it did end up on its side, relieving itself of its burdens. Alec, screaming underneath the bundles, pots, and pans that had been so carefully jammed around him, would have to be rescued. Mama and Bubbe would begin to blame each other for being careless at the same time they were hurriedly trying to rescue Alec, retrieve the picnic fixings, which were now headed in all directions, reload the wagon, and continue on our way.

After several hours, hot, sweaty and fretful, we would arrive at the park to join the traffic of other travelers like ourselves. Some would be unloading from trolley cars, and a few more fortunate families arrived in cars, while the majority of the picnic revelers arrived on foot. The gathering began to resemble a scene out of Ellis Island. Everyone carrying or lugging packages, children in arms or darting in and out between the legs of the adults in a spontaneous game of hide and seek. The sounds of Yiddish, Russian, Polish, and German peppered with fractured English filled the air until no one language was distinguishable.

Finding Papa was the next business at hand. The park was very large and filling rapidly with people. There was no telling how far he had walked to find a table for us. After searching for half an hour or more, we saw him waving his hands frantically above his head, whistling to catch our attention. We were so glad to be reunited with Papa after what seemed like forever that it took a while to get down to the serious business of unloading the wagon.

The careful engineering of unknotting the ties around the pots and bundles and freeing Alec was a nerve-wracking task. Alec, so close to liberation, was having a tantrum, but the knots wouldn't let go their hold. Mama, Papa, and Bubbe took turns trying to open knots that had tightened during the long hike. You must understand that at no time was it permissible to cut the ties. Rope and string had to be saved and used over and over again. Finally, Alec was free to try his fat little legs on the uneven surface of the grass, and food would be served at long last.

No sooner had the food been unwrapped than we attacked it. Everyone lightened up now that hunger was quieted. Even the struggle of the difficult journey to the park was forgotten and a humorous note was added in the telling and retelling of the challenges and unexpected events along the way. Alec began to nod in Bubbe's warm, soft lap and soon was sound asleep, the crumbs of his last mouthful of food hanging cutely from his chin. Himey had already curled up on a blanket, sucking his thumb, his bright blue eyes closed against the sunlight, and was drifting off into slumber. I was a big girl of five and no longer napped during the day. Mama and Bubbe began to clean up the debris and settled down to sip warm tea. They were free from responsibility for the brief moment.

As my Papa reached for the Yiddish paper, I held his hand and begged him to read to me. *The Forward*, a Yiddish daily newspaper, ran chapters of fiction every day, of unrequited love, broken trusts, and disappointments, not too unlike today's soap operas. Each installment was a melodrama of hardship, desertions, and unkept promises that finished on a provocative note, to be continued the next day. There was also a classified listing that revealed an endless number of desperate appeals from abandoned wives and children, searches for lost relatives, pleas for help from destitute families and prayers to God for pity on a poor, hapless sinner.

Being read to by Papa was the best part of the picnic. Papa's soft, patient voice would lull me into drowsiness. He would sing Russian lullabies as I drifted off. I could feel Papa's even breath and the echoing sound of his voice through his chest, where I rested my head when my eyelids became too heavy to keep open. Warm against Papa's body, safe within the circle of his arm as he supported me, I could relax. Soon the paper would drop from his hands as he, too, surrendered to sleep. All was quiet. All was peaceful. All was safe for a little while.

The pleasant interlude was usually disturbed by Alec's

waking cries, which started a ripple of activity. Leftovers were consumed. My brothers would start chasing each other around the table and wrestling good-naturedly until Alec became overwhelmed by too much rough play. Bubbe would rescue him as Mama scolded Himey for being so rough. Papa would then reach for a ball in his pocket, and our energy was soon diverted to a game of catch. This was the one and only sport my father engaged in, and for a short time we were a team of ball players, dropping more balls than we caught.

The day had been full and long. When late afternoon approached, it was time to collect our belongings and sadly begin the homeward journey. Inevitably, the three of us children were not ready to leave, complaining that it was too early to go home. We begged and begged for just a few more minutes in the park. Our appeals were ignored. The return trip was somewhat easier, though, because Papa was there to help, and the load had been lightened. Alec did not have to sit in the wagon again. Bubbe carried him when his short little legs failed to keep up with the procession. Papa also treated us to a ride home on the trolley, sparing us from another grueling hike.

It was dusk when we descended from the trolley, well fed, pleasantly tired, and anxious to feel the comfort of our beds. The house was a welcome sight, though just hours earlier we had been eager and impatient to leave it. The red wagon and its contents were scarcely in the vestibule when Bubbe carried Alec up to his crib and began to undress him for the night. He was already sound asleep and offered no protest. Himey was carried upstairs

by Mama. He stayed awake just long enough to cooper-
ate as she put him to bed. I was the last one taken up the
stairs. Papa would pick me up, my sleepy head on his
shoulders and my arms tightly encircling his neck and my
legs dangling.

Although I was secure in his protective hold, while
Papa climbed up the steep stairs, I felt a delicious fear and
excitement as he carried me higher and higher, up to the
second floor of the house. On other such occasions when
I was wide awake, I would send out squeals of nervous
laughter and hold tighter. From the perspective of a five-
year-old, the ascent was equal to climbing a mountain,
with each step threatening safety and survival. Finally,
the precarious but exciting adventure was over. Papa
would put me to bed. The last thing I remembered was
the roughness of his face as he kissed me goodnight,
pulled the light covers up to my chin, and left as I surrendered to sleep and dreams.

The day had been a blessed interruption of the confusion and anxiety I usually experienced. I hoped there
would be other Sunday picnics so Papa would again read
the Yiddish paper to me and sing quiet Russian lullabies
until I fell asleep.

Atlantic City

With mixed feelings I pressed my face against the rear window of Uncle Harry's Chevrolet. I was going off to Atlantic City with Aunt Bluma and Uncle Harry on a vacation trip for my eighth birthday. Everyone was lined up on the sidewalk waving good-bye. My brothers were crying—Himey held by Papa, and Alec squirming in Bubbe's arms. Mama looked as though she were having second thoughts about this trip. Was she sorry to see me go? Maybe she regretted giving in to Aunt Bluma, who had manipulated her into a position where she could not say no. Mama was convinced that Aunt Bluma was filled with poisonous envy because Mama had three children, and she had none.

I was not an adventurous child, and the excitement of such a rare event began to diminish as soon as my family was out of sight. I sat back with a sigh, wedged between packages, bundles, boxes of dishes, pots, pans, bedding, and all the necessities to set up summer housekeeping at a rented bungalow in Atlantic City. There was scarcely enough room for me to sit. There were even packages tied on to the roof of the car and in the rumble seat. The car looked like a one-vehicle caravan. Shyly I had asked that the two bags holding clothes and my one and only doll be placed next to me, attempting to establish familiar space in a strange setting. I reached for my doll, holding her close, so the fear that had begun to nibble on the edge of my stomach would calm down. I tried to remember that I was quite grown up. After all, I was eight, and only big girls got to go on vacation to Atlantic City without their family. So, I tightened my lips and assumed an appearance of confidence I did not feel. I knew how to do this from experience. Thus I could fool myself into denying that hard edge of concern that threatened to upset me and spoil my vacation.

We had not traveled very far when Aunt Bluma and Uncle Harry began to argue about which route to take. Mama and Papa never talked to each other that way, and my fear intensified. I held my doll closer. I shut my eyes, trying to find the quiet place I would seek when I went to sleep at night. In that place there were no troubles or fears, and I could relax and drift into my familiar fantasy. Once again I would see the princess holding court, dressed in her beautiful flowing gown, surrounded by admiring subjects. Even in the noisy car my fantasy quieted me and I drifted off to sleep. My head dropped against the packages of clothing, and I was safe again. I did not awaken until we reached Atlantic City, and thus I was spared any more of the endless arguing and bickering that went on between Uncle Harry and Aunt Bluma.

The day was hot and sunny. An unfamiliar smell was in the air, and I later learned it was the ocean. Uncle Harry and Aunt Bluma were greeted by old friends as we started unloading the car. Aunt Bluma kept pushing me toward hands that wanted to touch me, rub my head, or even plant unwelcome kisses on my cheeks. She explained, not with a little pride, that I was her favorite niece and would be spending the summer with them. Finally I escaped to Uncle Harry and helped carry small bundles into the bungalow, which quickly became very crowded.

The bungalow consisted of a medium-sized room, serving as kitchen and bedroom, and an outside bathroom shared by other renters. I immediately began to worry. I often had to go to the bathroom at night. I knew I would be afraid to go out in the dark by myself. This dilemma reminded me that I had not been to the bathroom since we left Philadelphia. My bladder was full to the point of pain. As if she could read my mind, Aunt Bluma showed me the chamber pot under my narrow cot. I was horrified at the prospect of using the pot while my aunt and uncle were in the room. My stomach began to ache. I felt humiliated. My bladder didn't care. Fortunately Uncle Harry and Aunt Bluma started up another one of their arguments, and I wandered out to the bathroom and blessed relief.

Looking for an escape route from Aunt Bluma, Uncle Harry announced he was taking me to the beach. Ducking behind a large box of groceries I changed into the bathing suit Mama had bought me and pushed my bare feet into my sneakers, eager to start this adventure. Uncle Harry surprised me with a red tin pail and a small shovel. I had no idea what use they would be, never having been to the beach before. Nevertheless, I held on to Uncle Harry's hand tightly, the shiny pail and shovel in my other hand, as we walked to the beach. There were lots of laughing children with towels over their shoulders and pails and shovels of their own. I began to feel like Atlantic City was going to be fun.

Nothing had prepared me for the sight of the vast ocean and the roar of the waves. Suddenly I was anxious again. None of the other children seemed apprehensive. They were laughing and squealing with delight. Once again I put on my big-girl face of confidence, but held on more tightly to Uncle Harry. He spread out a blanket on the sand, now crowded with more people than I had ever seen in my life. We sat down and Uncle Harry offered me a baloney sandwich. I discovered I was famished. The sounds of playful children and laughing, shouting adults distracted me. I became more interested in this fairyland by the sea. Sitting on the edge of the blanket because the sand was hot and rough, I began to dig, filling and emptying my pail just as the other children around me were doing. I was careful to check on Uncle Harry's proximity often, just in case the fear came back. But it didn't and when he invited me to walk toward the ocean, I was ready.

Everyone was in the water. Children were playing in the wet sand near the ocean and some were building sand castles, which I had never seen before. Holding on to Uncle Harry's hand I cautiously approached the edge of the shore, the cold ocean water surprising me delightfully when it wrapped itself around my ankles. I felt as though I might be swept out to sea as the water receded, but I was more excited than frightened. Still, I clung to Uncle Harry, but I was having a good time. Maybe this was going to be a good vacation after all.

The days quickly added up to weeks and I began to

settle down to a comfortable routine. I thought about home, but I could always distract myself. I didn't get seriously homesick. One day at the beach I even ventured into the water up to my thighs and had a great time running away when the waves chased me. It became a watery game of tag I thoroughly enjoyed. That day was also special for I found a ring in the sand. It was nothing more than a glass imitation of a diamond ring, but I quickly hid it, fearing someone would claim it. I took it out only at night, putting it on my finger in secret, dreaming about being grown-up and elegant.

In the evening we would stroll on the boardwalk and Uncle Harry would buy me a hot dog or an ice-cream cone. I was in heaven. The boardwalk was very, very crowded. Large wicker carriages, loaded with sightseers who were fortunate enough to afford the price of the fare were pushed by young men dressed in white shirts and pants. Such extravagance! The evenings were always filled with endless holiday spirit, and it became easier to be carefree. There were so many sights to see. The boardwalk was lined with brightly lit booths offering aromatic foods, cool drinks, and frozen treats. Vendors kept up a din, shouting their wares to window-shopping vacationers. There were souvenirs, clothing, games of chance, sideshows with scantily dressed dancers, and lockers to rent for those who did not have a bungalow of their own.

None of this fascinated me as much as watching the marathon dancers in the ballroom windows that faced the boardwalk. Crowds would gather nightly to stare at this bizarre sight. The dance would go on, day and night, nonstop torture, until there was one victorious couple standing. The one-hundred-dollar prize, a bonanza in those days, was enough of an incentive for poor people who were out of work or novice dancers who hoped to be discovered by some talent scout. The winners probably spent a good part of the prize on corn plasters and healing remedies for bodies that ached from all the dancing.

One night I had been so engrossed, watching the twirling couples that I didn't realize I had let go of my aunt's hand. With a gasp of panic, I realized I was alone, surrounded by a sea of bodies. No matter how I tried to navigate through the maze, I could not find my way out. Unashamedly, forgetting to be grown up, I cried out, "Aunt Bluma, Aunt Bluma, Uncle Harry. Where are you?" They did not respond. I was lost in Atlantic City, among strangers who paid no attention to me. In my panic I could not remember where the bungalow was and became more terrified when I realized I was a long way from home in Philadelphia. Just when I felt I would be trampled by the mob around me, a policeman stooped down and asked if I was lost. I became tongue-tied, too terrified to answer, but the situation was clear to him. He took my hand, and walked me around the vicinity of the ballroom on the chance someone would claim me. No one did. I was getting more panicked by the minute. By now I had a loud case of hiccups from crying so much. I understood that the policeman was taking me to the police station. How would Uncle Harry and Aunt Bluma ever find me there?

The policeman bought me a large ice-cream cone, sat

me down on his big oak desk, and began to make phone calls. The ice cream actually did calm my hiccups and soothed me, but I was close to hysteria between licks. I had no idea how long I was at the police station. It seemed like an eternity before Aunt Bluma and Uncle Harry mysteriously appeared in the doorway. Uncle Harry ran toward me, even as Aunt Bluma began to scold me for being a bad girl and getting lost. A new supply of tears gushed out of me. I hid my face in my uncle's jacket and said I wanted to go home to Mama, Papa, and Bubbe. I wanted to go now, tonight. I had had enough of Atlantic City. All the way home they tried to assure me that I would feel better in the morning. I slept fitfully, awakened by nightmares of being trampled by bodiless legs.

The next day was no better. Unable to calm me down, Uncle Harry and Aunt Bluma had one last argument about what to do with me, Aunt Bluma insisting that I stay and get over my panic, Uncle Harry just as firm that he was going to call my Papa to come get me. Thank God this was one argument Uncle Harry won. Not only did Papa come for me, but he stayed a whole day before we went home, a brief vacation for him. We played together in the ocean. He lifted me on his shoulders. I squealed with delight when the waves reached up to his chest, soaking us both. I had never seen Papa so playful, with a smiling face, released from his worries and hard work.

The trip home was like another fairy tale come true, for I had my Papa all to myself. It was my first train ride. We ate sandwiches from the dining room. We put our heads close together as we looked out the window and Papa pointed out the sights along the way. I wished the train would just keep on going and never reach the station.

Caught up in this holiday spirit, I brought out the glass ring I had found and Papa placed it on my ring finger. Papa and I laughed when the ring kept falling off because it was so large for my small hand. Suddenly my laughter was interrupted when I became aware people were looking at us and smiling. Self-conscious with so much attention I became quiet. Papa quickly sized up the situation, understanding my shyness and whispered, "They think you are all grown up and you are engaged." I looked up adoringly into Papa's laughing eyes and thought to myself, "Someday I will be grown up and engaged to somebody just as wonderful as my Papa." But for now my special time with Papa was coming to a close. Placing the ring back in my pocket, I picked up my doll and held on to Papa's hand as we left the train and boarded the trolley car for the short ride to Stanley Street and home.

My brothers ran out to greet me. I had to free myself from them to run to Mama, forgetting to be afraid of her as I hugged her. She was glad to see me, too. Then there was Bubbe waiting for me with open arms. It was only when I was safely held in her soft, warm embrace that I broke down and cried. I told her how scared I had been when I was in Atlantic City, and I never wanted to leave home again.

Still I did not want to forget all the events of that summer. I often daydreamed or put myself to sleep with memories of Papa playing with me in the ocean. I held on to the image of happy Papa with a smiling face. For a long time whenever I was scared at night, I would remember how Papa had rescued me from Aunt Bluma and Uncle Harry and knew he would always be there whenever I needed him.

The Insurance Fire

For children raised in poverty there are memorable occurrences that mercifully interrupt the daily struggle of being poor. Such an event was Passover in our house; with it came special foods eaten only during that holiday. Because this holiday lasted a whole week and groceries had to be ordered well in advance, delicious meals and treats were guaranteed. The challenge of feeding our family of six always weighed heavily on the adults. As children, however, we were unaware of the hardships that often threatened the frantic preparations for this special holiday. One such Passover will always be a reminder of the dark Depression years and Mama's and Bubbe's heroic measures to provide the necessities.

During the period my Bubbe lived with us, from the time I was born until I was thirteen, the exciting holiday rituals were repeated every year. Household duties were clearly defined and separated; Bubbe was confined to the cooking, and Mama was responsible for the cleaning, shopping, and disciplining of us children. Disputes were seldom resolved, often smoldering in silence until time blurred memories and the tension eroded. As this particular Passover approached, however, Mama and Bubbe became a coordinated team as they worked together.

Money was even scarcer that year, for Papa had been

out of work a long time and the small repair jobs he did were few and far between. Even when he found work, his labors were not always rewarded with money. Often he would bring home some articles of clothing or food in exchange for a day of hard work. How in the world would this Passover be paid for? While most of the food staples could be added to the already growing list of charges that the local grocery lady carried for our family, asking for more credit was always a shameful option for Mama.

There was no escape. Passover was fast approaching, and preparations had to be made. The responsibility fell to the women of the house. Papa was to be spared this torment. He had enough worries.

Bubbe and Mama devised an evil plan that year. Did they have the courage to carry it out? Desperation cast them in the role of conspirators. They put their coping skills together and joined in a plot that was abhorrent to them. They were going to cash in on the small fire insurance policy that Mama paid for with weekly twenty-five-cent installments. Somehow the payment was always made. I don't remember ever being threatened by fire, or even seeing a fire, in any of the neighborhoods we lived in. But the persistent insurance salesman convinced Mama that no one was safe without a fire insurance policy. The salesman would make his weekly visit, collect the money, and note it in his record book. Our house was then safe for another week. Now it was time to collect, but how?

Mama and Bubbe would not dare to burn articles of clothing or bedding; we barely had enough to keep us even reasonably warm and dressed. What could be destroyed by fire yet not deprive us of one more basic necessity? After going through a very small list of options, the choices were narrowed down to two family treasures. The first was the silver candlesticks that were used every Friday night for the Sabbath blessings and for holiday celebrations. They were markers of our traditional values and rituals. At no time would they be sold, for without them we would be nothing but poor "trash" in the eyes of other Jewish Orthodox housewives. We would be spared that humiliation as long as we held on to the silver candlesticks. We were not as poor as the Schneiders or the Levys, who had really fallen upon hard times. They were forced to sell their silver candlesticks when illness and untimely death necessitated such a desperate act.

The second treasure was the only pure linen tablecloth Mama had ever owned. It, too, had been purchased years ago, also on the installment plan, and we proudly displayed it on holidays. After each use it would be carefully washed, starched, pressed, and placed in a special pillowcase for safe keeping. With much painful deliberation, the decision to give up this treasure was made. The tablecloth would have to be sacrificed by fire for Passover.

Bubbe and Mama began to rehearse their plan. They could be seen whispering together, spreading out the linen tablecloth and placing the silver candlesticks on top of it. They practiced aiming the dripping hot wax from the lit candles on to the cloth, burning it in such a way that the act of arson would not be suspected by the insurance salesman. Their behavior was all very mysterious and unusual. Passover was still weeks away so they could not have been setting the table yet.

I peeked through the open doorway of the dining room, wondering what secrets they could possibly be sharing. When discovered, I was scolded by Mama and sent out of the room. As soon as I had gone I could hear them whispering again, their backs to the door, huddled close together, bending over the table and examining the tablecloth. What were they plotting? What disaster was about to befall us now?

When I awoke the next morning Bubbe and Mama were already in the kitchen, though there was no sign that breakfast had been prepared. There was a strange smell in the kitchen. Something had burned. Although it wasn't Friday, the silver candlesticks with smoking candles were in plain sight. Then I saw the linen tablecloth, crumpled in a heap on the table with a large blackened hole burned through it.

I would have expected Bubbe and Mama to be very upset about such a loss, arguing about who had been so careless about how they were ever going to replace this special linen tablecloth, and how much money it cost, and how hard it had been to pay for it, and on and on and on. Strangely, none of that was happening. They were both quiet. Their eyes did not meet as they busied themselves tidying up the room. In all innocence I asked what had happened to the tablecloth. Even at the tender age of six, I knew what a special property it was.

Mama immediately turned on me, threatening to slap my face if I ever mentioned the tablecloth again, but I could see tears in her eyes. Bubbe tried to comfort me and assured me that nothing was wrong. She explained that the candle had set fire to the tablecloth and burned a big hole in it. "But Bubbe," I said. "It is not *Shabbas*. Why was the candle lit?" Before she could answer, Mama tried to carry out her threat of punishment, and only Bubbe's quick reaction saved me from another undeserved attack. Bubbe picked me up and said something in Russian to Mama, which I did not understand. It had some magical effect on Mama. She silently left the room.

I tried to put this episode out of my mind, but I could make no sense out of it. I was afraid to bring it up again, so I watched and waited. Sure enough, several days later the whispering started again and the tablecloth was retrieved from its hiding place. Both Mama and Bubbe seemed to be very nervous as if they were silently looking over their shoulders, though no one was behind them. When the doorbell rang that day, Mama looked frightened. She opened the door and greeted the insurance salesman. He was a big man and he smelled of bad cigar smoke. I did not like him. He had a habit of pinching my cheek with his thick fingers.

Mama immediately began to talk fast in Yiddish, which I understood. She explained how Bubbe had set the table for *Shabbas* last week with the linen tablecloth and the silver candlesticks and how the candles were allowed to burn during the Friday night meal. None of this was unusual thus far, but then Mama said that Bubbe had forgotten to remove the candlesticks and the burning candles from the table as she busied herself in the kitchen. Mama said she was upstairs putting the children to bed when she heard Bubbe scream out. When she rushed downstairs the tablecloth was burning and Bubbe was putting the fire out with a kitchen towel, but it was too late. The damage was done and the tablecloth was ruined.

I knew this was not true. Why was Mama lying to this man? I watched in silence as the man examined the evidence. Mama told him Passover was approaching and the linen tablecloth had to be replaced. She wanted the insurance to cover this accident.

The insurance salesman became very officious. He stopped joking and laughing. He complained that there had been several losses that week and the insurance company would be hard-pressed to pay for one more claim. Mama ignored him and pushed on. She was a policyholder in good standing, had always met her payments on time, and now it was time to collect. Whether it was desperation or sheer courage I will never know, but in a matter of minutes Mama changed from a guilty conspirator to a righteous, demanding policyholder.

The insurance salesman could not persuade her to cancel her claim. Reluctantly he surrendered, filled out an official form, and told Mama to sign it. Mama could not write her name, but she was so energized by this victory that she made her X with an air of confidence. To her surprise, the insurance salesman paid her several dollars right on the spot and then left, after warning her to be more careful, threatening to cancel the policy if she made another claim.

After he was gone Mama and Bubbe sat in the kitchen, not speaking for a long time. Then Mama rallied, counted out the money, and told Bubbe she was going to the grocery to place the Passover order. She would not have to ask for credit this year.

So it was that the family was saved from a bleak, bare Passover that year because of Mama's and Bubbe's courageous conspiracy. I looked for the tablecloth for days, wanting to inspect it more closely, but I never found it. The evidence had been destroyed completely. It was a long time, however, before an unexpected ringing of the doorbell didn't cause Mama and Bubbe to catch their breaths and cast questioning glances at each other. Had they been found out after all? What authority was waiting on the other side of the door to confront them with their guilt? It never happened. They were safe. That Passover was an abundant and joyous holiday.

We Move to Brooklyn

Mama and Papa seemed more worried than usual. They were staying up late, talking in private, sometimes with Bubbe and sometimes after she had gone to bed. Papa went to the candy store often to use the public phone; that in itself was ominous because the phone was reserved for calling the doctor, but no one was sick right now. I could tell something serious was happening or about to happen. For a long time Papa had been coming home empty-handed and depressed after searching for work all day. I noticed that Mama's worried expression was becoming etched into the deep furrows of her brow. Bubbe was quieter than ever, and when I asked her what was the matter, she would not answer at all or say things like, "You don't have to worry about this. Everything will be all right." Everything obviously wasn't all right and her unconvincing words did little to quiet the anxiety building inside me.

Weeks went by with Mama's temper getting shorter. At the end of the day when Papa came home dirty, tired, and dejected, Mama and Papa would look at each other in silence and then part if someone came into the room. All I could do was wait and get more and more uneasy. Then something did happen. One Saturday morning when I came down to the kitchen, it was filled with card-

board boxes. Bubbe was wrapping the dishes in newspapers and carefully placing them in the boxes. This time
Bubbe did not avoid my questions and told me that we
were all moving to Brooklyn. I had never even heard of
Brooklyn. We were not a family that traveled anywhere.
Even an excursion to the park, requiring transportation
on the trolley car, was an unusual event. How could we
possibly be going all the way to Brooklyn?

Little by little I began to understand that moving
meant we would never be coming back to our home in
Philadelphia. Now I had a real reason to be fearful and
anxious. Where would we live? Where would I go to
school? Would I ever again see my beloved teacher, Miss
March, or play with my best friend, Sissy? Could it be
that I would never again see Aunt Bluma and Uncle
Harry, who always made such a fuss over me? I could
always count on Aunt Bluma to sew or knit a new outfit
for me for the holidays, even if it did make Mama mad.

By now I was fretting and crying, but I stopped short,
stifling the next sob when Mama came into the room
with Alec and Himey behind her. The boys were too
young to understand the magnitude of what was happening. They were not the least bit concerned and were
more interested in breakfast than in the unusual scene in
the kitchen. Bubbe fell silent, but Mama finally began to
talk. She told us that Papa had not been able to find work
for so long and now he had been offered a job with his
brother, Leo, in his sewing machine repair shop in New
York City's garment district. Everything was getting very
complicated. I was not comforted by this information. It
was all happening too fast.

The next few weeks disrupted our strictly organized lives completely, and from day to day I did not know what I would find when I came home from school. I felt like an intruder, always in the way. Boxes were piling up in the living room and bedrooms. Mama quickly got tired explaining why I couldn't have my one doll, or where my sneakers were, and why I couldn't use the skates. Even worse was Papa not being home for days at a time. He would take the train to Brooklyn to look for a place for us to live, and each time he left I feared I would never see him again. I clung to him tearfully, begging him not to leave. Though he promised we would all be together soon in Brooklyn I could not believe him. Brooklyn could just as well be on the other side of the world. It was no use turning to Mama for help. My questions would only make her angrier. Bubbe was no help. She was used to doing as she was told and kept on packing.

Finally, one day Papa came back from Brooklyn and said he had rented an apartment for us. What was an apartment? I had lived only in houses with big backyards and lots of room to play and run outdoors. Somehow I knew life was about to take a turn for the worse as the packing became more frantic. I knew the day of our departure was imminent, and my heart beat more rapidly.

Papa came back from Brooklyn to supervise the loading of the big moving truck that arrived with him. All the neighbors stood in their doorways watching. Some of the kids approached shyly, wanting to know where I was going. I could not answer. When my dearest friend, Sissy, came to say good-bye, my heart all but broke, and I hid my face in Bubbe's apron.

Finally Aunt Bluma arrived, teary and sad as she kissed me and my brothers. She began to wail as she said good-bye to Mama, Papa, and Bubbe. Aunt Bluma also must have believed we would never see each other again, as she clung to Mama and they both cried. This was a very serious situation, for nothing short of a catastrophe could ever bring Mama and Aunt Bluma together. Even Uncle Harry took a day off from work to visit us for what I was sure would be the last time.

Finally, the truck was loaded, with our furniture, boxes, and several large packages strapped on top of the roof. The driver squeezed into the well-worn seat in front of the steering wheel while Mama, Papa, and Bubbe crammed into a long, narrow bench next to him. Each held one of the children on their lap. As soon as we pulled away from the sidewalk, I began to feel squashed and claustrophobic, but I was grateful to be sitting on Papa's lap, pressing against him for protection. It was an old truck and not really up to such a challenge. It groaned and sputtered every time we stopped in traffic, only to resume its complaining sounds as soon as we were once again on our way.

Mama and Bubbe had their hands full trying to quiet my two younger brothers, especially five-year-old Alec who was a squirmy, active little boy and ready to get out every time we stopped. Once, much to my relief, we got an extra long break when the truck gave up like some worn-out dragon, with steam coming out of its radiator. The driver cursed and complained as he climbed down. The radiator gushed like Mt. Vesuvius when he removed the cap. I was hoping we would never get to Brooklyn, but in all too short order the motor cooled down, the driver gave the radiator a long drink of water, and we were off again without any further mishaps. A miracle.

After what seemed like an interminable period of time, the driver announced we were going to cross the Brooklyn Bridge and soon we would actually be in Brooklyn. We then drove through many narrow streets lined with tall, connected, brick buildings. There were no spaces between the buildings that rose out of the cement sidewalks like cliffs overlooking a narrow ravine. The buildings were four stories high, and every window was wide open in a futile attempt to capture any slight breeze. It was a very hot day. That did not stop hoards of dirty, laughing, jeering children from racing around us and pointing fingers as we struggled down from the truck, trying to stay close together.

The sidewalks were lined with overflowing garbage cans emitting a foul odor to join the hot, humid air. Cats and dogs seemed to be underfoot everywhere, searching for food in the garbage or dodging street traffic. There were four stories of metal stairways and landings underneath the windows. I later learned these were fire escapes. I figured there must be a lot of fires in Brooklyn. I had never seen anything like that in Philadelphia. I thought it would have been virtually impossible to use the fire escapes if there was a fire. The iron railings were hung with laundry, and the landings were crammed with storage boxes and household objects.

The apartment Papa had rented for us was on the ground floor, in the rear of a tomb-like dwelling. There were three small bedrooms and a small kitchen with a large washtub covered with a slab of plywood that doubled as a counter. Later, to my horror, I learned that the washtub was also the bathtub for the whole family. The bathroom was a tiny closet with barely enough room for a small sink and a toilet that had a water tank attached to the tin ceiling. All the rooms were on one floor. I was totally confused, for I had never seen a home that did not have an upstairs where everybody slept. I had always relished the small space of privacy this offered me in my room in Philadelphia. Now that, too, was gone.

The apartment was not much brighter than the dark hallway, and it smelled funny, as if earlier tenants had not been terribly clean. The kitchen linoleum was cracked and faded, and even in broad daylight one could see the population of cockroaches that shared our cramped quarters. Soon Mama and Bubbe would have to attack this gloomy, smelly place with strong soaps and bleaches to make it livable. But now they were both overwhelmed and began to cry, holding on to each other. Papa stood by, unable to offer any words in his own defense. Clearly it was the very best he could do, given that we were destitute and he had to borrow money from Uncle Leo for the move. Papa tried to cheer everyone up by reporting that he had cleverly gotten the first month's rent free from the landlord, and as soon as he began to make a steady wage we would move again to a better apartment.

So we became the newest inhabitants of one of the worst slums in Brownsville. In spite of that, the boys quickly adjusted and soon were playing ball in the street and chasing each other in endless games of tag. Fights broke out frequently among the children. Inevitably the mothers of the young warriors would join the fight and start arguing. These conflicts fostered distrust and hostility among the adults, but the kids would be pals again even as their mothers were still locked in battle. In time even I had a new friend to play house with, though I longed for Philadelphia, my big backyard, and my friend Sissy.

After a long, hot summer in this airless apartment, the first day of school arrived. Himey and I were to be tested by the principal to determine the classes in which we would be enrolled. I had completed the third grade in Philadelphia and was ready to take my rightful place in the fourth grade, but that was not to be my fate. I was unable to pass the long division arithmetic test, for I had not been introduced to that level of math in Philadelphia. To my humiliation I was to repeat the third grade. Even Mama pleaded with the principal, for to be kept back carried a terrible stigma. Only dummies or bad kids got kept back. Mama's words fell on deaf ears. I hung my head in shame, convinced that I was indeed stupid, and everyone would know it. I approached the first day of school with dread. My stomach was upset and my head ached, but I knew I had to go.

It soon became apparent life in Brooklyn was not free from worry either, so why did we leave Philadelphia in the first place? Papa worked very long hours, and Mama was just as worried and angry. In addition, when we moved Mama still owed the Philadelphia Electric Company for a steam iron she was paying for on the installment plan. She was terrified the bill collector would find her, shame her, and take her off to jail. No such thing ever happened, but Mama could not be convinced that the authorities would not come after her for the $4.23 she owed the company.

After a year, Papa earned a raise, and we moved up to a third-floor front apartment, with the luxury of a complete but cramped bathroom. At least it had a lock on the door, and I didn't have to worry about my brothers watching me take a bath. Some things did not improve, however. The same cockroaches from downstairs seemed to follow us upstairs, or were cousins of the downstairs roaches. The battle with them went on in spite of the fact that an exterminator arrived every month with evil-smelling stuff that killed off the first layer of intruders. The next generation, however, appeared in a matter of days.

The next year Papa found a larger apartment around the corner on Saratoga Avenue, with windows that faced a small yard with some trees. There was a narrow court-yard, which acted as a buffer from the sounds of traffic. Also, if you didn't make too much noise, the neighbors would not complain when you played house in the court-yard with your friends. That was my favorite game, and I always got to be the Mama. I would give orders to my playmates, who were the children in my imaginary family. I was just as stern and demanding as my own Mama, expecting the "children" to obey me without question. Such satisfaction was short-lived though, for at home I was still the unfortunate recipient of Mama's quick temper, but life was becoming less stressful. Mama was not worried all the time, now that Papa was steadily employed. We were no longer hungry, and there was often enough money for new holiday outfits for the children, if not for the grown-ups.

The monotonous routine of our daily lives was interrupted a couple of times a year when Aunt Bluma and Uncle Harry would arrive from Philadelphia. Mama and Bubbe would frantically get the house ready for their visit. Mama would complain about the expense of feeding them for three days, and she resented the extra work. The fact that Aunt Bluma would bring bags and boxes of groceries with her did not make it any easier for Mama. Mama still hated taking Aunt Bluma's charity. The rest of us were delighted to have this welcome interruption. The visits were filled with Uncle Harry's pranks, which kept us in stitches. In addition, Uncle Harry would drive up in his latest Chevrolet. There would be car rides to exotic places like Coney Island or Camden, New Jersey, where Uncle Harry could get whiskey cheaper, much to Aunt Bluma's consternation. Uncle Harry would tease and joke until even Aunt Bluma could no longer hold back her laughter.

I was thirty-one when my husband and I and our two children left Brownsville and moved to Canarsie, a residential section in Brooklyn. We bought one of the neat brick row houses on Farragut Road and finally escaped from the tenement slums of Brownsville. We lived downstairs in a long, spacious apartment and rented out two smaller apartments upstairs.

I became a landlady, a role that was totally foreign to me, and in which I was very uncomfortable. Remembering the suffering of the little girl in Brownsville, the suffocating summers and freezing winters, and the dark, cramped apartments, I tried to be a sympathetic landlady. I turned the large basement into a play space for my children and those of the tenants. The street was wide, and there was an open lot at one end with grass, trees, and a small creek where all the children fished for tadpoles. The air was clean, and there were cool breezes during the hot summers.

I had finally escaped from the slum I had lived in most of my life, and with that escape came an additional, unexpected blessing. There were no cockroaches. We lived in that house for five years, and I never did see a bug of any kind. Finally I relaxed whenever I got up during the night and turned on the light in the kitchen or bathroom. Still I would automatically let out a sigh of relief when no roaches appeared. I felt rich and safe, and there was always food in the refrigerator.

I often remember, with greater understanding and compassion, how Mama and Bubbe never gave up the battle to keep us clean and fed, and what hardships my Papa endured during the Depression years. Yet, in spite of those oppressive times, they never stopped trying. Somehow we had all survived. The hard lessons of those years became part of my survival education. I was determined to spare my children the devastation that was part of my life when I was growing up in Brownsville.

A 'Shtetl' in Brooklyn

After we moved to Brooklyn, life was never the same. Nothing could have prepared us for this dramatic change and the scene that awaited us when we arrived at Douglass Street. Sitting in the moving van with all our belongings, we were stunned into silence. Hours before we had left our poor but clean, quiet, orderly neighborhood in Philadelphia.

Suddenly we were dumped into a crowded, dirty bedlam in Brownsville—a slum neighborhood in Brooklyn. Every window facing the street in the four-story apartment building seemed to be filled with people watching us unload our shabby belongings. Dirty, shouting kids were everywhere, getting in the way and paying no attention to the truck driver as he struggled to unload the truck. I was overwhelmed and horrified. This could not possibly be my new home. Mercifully, I did not know it would be decades before I could escape from Brownsville. I lived there from the time I was nine years old until I was thirty-one, married, and with two children of my own.

Looking back at that period of my childhood in Brownsville, I can still remember the shock of having to adjust to the overcrowded, filthy, and noisy neighborhood that was to be our new home. The tenement buildings housed thousands of people on one city block. Gone was the slower pace of Philadelphia neighborhoods. Gone were the children who seemed calmer and less threatening than the mobs of aggressive city kids in Brownsville. Gone, too, was the luxury and privacy of our house in Philadelphia, separated from other houses by a spacious yard and alleyways. In our dark, crowded apartment in Brooklyn, my two brothers shared a bedroom, my parents had their own bedroom, and Bubbe had a tiny room just big enough for a folding bed and a small, makeshift dresser. I no longer had a room of my own, and for years slept on another folding bed in the living room. Survival was the order of the day. It was against this impossible background that Mama and Bubbe had to make a home for us while Papa went off to work for his brother in New York City.

Our apartment building, like all the others on our block, had a live-in janitor who did the dirty work of an absentee slum landlord. Our janitor, Mr. White, was as different as he could be from the European Jewish tenants. Mr. White was a black man. He was "the different one" to the Jews he lived with, away from any community of his own. Though Jews are no strangers to persecution and prejudice, in private they felt superior to Mr. White. When dealing with him, however, they treated him with a veiled respect they did not really feel and addressed him as "Mr. White." It probably did not fool him. He knew that behind his back he was referred to as "the *shvartzer*," the black one. Often the tenants forgot that Mr. White had a good Yiddish vocabulary. He had acquired it after living in the Jewish ghetto for years.

Mr. White occupied a very small, dark, and airless apartment behind the stairwell in our building. He lived rent free in his small cave with his wife. He was given a meager stipend, which was his only source of income. Mr. White held down his menial job; he was no burden on society and was always willing to be helpful, carrying heavy packages, or bringing up your mail if you were ill. In return, the Jewish housewives would give him some food or small change as a tip. He was a good soul and a friendly man. Mr. White, too, was a survivor, though he had acquired different skills than his aggressive, verbal, Jewish neighbors. It was not in his nature to challenge, resist, or question. He kept to himself and, when he could afford it, found solace in a bottle of beer or wine.

The candy store was probably the most important store in the neighborhood. It doubled as the local community center. It was the hub of social activity. There were always clusters of men, boys, and girls, who gathered at the candy store, while the women remained at home, cooking, cleaning, and taking care of babies. Here, dates were made, and young lovers shared rich malted milks. Fast-talking, gum-chewing bookies and small-time racketeers posted themselves near the public phones and did a brisk business. Younger kids waited for the phones to ring and would call apartment tenants to the phone for a three-penny tip. These stores usually had a small apartment in the rear where the proprietor lived with his wife and children. This living arrangement was a convenience for the store owner's wife, who did double duty when she balanced the newest baby on her hip to answer the phone or expertly mixed frothy ice cream sodas for five cents.

The corner drugstore, another gathering place, often offered the only medical advice and treatment that the tenement poor could afford. The druggist, as he was called, was an esteemed professional. He could prescribe medication for a boil as easily as he could diagnose a hernia. Minor injuries were treated on the spot with a splash of peroxide and a painful swabbing of iodine. Women would discretely seek out his advice for miscarriages or missed periods with the assurance that their secrets would be safe with him. The druggist was like a combat medic on the battlefield of the slums.

Papa and I had an ongoing relationship with our neighborhood druggist. Every Saturday Papa would take me to the drugstore and solemnly weigh me on the scale for a penny. Then Papa and the druggist would have a discussion about which tonic might be most effective in tempting my feeble appetite and putting some flesh on my bony frame. Bubbe, also, would go the drugstore to buy bottles of hair tint, hiding her purchase in the deep pockets of her clothing for fear the neighbors might discover that she colored her hair.

Mrs. Reitzen ran the local grocery store on the corner. A widow with two children and an elderly mother who was dependent on her, this mild-mannered, sweet woman was at her post before sun up and well after dark. She was a familiar figure as she commuted between her little store and her apartment, which was halfway down the block. She did what appeared to be good business, but many of her customers, my Mama among them, didn't always have enough money to pay for groceries. Mrs. Reitzen generously offered credit, adding the latest purchase to your account. The accounts consisted of strips of white butcher paper with a name, a date, and the amount of the purchase being charged. These were placed on a large spindle file, which she would leaf through whenever she recorded another debt. I don't know how she stayed in business. I don't remember her ever asking anyone to pay their bills, nor did she refuse credit to her regular customers. Mama would often send me to the grocery for small purchases in order not to face Mrs. Reitzen when our account was long overdue. I soon caught on to this and felt very shy whenever I would tell Mrs. Reitzen, in a whisper, "Mama said to add it to our bill."

Our neighborhood barber happened to be a cousin of my father's, but we called him Uncle Benny. His shop was next door to Mrs. Reitzen's grocery. He proudly displayed initialed shaving cups for his steady customers and signs that advertised his ability to perform cupping as an alternative form of healing for a variety of ills. Every four or five weeks, Papa would get his hair cut at Uncle Benny's barber shop, and if he could afford it, he would have "the works," consisting of a haircut and a professional shave—a sheer luxury for Papa. He would fall asleep under hot, steaming, moist towels draped over his face, as he lay back in the reclining barber chair. He would be awakened when Uncle Benny removed the now cool towel and began to briskly massage Papa's face, finishing off this treatment with a splash of perfumed aftershave lotion. I loved being the first one to be picked up by Papa when he came home from the barber; his face was smooth, clean, and shiny. He smelled so good, it made my head spin.

As children we were also taken to Uncle Benny's barber shop. We were given lollipops for sitting still when he cut our hair. Mama would wait from one holiday to the next before she felt obliged to get her hair cut, not wanting to spend any money on herself. Benny was a friendly, joking man and always made a fuss over us when we came to his shop. We were not just ordinary customers. We were family.

Thursday was a particularly busy day in Jewish neighborhoods. It was the day before *Shabbas*. *Balaboostas* were out early in the morning, rain or shine, in search of the best bargains for the *Shabbas* meal. My Mama would join the army of shoppers, hoping to be first in line at the fish market.

Tony, the proprietor, was a young, very good-looking Italian who spoke Yiddish fluently, knew everyone's name, and joked and teased constantly, bringing smiles to the careworn faces of the poor, hard-working housewives. Every one of them wanted the center cut of the fresh carp, leaving the head and tail for later customers. Tony good-naturedly ignored such outrageous requests, as he sliced and expertly filleted fish that had been alive minutes earlier. Everyone went home happy. No one could be angry at Tony.

The kosher butcher shop was already filled with impatient housewives, no matter how early Mama arrived. *Balaboostas* wanted a chicken that had been freshly killed and was still warm to the touch. Fights broke out when the butcher insisted he would not slaughter another chicken until every fowl on the table was bought and paid for. He marched behind his meat case, looking down from his platform with the unlit stump of a cigar in his mouth, wiping his hands on his blood-smeared apron. It would be a waste of time to go anywhere else, so the housewives would grumble, settle down, and make their purchases.

No sooner was the standoff with the butcher resolved than those who had an extra five cents that day would start pushing to be first in line for the services of the woman who plucked the chickens. The "chicken flicker" was a sight to behold. There she sat, her head covered in several layers of scarves, her long sleeves tied at the wrist with string, the collar of her dress pinned under her chin; all this in a futile attempt to keep the chicken lice from attacking her as they were evicted from the chickens. She was surrounded by the loud, demanding housewives, each clutching a dead, limp, warm chicken that at times was aimed at anyone who tried to get in her way. Ignoring the angry voices, the chicken flicker sat hunched over her task in a cloud of flying feathers, furiously plucking away as though her life depended on it. She only stopped long enough to take useless swipes at the lice that were everywhere. No sooner was she through with one chicken, returning its naked body to its owner in exchange for the well-earned five cents, than an argument would break out among the impatient women, each one gesticulating with her dead chicken, wanting to be next, in order to escape this infested environment.

Sometimes there was enough money for Mama to make a stop at the "appetizing store" where all the fat, succulent, aromatic, smoked fish were arranged in a refrigerated case. A juicy, smoked whitefish or a piece of smoked sablefish for Saturday's breakfast might join the packages in the shopping bag that was beginning to get heavier and heavier. The store was also filled with imported nuts, candies, dried fruits, and sweet *halavah* from mysterious lands on the other side of the world. Only when Uncle Harry came to visit from Philadelphia, bringing my brothers and me some spending money, could I buy some of these foreign delicacies. Most of the time, when I accompanied Mama, I could only lean against the glass case, salivating until the storekeeper scolded me for leaving fingerprints on the glass. Mama would emphasize his scolding with a scowl that immediately awoke me from my mouth-watering daydream.

The local dairy store was next, stacked with trays of fresh eggs, huge wooden tubs filled with bulk sweet butter, cream cheeses of all flavors, sliced mild Jewish cheeses, and huge metal containers of fresh sour cream that you could measure out and take home in your own container. It never ceased to astonish me how the dairy-store lady would quickly and artistically carve out just the right size and weight of the bulk cheeses and butter, whether the order was for an eighth of a pound or a whole pound. These were the days before storekeepers thought of handing out numbers to customers to maintain some fair system of service, so there was a lot of pushing and shoving and angry challenges when the storekeeper called "next."

No matter how familiar and accommodating the local storekeeper might be, if you wanted a real bargain, you took the trolley to Rockaway Avenue. There the scene was not unlike the open markets in the Russian *shtetls* with pushcarts overflowing with merchandise of every description. Storekeepers, not content to stock their inventory to the ceilings in their stores, extended their business space outdoors on steps and layers of boxes. Clothing was hung overhead from awnings and precarious makeshift racks in order to compete with the street peddlers. Aggressive storekeepers would actually reach out into the heavily populated streets and pull you into their stores to make a sale. When I was twelve, Mama bought my first bra, to my humiliation, from one of the pushcarts, for five cents. The pushcart peddler made some lascivious remark about what a big girl I must be now that I had a new brassiere. I wished I were dead, as I ducked my red face behind my Mama.

There were stores that sold only kosher pickles. The pickle lady would stand guard over her barrels, advertising her specialty with loud invitations. Summer or winter she wore the same outfit, the weather determining the number of layers. Her sleeves were rolled up above her elbows so she could dip into the brine-filled barrel, reaching for the biggest and best pickle, just for you. In the winter the brine was freezing, but the pickle lady never blinked as she repeated her routine throughout the day, her hands and arms beet red from the cold. In the summer heat she would be surrounded by clouds of flies circling her barrels. She would attack them with her handy flyswatter, but no sooner would they leave than another battalion arrived, and her losing battle would be repeated.

Next to her would be the herring lady, who stood guard over her barrels of *shmaltz* herrings. Her sleeves were rolled up as well, for she would dip her arms into layers of herring, bringing up a carefully selected prize for her customer. At times some fussy *balaboosta* might reject her offering and insist that she search deeper in the barrel for a bigger, better herring. Often a fight would erupt, for the peddlers and storekeepers were very aggressive. They catered to customers only up to a point. They would easily become offended, and an argument quickly became a bout of curses and name calling until the attacked customer escaped. There were many such stores and pushcarts along Rockaway Avenue, however, and it would not take long to find someone who was eager to wait on you and, if you were lucky, for two cents less. At the end of each challenging shopping excursion, the *balaboostas* would haul their heavy bundles up on the streetcar and stagger home.

The streets of Brooklyn were filled with activities that punctuated our daily existence. No holiday, no season, no event went unnoticed by neighborhood storekeepers, peddlers, insurance agents, and other street personalities, all of whom wove themselves into the rhythm of our lives.

Chilly winter days brought out the *knish* man. He would appear with the first touch of cold weather, as if he had been hibernating in some dark, warm cave, out of sight until he was called into service. Then he would become a familiar sight: an old Jewish man, dressed in layers of heavy clothing, a wool hat with flaps to cover his ears, gloves that had no finger tips and a long, soiled apron to top off his uniform. He wore his galoshes unbuckled, and they squeaked and rattled with each laborious step. He would stand guard at a corner with a well-worn metal cart on old baby carriage wheels. The cart had a tray of hot charcoal and two drawers, one filled with assorted hot *knishes,* the other with aromatic, baked sweet potatoes. I would save my pennies all week until I had five of them and then struggle with the decision over which tantalizing morsel to buy. With stiff, cold fingers the *knish* man would wrap my purchase in recycled orange or apple tissue paper covers. I would hold the hot treat in my hands for long minutes, warming my outsides before I bit into the precious morsel to warm my insides.

The *knish* man's summer counterpart was the Good Humor ice-cream man. He announced his arrival with musical chimes you could hear long before his truck appeared. He was dressed like a laboratory technician in white pants, a white shirt with a smart black clip-on bow tie, and a white jacket topped off with a white cap that had a crisp black peak. Even his shoes were white. His outfit bestowed upon him a look of professionalism more appropriately reserved for a doctor or dentist. His truck was filled with every frozen delight you could imagine; chocolate-covered pops, icicles, fudgsicles, ice-cream cones that had been dipped in nuts, and ice-cream sandwiches. Long before he opened up the refrigerated doors, which released a welcome blast of ice-cold air that momentarily conquered the steamy, humid temperature of the afternoon, he was knee deep in eager customers of all ages. Children and adults would come pouring out of the hot apartments. The Good Humor man was our Pied Piper. We would follow him anywhere and obediently line up as he dispensed his cold treasures. He also catered to customers who lived up on the top floors of the tenement buildings, those who could not make one more round trip of four flights of stairs, not even for ice cream. These women and children would lean out from the open windows as they lowered a small box or a bag tied to a cord with a note and exact change. Then they would wait for their order to be filled, sometimes carrying on a conversation with a neighbor or friend below. When the crowd began to thin out, the Good Humor man rang his chimes one more time, then briskly hopped into his truck and drove to the next corner, where he was sure to receive another warm welcome.

During the Jewish holidays, a solitary, dark-skinned Arab would suddenly appear outside the synagogue, pushing a cart filled with homemade honey-sweetened sesame candies, pistachio nuts, hot roasted chestnuts, and assorted exotic sweets wrapped in shiny papers. I never knew if he spoke English, or if he even spoke at all, because his transactions were conducted in silence. There he stood like a sentinel and did not leave until the sun went down, only to reappear the next day. This would go on until the end of the holiday. He would vanish as silently as he had appeared, probably returning to his family. I never knew where he came from or how he knew exactly when to return. I am sure we probably looked as alien to him as he did to us.

When the winter weather seriously set in with temperatures falling every day, and the streets were covered with the first snowfall, small glass-enclosed cases would appear outside candy stores. Inside were rows of charlotte russe, made out of white cardboard cups, fluted and lined with thin layers of sponge cake and swirls of fresh whipped cream, topped with a real maraschino cherry. The whipped cream stayed fresh and cool in the crisp, freezing weather. As it entered your mouth, it would dissolve with a delicate sweetness against your taste buds. At once, having tasted this delicacy, you were hooked. It was torture to pass the magical glass case day after day and not have the five cents to purchase this gossamer delight. No matter how long I had to wait for this exotic treat, as soon as the whipped cream touched my lips, all my senses were sated. Of course, I always saved the cherry for last.

The streets were also filled with familiar peddlers, repairmen, and salesmen who would sell almost anything on the installment plan. Every Friday you could be sure to find the horseradish man, who carried a small home-made grinder on his back and a box of fresh horseradish roots. His familiar call would invite the *balaboostas* to leave their kitchens long enough to buy some fresh, mouth-watering horseradish to go with the *Shabbas gefiltefish*. He was often followed by the man who would sharpen your knives, setting up his work space wherever his services were needed, sparks flying from his sharpening stone. Minutes later the familiar cry of the umbrella repairman would announce his presence. For pennies he would replace a rib on a broken umbrella, making it as good as new. An old wagon strung with cowbells, pulled by an old horse, would make its way down the street, the peddler shouting, "I buy clothes. I buy clothes." This was the junkman. Often the few pennies you got for an old pair of shoes, an old pot, or a pan would go a long way toward buying some item of food for the day. The newspaper man who sold the Yiddish paper, *The Forward*, would march up and down the street in all kinds of weather, an old rope over his shoulder creating a sling that held his papers in place. This poor man stuttered and was greeted with hurtful jokes and laughter as he shouted, "*F-F-F-Forward, F-F-F-Forward*. Who wants a paper for *Sh-Sh-Shabbas*?" No one, however, would ever buy their paper from anyone but the *Forward* man.

There was a parade of installment-plan salesmen who would knock on your door and tempt *balaboostas* to buy their wares. Linens, clothing, kitchenware, and small handmade rugs with oriental scenes were a mark of style in those days. Every poor apartment had several hanging on the walls in the living room. These peddlers would then return every week for their twenty-five-cent installment payment. Even insurance was bought and paid for in this manner. When Mama did not have the money for the weekly payment, she would pull the blinds down and lock the door as soon as she saw the salesman coming up the street. In silence she waited out his persistent knocking.

None of these creditors was ever as zealous as the little rabbi who would insist upon leaving a small metal box in which you were to make daily deposits for Jewish orphans. In Yiddish the box was called a "*pishka*." The rabbi, dressed in his official black hat, his forelocks draped over each ear, a full beard, and a long black coat, would carry a worn leather briefcase that seemed to hold an endless supply of *pishkas*. Once you accepted a box, and you really had no choice, the rabbi would write your name down in his ledger and thereafter would stop by weekly to collect your donations. We were so poor it was often difficult to deposit pennies every day. The rabbi would give Mama and Bubbe a tongue-lashing for not being charitable enough. He would leave with a warning that they just had to do better next time.

There was also a procession of street musicians: violinists, clarinet players, and a one-man band who played a harmonica on a frame in front of his face, an accordion and cymbals strapped between his knees. These performing artists would play in the small courtyards on a Sunday morning, sending up a serenade through the tightly stacked apartments. Soon windows would open, and pennies wrapped in bits of paper would shower down on them. In this way people showed their appreciation of this pleasant interruption of the work week.

There were playful treats for the children as well; trucks with small merry-go-rounds would appear in the summertime. For two pennies you could mount your horse and be in hot pursuit of the horse in front of you in a matter of minutes. There was much laughter and taunting of the unfortunate children who did not have the price of admission. They encircled the truck with sad faces, some unable to hold back the tears.

Summertime was the best time of the year. With the end of the long, cold, confining winter and brief daylight came mild weather and long hours of sunshine. The amount of time children were allowed to spend outdoors increased. We had one pair of roller skates for the three of us, causing many quarrels and tears. When you finally got your turn, the freedom of going downhill on your skates, with the wheels carrying you faster and faster away from the confines of home, was absolutely exhilarating. Broken skates were recycled by the older boys, who would construct wooden scooters with noisy, discarded roller-skate wheels to compete in soapbox derby races. But no matter how many activities took place during the day, everything came to a halt when fathers came home from work, and families sat down to eat supper together.

The caravan of characters was endless and became part of the family scene. They interrupted the drudgery of our lives and often knew as much about us as our own families: who had died, who had been born, who had married, and who had run away with someone else's spouse. Gossip was rampant, often distorting and exaggerating information out of all proportion. Juicy tidbits were repeated from one neighbor to the other. The familiarity of our surroundings and the repetitive weekly and annual events went a long way, however, to provide a sense of security in the struggle to survive during the Depression. Everyone knew everyone else. In that respect, the teeming, crowded streets of Brooklyn were no different than the small *shtetls* in Europe. In spite of the crowded conditions and the poverty that stalked everyone, there was little crime, and no one was ever mugged or attacked where I lived. It was safe to walk the streets after dark and for children to play outdoors in the long, hot, summer nights.

Life was hard, it was true, but everyone was in the

same boat, and there was no division by class or economics. There was only one class: the poor class. Socialization was swift, and most of us acquired an awareness, which developed into coping skills that lasted a lifetime. Having survived life in the streets of Brownsville, it was easier to find your place in the rush and pressure of the big city. The streets were classrooms and training grounds that sharpened our wits and hardened our bodies for the future battles. Many never left the neighborhoods, living out their childhoods, marrying neighbors, and establishing families and households in the same buildings where they had been raised and where their parents and grandparents might still live.

Life in the *shtetl* in Brownsville went on uninterrupted until the end of World War II. The long-awaited peace and the prosperity that followed made it possible for many *shtetl* residents to migrate to the suburbs of Long Island, repeating the journeys of their parents and grandparents who had left their homelands for a new life in golden America.

Summertime in Brooklyn

I didn't know why Mama's short temper became even shorter as summer approached. I loved the summer. The hot, humid days turned the city streets into playgrounds. I was released from heavy winter clothing and long school days. I was free to spend hours outdoors, away from Mama's scolding and punishment. The boys played game after game of stickball and ring-o-levio. Girls engaged in tournaments of hopscotch, or just hung out with favorite chums. The sun did not set until 9:00 P.M., and sometimes it felt like bedtime could be put off until the next day.

Summer meant more work for Mama and Bubbe, but we children were oblivious to that. Mama would chase furiously after every muddy footprint with her mop as we kept up a lively traffic in and out of the apartment. The more vigorously we played outdoors, the faster laundry accumulated. She washed and ironed every day. She turned off lights, closed doors to keep the flies out, and picked up after us as soon as we left the room. There was also the ongoing battle with the old icebox that could not keep up with the demands of summer heat. Food spoiled quickly, and a block of ice, which had lasted at least two days in the winter, now must be replaced daily. As a result, the pan under the icebox overflowed frequently. Out would come Mama's mop again as she scolded and cursed, perspiration glistening on her face.

The crowded, noisy city streets offered little space for playing quiet, make-believe games with your best friends, but the courtyard of our tenement building created a sense of privacy, and the brick walls cast a welcome shade, giving us some respite from the bright summer sun. It was against that background that ongoing soap-opera dramas were played out. I was always the princess or the queen. As soon as I fashioned an old baby blanket into a royal cape, I immediately assumed the authority of my position. I dictated who was to be the Mama or Papa or the children or the servant in the drama. Out would come the broken doll carriage and the hand-me-down doll with one eye and no shoes. An old box of chipped and cracked dishes served lunches and teas. Seldom were there any special treats available during these pretend meals. That never stopped us. Our imagination created feasts and banquets. The scarcity of any real props never discouraged us. Our imagination helped elevate us from dreary reality.

Sometimes the heat of the day would be interrupted by a daring boy who would open the corner fire hydrant with a wrench, his boldness punctuated by a mischievous wink. He was an instant hero. Off we would go running to Mama, pleading with her to let us take our clothes off and play in the cold, gushing fountain. Mama, often so drained by the heat herself, would quickly give us permission to undress down to our underwear and join the other children. No child in the whole neighborhood had the luxury of owning a bathing suit. The squeals of delight and the daring feats by the older boys playing leapfrog over the spouting fire hydrant added to the icy refreshment of the water. The grownups hanging out of the tenement windows seemed to enjoy the sight of such sheer joy. Even the local policeman walking his beat stood back away from the spray and smiled at the carnival-like scene. Dogs would join us, barking and nipping at wet ankles, and even venturing into the cold water themselves.

All good things must come to an end and when they do it is always too soon. Mothers would start calling from windows, ordering their kids to come home now before they caught their death of cold. It was hard to hear anything above the noise of the water and laughter and shouting. It was also easy to pretend you didn't hear your mama calling. Sometimes you could extend this joyful respite for fifteen minutes, or even half an hour. Ultimately, however, an angry mother would leave her post at the window and come down to the street. There she would grab her child by an ear or the back of the neck and drag her captive home.

Although I was deathly afraid of my Mama, even I would not always hear her the first time she called me. Suddenly she would appear, her eyes angry and her mouth spewing a nonstop attack as she approached. She had to keep her distance, though, to avoid getting drenched. It only made her angrier as she tried to round us up. No sooner had she caught the attention of one of my brothers than the other would duck and disappear from her view. They seemed to be able to put off the inevitable moment of her grasp. I was an easier target. In fear I would stop dead in my tracks. Mama would grab me by my arm and drag me all the way home, my bare feet scorching on the hot pavement. Didn't I hear her calling me through the window until she was hoarse? Didn't I have enough sense to come out of the water before my lips turned blue and I caught pneumonia?

By now Mama was roughly rubbing my cold body with a towel, interrupting herself frequently to run to the open window and yell at my brothers to come home this minute. Her demands continued to fall on deaf ears, which made her angrier and rougher as she turned back to me. Finally, dry and bruised and dressed again, I was told to sit still and not get dirty as she ran down to the street again to get my brothers. Even they could not avoid Mama's reach forever, and soon they too would be subjected to her verbal tirade and a couple of whacks across the side of the head. They recovered quickly, however, escaping from her scornful ministering to the small room they shared, where they could be heard whispering and laughing.

Being the oldest and the only girl, I was never included in my brothers' close relationship. I would listen to their laughter and wonder how they could be so happy in the same family where I felt so miserable and alone. How could they joke about Mama's anger when I felt so vulnerable and victimized? This was often borne out by the more frequent attacks and scoldings Mama aimed at me. Yet, during the freedom of summer I could even forget about my loneliness. I knew I could soon escape to the street.

Roller skating was something else I loved to do in the summer. The skates clamped onto your shoes, tightened by a key worn around your neck on a string. We owned only one pair of skates, and most of the time I was over-ruled by my brothers, who assumed ownership. There were times, however, when I could go off by myself, quickly attaching the skates to my shoes. Even as I skated to freedom I could hear Mama's warnings not to tear my clothes, scuff my shoes or, God forbid, get hurt.

It was a struggle to tighten the skates on your shoes just enough so they would stay on as you raced along the sidewalk. If you tightened the clamps too much they would cut into your shoes and separate the soles or tear into the canvas of your sneakers. When that happened all hell would break loose for there was no money for an extra pair of shoes. Those dire circumstances did not dampen the joy of skating, nor did the pain of the sharp metal of the clamps digging into my feet. Even when I had a boil on my big toe, which for some reason I had frequently, I would skate. Mama complained at the time it took her to treat the boil. In addition, a hole would have to be cut out of my sneakers to accommodate a huge bandage that had been soaked with an evil-smelling, dark ointment. I must have been a sight, my skates digging painfully into my big toe. Often by the time I got home the bandage would be streaked with blood. This angered Mama, and she would threaten to never let me go skating again. Though I may have been grounded for a while or even physically punished, I always looked forward to skating. I quickly forgot the punishment or the pain of the bruised toe once I was as free as the wind.

Another game I happily engaged in during the summer nights was playing Tarzan. As kids we were all influenced by Tarzan on the movie screen as he went swinging through the jungle. He emitted his bloodcurdling call for all the world to hear. I somehow acquired the ability to mimic that call with such accuracy that I was always the one who played Tarzan. I would cup my hands around my mouth, raise my face to the sky and transport myself to the jungle with the most powerful and commanding sounds I could release from my vocal cords. It was as if all my pent-up fears and repressed feelings had finally found release. My friends would cheer me on. Tired grown-ups looking for a little peace and quiet after a hot day did not appreciate my efforts. Shouts and curses rained down on us through open windows as we smothered our laughter with our hands so as not to reveal our hiding places.

Last but not least of the excitements of summer was sleeping on the roof. If you have never lived in Brooklyn during a heat wave, you probably have no idea how exhausting it can be. The brick buildings soak up and hold on to the relentless heat. The walls inside the apartments are literally hot to the touch day and night. If you could afford an electric fan, it only circulated the stagnant air. It seemed impossible to sleep indoors on those nights.

I remember one night in particular when there was a major evacuation from stifling, crowded apartments to the black, tarred rooftop. Mama, Papa, and Bubbe carried our mattresses up to the rooftop, while we children carried the pillows. Newspaper had to be spread under the mattresses for the tarred rooftop was filthy and blackened everything that came in contact with it. We were all exhausted after many hot, sleepless nights and quickly collapsed on the mattresses, though there was little room and no privacy. All of the twenty families who lived in our building were on the roof that night. The older children were constantly being warned to stay away from the edge of the roof. Smaller children were held tightly. At least there was a breeze. Even the avaricious mosquitoes were tolerated. The magic of sleeping under the stars was not unnoticed. Fretful babies became quiet. Soon everyone slept in blissful oblivion. Forgotten were complaints, worries, disagreements, and the heat.

Suddenly, without any warning, in the still, dark, early hours of the morning, storm clouds quickly hid the sparkling stars and the bright moon. We were awakened by a loud thunderclap, followed by silver streaks of lightning and a sudden downpour. Sharp cries filled the once silent night. Everyone scrambled to gather belongings, then pushed toward the single exit from the roof. Hysterical and desperate, everyone rushed toward the door. We pushed and yelled, trying in vain to protect ourselves from getting soaked. Mattresses were pushed ahead like cumbersome shields. Mothers desperately tried to herd their children in front of them to keep them from falling off the roof.

Miraculously we got to our apartment, totally exhausted and covered with sticky sweat and black grime from the tarred roof. We were all drained, but tempers were flaring. It was four o'clock in the morning. Further sleep was impossible. To add to our distress, the windows had to be closed against the storm. The apartment literally began to steam. The rain was fierce, and a hot, humid wind was whipping the storm into a frenzy accompanied by thunder and lightning that shook the old building.

I was covered with damp, salty perspiration that stuck to my hair and the flimsy nightgown I was wearing. Every space of my exposed skin was covered with black tar soot, punctuated with mosquito bites that were too numerous to count. They spread out over my skin in itchy welts. Terrified of the thunder and lightning, I covered myself with a sheet. I would not come out until the storm had passed. Finally, Mama could open the windows, and the apartment was filled with a fresh, cool breeze that followed the storm.

We all began to calm down, exhausted from the trial of the adventure of sleeping on the roof. Hands and faces were washed. One more drink of water was gulped. I passed out, dead to the world, and slept soundly until the hot sun began to stream into the window in the morning. As I woke, I could already hear Mama complaining to Bubbe about having to bathe the three of us and all the washing and cleaning she had to do on yet another hot day. This was absolutely the last time she would let us sleep on the roof. At the moment, I was not at all eager to repeat that experience either.

Later, I was able to escape to the street again and meet with other bleary-eyed kids who had barely made it through the night. All was soon forgotten, however, as we resumed our games and fantasies. After all, this was summertime in Brooklyn, and it was many weeks before school would start again. Another long, bright, free day awaited me. Perhaps I could grab the skates before my brothers realized they were missing. I could be off, skating rapidly, creating a breeze against my face, once more escaping from home. Summertime was not over yet.

Papa's New Teeth

When I was that little girl in Brooklyn during the Depression years, I learned early not to ask for anything that had a price tag attached to it. After the paying of rent and keeping the family fed and clothed, there was nothing left over from Papa's meager earnings. Mama would often have to humble herself and go to the local grocery lady, who was also our neighbor, for credit. It was a bitter pill for Mama to swallow. Every single family on the block was in the same life-and-death struggle, but Mama was stoic, proud, and very private.

Under these difficult circumstances, doctor visits and dental care were unheard of, outside of emergencies. As a result, we walked around with cavities in our teeth, and most illnesses were treated with purging enemas, alcohol sponge baths, and old-world home remedies. Many of them actually worked. One of Bubbe's unique contributions to our health care was to sew small sacks containing evil-smelling camphor cubes, which were then pinned on our underwear. This was guaranteed to keep illness and evil spirits at a distance. It was probably effective in warding off bacteria, because no one would dare come near you because of the strong vapors that were released every time you moved.

I don't remember going to the dentist until I was

about ten, and then only because I was sent home by the
school nurse when she discovered I had an abscessed
tooth, which had to be pulled. The public school system
attempted, against impossible odds of poverty, fear, and
ignorance, to enforce hygienic and health standards. To
be sent home by the school nurse with a note instructing
parents not to send the child back to school until the
medical problem had been solved was a very threatening
and humiliating experience and tantamount to being
found guilty of committing a crime. Even though a doctor's house call cost only $3.00 in those days, since we
could not even afford the expense of toothbrushes and
toothpaste, medical care was out of the question. I don't
think Papa, Mama, or Bubbe ever saw the inside of a
doctor's or dentist's office. They came from long-suffer-
ing stock and just endured hardships, resigned to making
the best of things. After years of such neglect, however,
Papa's poor teeth gave up entirely one day and something
had to be done.

I don't remember paying much attention to how
Papa's teeth looked. He smoked Camel cigarettes, which
even Papa could afford because they cost only a penny
for two cigarettes. His fingers and teeth were stained by
the tobacco, but his smile was warm and adoring when
he looked at me. I didn't even mind the smell of the stale
tobacco on his breath. He was just my own Papa. He
must have developed multiple dental problems over
time, and the cheapest, most expeditious solution was to
extract all his teeth and replace them with dentures.

I always knew there was some trouble brewing when
Papa and Mama began to whisper. Such secretiveness

would create a chilling sensation in my chest as I wondered what disaster was on its way now. Were we going to be put out on the street because Papa had not been able to pay the rent? Was Papa out of work again? Whatever the crisis, it was never discussed in front of the children, so each incident carried the threat of the apocalypse. When faced with an inevitable problem or emergency, Mama and Papa would lie, assuring us that everything was all right. This created much confusion, for they continued to look worried. Part of me wanted to believe them. Part of me never believed them. Was I being shielded from an approaching disaster or were Mama and Papa stalling to avoid having to deal with anxious, crying children? Such situations were not the basis on which trust and security could flourish.

It was with much relief that I learned the whispering this time was about Papa going to the dentist to get new teeth. That sounded like a great idea and not at all a crisis. I never did know how Papa arranged to pay for his new teeth. Perhaps he had found some starving, novice of a dentist who agreed to let him pay his bill on the installment plan. Papa had no choice. His teeth were rotting, and he was in pain. He tried to minimize the seriousness of the situation by joking about what a dashing fellow he would be, and saying that he would bite my tush as soon as he got his new teeth. I squealed with delight.

When Papa left for the dentist, the farewell scene was probably not unlike the time Mama had to go on to America and leave Papa in Romania for a whole year. I began to get worried. This did not look like a whole lot of fun. There was much crying and clinging and then the final painful separation. It was as if they would never see each other again. There was no consoling Mama that afternoon. Time passed slowly with Mama frequently looking out the window for Papa and pleading with God to spare him and send him home soon. Finally, Mama sat down, a cold compress on her head, her hands in her lap, staring at the wall, and just waited. Hours later Papa stumbled into the apartment. He looked near death, ashen and weak. He could not speak. All his teeth were gone. Blood spurted from his torn and ripped gums. He looked as if he had been beaten by some crazed attacker.

Mama, galvanized into action, began thanking God for sending Papa home and placed a pillow on the couch, insisting that he lie down immediately. She scolded us if we got too close to him, perhaps trying to spare us the horror of Papa's battle wounds. He lay there, blood drooling out of his mouth, staining the pillow as Mama applied a cold compress to his jaw. An icebag would have brought him more relief, but we did not have an icebag, and Papa refused to let Mama ask for a block of ice on credit. He just would not hear of it. He downplayed his pain and assured her that he was already feeling better. As if to prove that, he struggled to make his way to the bathroom where he could be heard gargling and rinsing his mouth with salt water. The sounds of all that spitting made me feel sick to my stomach. When he lay down again on the bloodstained pillow, I was overcome by the memory of my little brother Himey and how he looked when all his teeth had been extracted.

The smell of the blood and the sight of my father's

face swelling and becoming discolored fascinated and horrified me at the same time. Would he ever look like my Papa again? Would the bleeding ever stop? It scared me. I tried to comfort myself, remembering that Himey's teeth had eventually all grown back. I wondered how long Papa would have to wait for his teeth to grow back. Mostly I wondered how long it would take for Papa to look like Papa again. Since nothing was ever explained, and I had only my childhood fears and fantasies to plague me, reality was distorted out of all proportion. There was nothing to do but wait in fearful silence.

For two weeks, Papa, without a tooth in his head, went to work and did not even take the lunch Mama always packed for him, for he could not chew at all. When he came home he would try to be the old cheerful, loving Papa, but I could not understand a word he said and was afraid to get too close to him. I began to have nightmares about Papa's teeth. I would wake up in a cold sweat, wondering whether I might be next. Would Mama take me to the dentist and have all my teeth removed so she wouldn't get any more notes from the school nurse?

Days went by and still no sign of Papa's new teeth growing back, though the swelling and discoloration on his face did finally subside. One day he announced he was going to the dentist that very afternoon and that when he returned he would have his new teeth. Is it possible he could grow a full set of teeth just by going to the dentist? I waited some more, trying to hide my impatience so as not to annoy or anger Mama.

Time moved slowly. I kept opening and closing the window, looking for Papa, until Mama slammed the window shut and chased me out of the house. There I sat, on the stoop of our apartment house, facing the direction of Papa's arrival. He had a very special way of swinging his shoulders when he walked, and I had long ago learned to recognize his gait from a distance. I loved waiting for Papa to come home from work and would stand at the corner, watching for that familiar, beloved silhouette. Finally, there he was, his shoulders swinging with each step.

I ran to the corner to be the first one to greet Papa and see his new teeth. But my joy was short-lived. The hollowness of his cheeks was gone, his lips no longer looked shrunken, and he seemed more like Papa at first, but as soon as he smiled broadly, revealing his new teeth, I recoiled. This man looked like my Papa, walked like my Papa, but was not my Papa at all. His parted lips displayed a mouth jammed full of large, stark-white teeth that filled every space in his mouth, and clicked when he talked. I was terrified at this unexpected transformation and was not entirely convinced it was Papa at all. I ran home in tears, straight to my Bubbe whose soft arms stifled my cries. Papa was close behind and met Mama at the door. I peeked out behind Bubbe and there was that skull face again, but this time it was talking and smiling at Mama. Mama recoiled in horror. She even covered her face with her hands and began to cry loudly. She couldn't bear to look at Papa either.

Poor Papa put aside his own struggle to keep the large, porcelain teeth in place, displaying a smile that bordered on a leer. He held Mama and promised her he would take the teeth out and never wear them again. Far from calming my mother, it only resulted in escalating her wailing and she began to wring her hands. With tears running down her face she told him he had to wear his teeth, they cost so much money, she would get used to the way he looked. She was sorry she was so upset. So they held each other as my brothers and I watched from a safe distance, not understanding this bizarre scene at all.

Everyone was exhausted from the stressful day and settled down early that evening. During the night I had to go to the bathroom and was totally unprepared for the grotesque sight of Papa's teeth, immersed in a glass of water, which was resting on the sink. My heavy-lidded, sleepy eyes opened wide as I made a mad dash for the door. Nothing could convince me that had I stayed a moment longer, the teeth would not have jumped out of the glass and pounced on me for disturbing their privacy. That night I lay awake for a long time in fear of the teeth, afraid to go back to the bathroom and trying to prevent my poor bladder from humiliating me during the night.

Papa did keep his teeth, but it was some time before Mama could look at him. It also took some time for me to return to my special place on his lap without the fear that his teeth would jump out of his mouth and bite me. A few times I had actually seen the teeth leap out of Papa's mouth while he was eating or talking.

Eventually castanet clicking of the teeth settled down to an intermittent lisp that was hardly noticed at all. Mercifully, time and familiarity lessened the impact of this family trauma. I could walk by the teeth in the glass and not notice them. I even grew to like the way my Papa's teeth sparkled. Years later when a couple of teeth became chipped, Papa refused to have them repaired. He said now he looked more natural; actually it was too expensive to go back to the dentist. The false teeth became discolored by tobacco stains, and in time the frightful ordeal of Papa's new teeth became blurred and the whole family settled down. We never talked about it again.

The Rebellion
of the Furnace

There were few comforts or considerations that tenement landlords were compelled to provide their tenants in the 1930s. Their motto was to do as little as possible, avoid all contact with the tenants, and collect the rent the first of each month. Some basic necessities, however, were dictated by the Board of Health. For instance, hot water all year round and heat during the bitter cold East Coast winter months were to be provided for the monthly $40.00 rent.

These ancient, neglected buildings owned by absentee landlords were always in disrepair. Small problems developed into major disasters in time, causing much discomfort and hardships for the poor, powerless tenants. Such a problem was the furnace in our building. It was a relic well on its way to achieving antique status. During the winter it seemed to stamp its cast-iron foot and go on strike as soon as the weather threatened freezing temperatures. The janitor would, nevertheless, optimistically fill the furnace's belly with newly delivered coal, hoping for the best, but after much laborious wheezing, choking, and coughing up of smoke, the furnace would usually quit altogether.

The janitor, who had no mechanical skills at all, would go through a routine of emptying the freshly laid coal, rattling the draft, and poking around in the dark cavern of the furnace, faking an internal inspection. He would then make one more effort, refill the furnace belly with the coal, and attempt to ignite it, to no avail. This time the furnace did not even bother to wheeze or choke. It just simply refused to respond at all. Not a sound. It was stone cold. The janitor quickly accepted defeat, glad to creep to his dark living space, hoping to avoid meeting any of the angry tenants along the way. He would then take a few long drafts from his whiskey bottle and settle in for hibernation while hell froze over all around him.

A winter morning in 1933 was no different as I awoke to a freezing room, with dim light barely making its way through the window. The room was so cold that frozen crystals clung to the inside windowpane, creating prism designs on the glass through which the morning light reflected. Wrapping the blanket around me so that only my nose peeked out from beneath the warm folds, I made my way to the window and my eyes opened wide with excitement.

It had snowed so hard during the night that snow-drifts had piled up on the sidewalks and steps. My warm breath melted some of the crystals on the window. I pressed closer to get a better view of the magical snow that continued to drop silently to the ground, transforming everything with its cold, white downy feathers. The anticipation of playing in the snow, making snowballs, taking my turn on the broken sled, which only leaned slightly when it went down hill, threatening to toss you into the snow, was so tantalizing. I forgot about the freezing room.

I dropped the blanket, dressed quickly, eager to go downstairs to gulp down my breakfast. I was already rehearsing my appeals to Mama to let me go out, promising to keep my coat buttoned and my scarf on so I would be sure not to catch cold. In my excitement I had not noticed that the radiator was silent. There were no promising gurgles or hiccups announcing the arrival of heat this morning.

Mama, Bubbe, and my little brothers were already in the kitchen. Papa had left earlier for work. Mama appeared to be in a foul mood already. We had not even had breakfast yet, and she was already angry. What was she angry about now? I didn't have long to wait for the answer, for no sooner was I seated at the table in front of a steaming bowl of Bubbe's oatmeal when Mama picked up a large serving spoon and began to beat the old heating pipe with such force that peeling paint and rust began to fly in all directions. There was absolutely no heat this morning, and Mama hoped the noise would arouse the janitor to hurry to the basement and fire up the furnace.

That done, she returned to the table, first coaxing and scolding me and my brothers to eat our cereal while it was hot. We busied ourselves with breakfast, talking about the fresh snow and making plans to go outdoors. Mama immediately began to warn us of the danger of playing outdoors in the snow. You would surely catch a cold, you would slip and, God forbid, break a leg, you would get hit in the eye with a snowball, you would soon be soaked to the skin and your hands would freeze, and your fingers would fall off, God forbid. Her warnings and threats did little to dampen our enthusiasm. We begged to be allowed to go out for just a little while.

The kitchen remained icy cold and Mama attacked the pipe again with renewed vigor, this time using a hammer. As if this were an invitation for all the other housewives in the building to join in this attack, a cacophony of ear-shattering blows resounding through the old heating system began to shatter the cold, which was beginning to penetrate our clothing. The walls in the old building began to shake with the fierceness of this open warfare. It was becoming evident that the furnace was broken again. There would be no heat on what promised to be the coldest day of the winter.

Mama had whipped herself into a fury, and she began to curse the furnace, the janitor, the landlord, and herself for having such bad luck. Bubbe stood helplessly by, attempting to calm her, but once Mama was in high gear, she seldom stopped. Perhaps anger was warming her up, for her face had become quite red. Adventures in the snow would have to wait. This was no time to ask Mama for anything.

Mama put on an old housedress over her nightgown, which trailed out beneath the faded dress, wrapped herself in my father's old sweater, and marched herself down to the janitor's dark basement apartment, quickly joined by other tenants. In the meantime, Bubbe began to dress us in our outdoor winter clothing, for the temperature in the house was freezing. Then she lit the oven and the stove, attempting to take the chill out of the air. No sooner had she done that than the mice and roaches that had been huddling together in the insulation of the oven doors began to run for their lives, my Bubbe right behind them with her broom.

In time Mama returned, reporting on the angry housewives and how they attacked the janitor, waking him from his drunken stupor. For a moment it appeared that the reason there was no heat was that the janitor had passed out and had not lit the furnace. That optimism was short-lived as the janitor struggled with his slurred speech to let them know that he had already given up on the furnace. He had tried to make it work earlier, and it just would not.

This poor black man had spent all of his working years in old buildings in Jewish ghetto neighborhoods and had acquired a good knowledge of Yiddish, and so the barrage of Yiddish expletives rained upon him by raging housewives did not fall on deaf ears. His fractured Yiddish, dramatically slowed down by the effect of the alcohol he had consumed, defied translation. He struggled mightily to make himself understood and defend himself. He wearily insisted that the furnace had needed repair since last winter but the landlord had refused to heed his warnings that this bucket of bolts was ready to collapse again. The landlord had heard this story before but was determined to get away without correcting the multiple problems of the overburdened and neglected heating system for one more winter. He knew he could escape to Florida, avoiding the bitter-cold Brooklyn weather altogether as well as the sharp tongues of the freezing, furious tenants. Now the landlord was nowhere to be found. We would have to wait until he turned up.

Resigned to their fate once more, in impotent rage and with chattering teeth, the women had returned to their apartments, defeated again.

Mama began to cry as Bubbe put her old, worn winter coat around her. Her rough, red, chapped hands covered her face as she surrendered to the futility of life in the tenements. She cursed the landlord, she cursed the janitor, and she cursed herself for having such a miserable life. What, after all, had she done to deserve such a fate. This last statement was always addressed to God as she raised her face and her arms up to the ceiling and pleaded with Him to have pity on her. This did nothing to solve the problem. There was nothing anyone could do.

Bubbe, ever our champion, suggested to Mama that she might as well let the children go out and play in the snow or else we would just be underfoot. Exhausted, Mama agreed and began to bundle and swaddle us into so many layers of clothing that it was impossible to bend or turn without losing your balance. You would then land on your back, as helpless as a turtle in its shell, unable to get up. Nevertheless, we were excited to get outdoors, and I didn't even complain as one more diaper pin was placed under my chin, tightening the rough fabric of my coat under my neck, making it impossible for me even to breathe freely. It was worth enduring such treatment, however, to be allowed to escape and play in the snow.

After a couple of hours outdoors, exhausted, our hands almost blue with cold, our old galoshes no longer able to protect our feet from the melting snow, our noses running, we returned to the apartment. I had forgotten about the furnace not working and was looking forward to warming myself by the hot radiator. It was not to be. When I entered the house no current of warm air greeted me. It was as cold indoors as it was outside.

Mama and Bubbe had busied themselves, stuffing newspapers into every crack around the windows. They had placed towels and rags under doorways and the oven and stove were on full force, using up the oxygen in the room, but the cold clung stubbornly to the apartment. Bubbe huddled us around the oven as we undressed. Mama began to complain about how wet we were, scolding that we would not be allowed out again. Even the dry clothing I put on did nothing to warm me, and my teeth began to chatter.

Bubbe made hot cocoa for all of us, a welcome treat under the circumstances. Mama then roughly wrapped us in blankets and told us to sit still and not to remove the blankets or we would catch pneumonia for sure.

This scene was repeated during four interminable, freezing days. The snow finally stopped, but it had ceased to be an inviting attraction. We were too cold to leave our blankets and the scant warmth that came from the oven. The tenants, totally defeated and resigned, finally stopped cursing the janitor who, after all, was not the cause of the problem. Families could be heard arguing and shouting as tempers wore thin.

Finally, on the afternoon of the fourth day, a lumbering, noisy, repair truck arrived. I ran to the window to watch. Mama took to the hall again and joined others marching down to confront the janitor, who was now in the cellar with the repair man. They tried to extract a promise that heat would soon be restored. Though no such promises were forthcoming, we felt a bit optimistic as we heard the sounds of hammering and scraping coming up through the cold pipes.

We listened intensely for even the faintest sounds of restored life from below. Finally the old rusty pipes and radiators started to fuss, sputter, and hiccup. Small clouds of steam began to escape from the steam valves. The furnace that had remained silent in the dark cellar for days, like an old dying patient, was resurrected one more time. Though the apartment remained cold for hours after, the radiators got hotter and hotter. We were heartened by the noisy steam valves as we began to feel warmth in our frozen bones. Tempers calmed down, noses stopped running, and life returned to a more comfortable pace.

The Painter Is Coming

It was still months before *Pesach*. Already Mama and Bubbe were caught up in the frenzy of preparing the house for my favorite holiday. The painter was coming early this year. Last year he painted the kitchen and bathroom and it took only a couple of days. This year he would be in the house for at least a week. He would paint the entire apartment.

Before he arrived, a clear path had to be prepared for his ladders, paint buckets, and brushes. All the furniture had to be moved to the center of the rooms and covered with sheets. Floors were swept clean of dust balls that had gathered in dark corners under beds and behind heavy furniture. Brooms covered with old pillowcases brushed away the cobwebs from the ceilings. Clothes had to be removed from the one closet that served our entire family. This in itself did not take very much time, because we did not own many articles of clothing. The most time-consuming job was clearing the kitchen cupboards of dishes, utensils, and groceries stored on shelves and in drawers. Mama and Bubbe seemed to be everywhere at once, rushing from one task to another.

When all was ready for the painter, his first act would be to open wide all the windows to send the strong paint odors, loaded with lead and other toxins, into the icy outdoors. The stove and oven would be lit every day, but this did little to keep freezing wind from invading every room. When the oven heated up, it was not unusual to see a sleepy family of mice scattering for safety. City mice love to build nests in the asbestos insulation inside oven doors, living there safely until the oven is lighted.

Another problem could be predicted to develop during this turmoil. Cockroaches that had set up permanent housekeeping under shelf paper and behind dishes and utensils would be disturbed. Soon they could be seen everywhere, scurrying to escape Mama's well-aimed broom or rushing to avoid the death blow of her shoe. Like their neighbors the mice, these roaches did not venture out in daylight, staying out of sight, waiting in their dark bunkers for the night, when they would invade the kitchen in battle formation, searching for and finding bits of food on which to gorge themselves. You entered the dark kitchen at night at your own risk. If it was necessary to turn on the light, you had to retreat quickly to avoid being rushed by roaches skating across the linoleum floor to their secret hiding places.

These roaches were highly intelligent, although disgusting creatures. When the painter disrupted their daily routines, they would evacuate and invade another defenseless apartment, doubling that roach population. After the paint job, there would be a blessed short period when roaches seemed to disappear, but as soon as they were disturbed by tenants moving in or out of the building, or by preparations for the annual paint job, they would migrate to the next unsuspecting household and take over. Thus they would enter and exit apartments during the year like displaced persons, seeking shelter wherever they could find it, ignoring the fact that they were never, ever welcome.

Months before *Pesach*, there would be a noticeable increase of activity in the apartment building as the housewives began to vie for the painter's favor, attempting to be first on his schedule before the onset of the holiday. There were twenty families living in this ghetto building, and each housewife's needs were more urgent than her neighbors. They gave the painter no peace until he fixed a date with each of them. In our building, Mr. Borsack, who lived just above us, was also the painter and was always treated with great deference. Woe be unto you if sometime during the year you had a falling out with Mr. Borsack, his good wife, or one of his five mischievous sons. Fights would break out in the narrow hallways, and neighbors would besiege each other with complaints and threats if the Borsacks did not do something to control their wild bunch. The arguments would end with slamming doors. Silence would prevail once more. But now *Pesach* was approaching and it was hoped that Mr. Borsack would have long forgotten these confrontations. Each year he would take advantage of his exalted position. He would answer the housewives' requests with arrogant language or respond not at all as he disappeared amidst folds of heavy tarps, paint buckets, and ladders on his way to the next apartment.

Once Mr. Borsack was safely ensconced in our apartment, Mama would watch him closely, missing no chance to complain if he was not generous enough with his brush, or thin streaks of paint failed to cover a surface adequately. This was always a testy time. The challenge was to apply just enough pressure on Mr. Borsack to get him to repair the damage, but not enough to provoke him into a temperamental pout that would result in his storming out of the apartment, vowing never to return. This was not a rare occurrence. Mama would be left amidst the dust of plaster, dropcloths, and wet paintbrushes stuck fast to the lids of the cans. Out she would go, looking for Mr. Borsack, holding back her caustic tongue, pleading with him to be reasonable and finish the job. In all fairness to Mr. Borsack, the landlord provided him with the thinnest, cheapest paint, no better than whitewash. It took forever to dry, seemed to deteriorate as soon as he lifted his brush, and would disappear altogether after even the gentlest application of a good *balaboosta's* scrub cloth or *shmata*.

The year I was 13, Mama persuaded Mr. Borsack, with a $2.00 tip, to paint our apartment well before the holidays so that all would be ready for the first *Seder*. Everything was going well, even after days and nights of bitter cold and acrid paint odors that brought tears to our eyes and played havoc with our sinuses. Only the kitchen awaited Mr. Borsack's Passover treatment. Encouraged by the progress, Mama determined to convince him to work on one of the walls in the kitchen that, over time, had developed a big belly of loose plaster, barely holding together under the old oilcloth wall covering. Year after year Mama watched the belly get bigger and bigger, pregnant with plaster particles. This time Mama wore Mr. Borsack down, and he gave in to her. Before replacing the old wall covering with a new selection (more hideous than the last one), Mr. Borsack promised to per-form a caesarian on the belly and smooth out the wall. This was a decision he regretted as soon as he peeled away the first layer of oilcloth. Immediately a huge mound of broken plaster and a thick cloud of dust were released, revealing the open stud boards inside the wall and of course a few surprised roaches. Now Mr. Borsack was not only furious with Mama for talking him into this extra job, but he was also horrified. How would he explain his action to the landlord, who would not be inclined to deal kindly with him? All work came to an immediate halt. Mr. Borsack left, slamming the door behind him.

Days went by as we shivered in the freezing apart-ment while Mama and Bubbe tried to manage the daily needs of the family under extreme circumstances. Still no word from the landlord and no sight of Mr. Borsack. Mama was beside herself, wringing her hands, com-plaining to the four walls, appealing to them to provide her with a miraculous solution to this crisis that threat-ened the holiday preparations. Though Papa usually left such problems for Mama to solve, this time he went upstairs to talk to Mr. Borsack. Unfortunately, Papa fared no better than Mama and he returned empty-handed. He had been informed that the matter was out of Mr. Borsack's control. He was still waiting to hear from the landlord. A week later the landlord finally appeared and accused Mama of causing him much aggravation and expense. He demanded she pay for the damage before he would permit Mr. Borsack to return. This was out of the question, of course. Mama and Papa had no savings at all and could barely pay the $40.00 per month for rent. Only after the landlord agreed to let them pay for the damage with a $2.00 rent increase did he allow the paint job to resume. This was a dilemma of such magnitude that Mama had to hold her tongue and agree to his terms if we were to have a *Seder* that year.

When Mr. Borsack finally returned, he refused to talk to Mama. Nor was she eager to talk to him. She had been duly chastened and kept out of his way as much as possible.

The day finally arrived when Mr. Borsack gathered up his tools and left. Mama no longer needed to stay in his good graces. As he slammed the door, Mama said, "Good riddance," and applied herself to the job of restoring the household to sanity. She and Bubbe worked frantically to complete the holiday preparations.

The windows, which the painter had left open to keep from being asphyxiated by the evil-smelling, lethal paint fumes could finally be closed. This was done with cursing and scraped knuckles. Mr. Borsack had carelessly painted the wooden frames, which had frozen tight in the bitter winter cold. Mr. Borsack had also generously splattered the windowpanes with paint, revenge for the trouble Mama had caused him. With a sharp razor blade, Mama spent hours scraping off the paint, then cleaning the windows until they sparkled to her satisfaction. She frequently cursed Mr. Borsack and his whole family, forgetting how she had pleaded with him to paint our apartment, promising to do anything to make his work easier. Now all her pent-up frustration could finally be vented. She did not hold back. I stayed out of her way.

Meanwhile, the smell of Bubbe's good cooking struggled to overcome the lingering caustic odor. But every time the radiators, which now bore a fresh coat of paint, heated up, the acrid smell insulted the nostrils again. In an effort to help Mama forget her troubles, Papa surprised her by ordering new kitchen linoleum to replace last year's floor covering, now worn paper thin from Mama's relentless scrubbing. If you didn't look too closely at the flaws in Mr. Borsack's brushmarks, everything was clean, orderly, and ready for the holiday.

In time Mama's humiliation at losing the battle with the landlord was somehow transformed into a victory. Hadn't she finally gotten rid of the swollen kitchen wall? Soon the kitchen would be a hub of activity as Bubbe, surrounded by steaming pots and a hot oven, and producing a seemingly endless variety of Passover dishes, became the center attraction. Each year her *latkes* were more golden, her sponge cakes as light as feathers, and mouth-watering chopped liver, eggs, onions, and *matzoh brei* tantalized our appetites. Bubbe's wine grew richer and sweeter each time. *Pesach* was finally here.

The Sparrow

It stormed so hard last night I was sure Papa and I would not be able to go to the park today. I couldn't sleep, listening to the heavy raindrops attacking the windowpane as though they were searching for shelter from the storm. Finally, too tired to stay awake, I covered my head with the blanket, blocking out the fierce storm. In the morning my sleepy eyes greeted the bright sunshine in disbelief. The trees seem to be stretching their branches toward the sunlight. Papa and I will have our day in the park after all.

Filled with anticipation, I dress quickly, washing my hands and face. I try to be patient as Mama combs my hair this morning, even though she pulls hard through my curly tangles. I eat breakfast, careful to clean my plate so Mama won't scold. If I am a good girl, perhaps she won't find reason to spoil my day with Papa. I am relieved when Papa sits down for his breakfast. Mama won't make a fuss when Papa is in the room. He kisses all of us and reminds me he will take me to the park right after breakfast. I hold my breath for just a moment. Mama could yet spoil everything, but she doesn't. I relax.

As we walk out the door I promise Mama I won't take my jacket off, even though the balmy temperature is promising an early spring day. She warns Papa not to let

me roll down my heavy, white cotton stockings because
the weather might change and I could get a chill. He is
also not to allow me to run and get overheated. Finally,
we are on our way, out of Mama's reach. Papa is carrying a paper bag with two baloney sandwiches for our
picnic lunch. I am ecstatic while walking with Papa to the
trolley car stop.

I love walking with Papa. He holds my hand and
doesn't let go. When I walk with Mama I have to hold on
tightly to her hand because she walks too fast. I often trip
and fall. Then she gets mad. Not Papa. He doesn't take
such big steps, and even though I am a big eight-year-old
girl, he always carries me when I get tired. Sometimes I
ask him to carry me even when I'm not tired, so we can
talk with our heads close together. I love the way Papa
smells of cigarettes and the soap he uses when he shaves
every day.

I pulled on Papa's hand as soon as we got off the
trolley, impatient to walk through the archway entrance
of the park. The sounds of the traffic were quickly left
behind as I stepped on the deep, dewy carpet of grass.
The stillness was broken only by the sound of the breeze
coming in contact with the budding trees, releasing a
whisper that was carried from one tree to the next. I
wondered how long it would take for the trees to stop
whispering. When I asked Papa, he smiled and told me a
story about Russia, and how he would walk in the
woods, marking his path on the tree trunks so he would
not get lost. It was dark in those woods, but he was not
afraid. He loved the stillness too. I felt very close to Papa.

Our first stop was at the duck pond. The ducks were

as glad to see me as I was to see them. They immediately began to paddle furiously toward us, quacking to make sure we would know they were there. Papa had brought some stale bread and crumbled it into small pieces. The sun was warm on my back. I sat on a rock, scattering bread crumbs, making sure to offer some to the ducklings who could not keep up with the adults. Papa and I laughed as the ducklings dove into the water after the crumbs, their little feathered bottoms wiggling in the sunlight. All that feeding made me hungry, so we walked on in search of a spot for our private picnic.

Papa found just the right table and bench, under a giant tree, which cast a cool blanket of shade as we opened up our bag lunch. Immediately the aroma of the baloney made my mouth water. I wondered why I was never this hungry at home. I ate with gusto and could see that Papa was pleased. He took out the Yiddish paper from his pocket. This was always a special treat for me. The weekly romance serials were the forerunners of soap operas and just as compelling. Papa would read them to me in his soft, pleasant voice. I listened to words reflecting dramas too mature for me to really comprehend. But there was no mistaking the understanding shared between me and Papa.

Suddenly a soft sound at the other end of the table brought us out of the fantasy of the story. Something had fallen from the tree, but it was not a berry or a leaf. It was moving where it had landed. Papa and I quietly approached what looked like a small ball of feathers, moving with the breeze. Only when we got closer did I recognize a baby bird, sitting on spindly legs, barely able to support its tiny body. As we got closer it began to make little miserable peeping sounds. It was so weak and helpless. Any attempt to stand up resulted in its falling over on its back. Papa put his finger to his lips, cautioning me not to make a sound. We stood silently, like sentinels, making sure no harm would come to this tiny baby. Only when it stopped squirming did we sit down on the bench close enough to examine it. It cocked its head, as if no longer afraid. Papa left me with the little bird while he searched for a nest or for a distraught mother looking for her infant. But all was still, except for the peeping and the whispering trees.

It was getting late. We did not want to miss our trolley, but we could not leave the helpless little bird. Before I could even beg Papa to take it home, he reached into his pocket for his clean handkerchief and gently wrapped the baby in it, keeping up a stream of soft, soothing sounds that seemed to reassure the bird. Then Papa opened my jacket, placed the warm little package against my heart, and positioned my hand under this precious cargo. He told me not to close my fingers around the bird. I was sure my heart would jump out of my chest it was beating so hard. I caught my breath as I felt the bird moving under my hand. Papa praised me for being so careful.

On our way home Papa and I stopped at the junkman's store and he bought an old metal birdcage. Papa told me he would clean it well before it became the little bird's new home. I had confidence Papa could do all that. Somehow he would also successfully deal with Mama. She would surely object to "one more mouth to feed." But I had seen him increase our household with abandoned puppies and kittens despite Mama's objections. This was such a tiny baby, and I would promise to take care of it. Surely she would agree. My optimism began to fade when we came home and actually had to face Mama.

I held the little bird, wrapped in the handkerchief, in one hand; the other tightly clutching Papa's strong hand. Mama sized up the situation quickly. The first words that came out of her mouth were "No! Take that back where you found it." Mama had that determined look on her face, an expression I was very familiar with but one she seldom directed at Papa. Today she was not going to yield to him again and rescue another helpless creature. She almost blocked the doorway as she went on. "It has been scarcely a month since I got rid of the last stray dog you brought home. I told you then I will not let another animal in this house. I have enough to do. We just can't feed one more mouth."

Papa put the cage down. I stayed close to it, all the time gently cradling the sleeping bird. Papa began to soothe Mama and told her this time it would be different. There would be no cleaning up after this baby because he and I would take care of its needs, and it would be kept in the cage. I could see Mama begin to soften. I stood there, my heart racing and my mind trying to keep up with it. The bird began to stir in my hand. To distract myself I began to devise a plan for feeding the bird.

While Mama and Papa were still locked in negotiation, I quietly went into the kitchen with the bird and took a small piece of Bubbe's freshly baked bread. The chick began to peep loudly, opening its small beak as wide as it could, revealing a deep red mouth that hid its face completely. I chewed the bread into a sweet paste and placed the bird's beak between my lips. I let the sticky sweet mush drop into its mouth. Soon it was peeping and clamoring for food faster than I could provide it. Finally, it fell asleep in my hand, its little well-fed belly rising and falling with deep breaths.

I became aware of the silence now, and it filled me with renewed dread. I could no longer hear Mama and Papa but suddenly felt their presence. I don't know how long they had been standing in the kitchen doorway, watching me feed the bird. Nor did I have a clue at that moment whether Papa had won our case. Papa smiled, and I knew all was well. Mama was gruff, but she and Papa went to work cleaning the cage. Papa even made a little nest for the bird. I placed it in its new home as it slept soundly. I heaved a sigh of relief. The threatening situation was over. The bird could stay. Now I had to figure out how I would take care of it and not give Mama any reason for regretting her decision.

I took my parenting responsibilities seriously. I was determined to do whatever was necessary to protect the bird. My first challenge was keeping up with its demanding appetite. My small charge did not know the difference between daylight and darkness, and I had to be prepared at its first cries for more food, no matter what the time. I was a busy mama, and though I was inexperienced and sleep deprived, I found myself equal to the task. In a matter of days the fat little bird was supporting itself on stronger legs, hopping around on the floor of the cage. Its feathers had thickened to cover its body. It was beginning to look like a young sparrow. Instinctively I knew it was important for the bird to be warm. At night it curled up in its nest, but during the day I placed it on my shoulder, spreading my long hair around it, protecting it from an unexpected breeze. It soon learned to snuggle against my neck, chirping contentedly. It must have felt warm and safe close to me, and it tickled me with its nuzzling as it preened my hair. When it came time for the bird to take solid food, I offered it birdseed from my mouth. The smart little bird soon found its own way to the feeding cups in the cage and began feeding itself. My baby was growing up.

In a couple of weeks the bird began to strengthen its wings by flapping them furiously, but it could not fly. It was earthbound. Something had to be done to accommodate this next developmental stage. One day I sat on the bed with my fat, happy baby and decided to toss it gently up into the air. It flapped its wings but plopped down on the bed covers. Next time I held it in my hand, waiting for it to start its wing exercises, and when it began to flex its little muscles I gently tossed it up in the air again over the bed. This time the bird remained airborne for a moment or two before it landed safely. My bird began to get the hang of it as I gave it flying lessons for several days. Soon it was flying around the room, landing on my head. Even Mama marveled at my care of the bird and praised me. Papa and Bubbe were proud of me, too. I was delighted.

One morning I awoke to loud chirping and activity coming from the cage on the windowsill, next to the half-opened window. A sparrow had flown in, landing on the cage, causing all the excitement. My bird tried desperately to fly in its cramped quarters as the two creatures conversed in an excited foreign language. Immediately, I became sad and silent for I knew the meaning of that language. I knew the time had arrived for me to release the bird. I began to worry for its safety, even though I had taught it all it needed to know to survive. It could now fly, and it could eat seeds and greens. But it had never been outdoors on its own and did not know how to protect itself in dangerous situations. I had kept it warm and protected against my body. We were happy together. But not until a free sparrow landed on its cage did my bird become alive with a passion to be free—free to fly, and free to be in Nature with other birds.

It was with heavy hearts that Papa and I started out on a journey the next day, back to the park. I carried the cage, talking to my bird, trying to hold back the tears. Papa assured me I was doing the right thing and that the sparrow would really be happy to be free. We went to the same table where we had found my baby. With a lump in my throat I opened the cage door and called to the bird, as I had done so many times before. Responding to my familiar chirp, it hopped out and sat on top of the cage. It looked around and then flew to my shoulder where it sat for several minutes, playing with my hair. It flew up on a low branch and began to chirp timidly. From out of nowhere another sparrow appeared and they went through a little get-acquainted conversation. That accomplished, my bird flew back on to my shoulder but kept up the chirping dialogue with its new friend in the tree. There was no time for good-bye. Having found the freedom of its wings in open space, it flew away with its new friend into the vast green spaces of the park. It did not look back. I could see it no more.

I sat with Papa for a long time, the open cage reminding me of the empty space in my heart. But even in my pain I knew the bird had to be free in order to survive, and I had done the right thing. Papa picked me up and carried me home, talking in that same comforting way he had talked to the helpless baby bird when it had fallen out of the tree. I clung to Papa through my tears. I knew that one day I too would be big enough to find my own freedom. For now, Papa's arms would keep me safe.

Hot Dogs and Movies

Saturday morning. Not only is there no school today, but this is the day I go to the movies. The ominous cloud that hangs over me during the week suddenly lifts, and I am filled with joy and boundless energy as I jump out of bed and begin to dress quickly. I am almost 9 years old now and am allowed to go to the movies without Mama, but I must take my seven-year-old brother, Himey, with me. Even that doesn't diminish the excitement of the day.

There is a new Tarzan movie, and the continuation of the serial, which ended last week with the good guy tied up in a cave full of agitated rattlesnakes. The show will start with two cartoons, and there will be much laughter and clapping. The theater will be filled with children. It is only 7:00 A.M., and while there are many hours to wait before I can escape, I am filled with the anticipation of being freed from the confines of the house and Mama's watchful eyes.

Saturdays are special in another way. At about noon, Mama will send me to the delicatessen with some money and a note. The delicatessen man is to give me three raw hot dogs and six hot dog rolls. I must remember to ask him for two extra portions of mustard. I love to watch the man, his big round belly covered with a stained white apron that smells of salami and kosher sour pickles. He pours the mustard, never spilling a drop, from a big jar into a waxed paper cone. He then seals the open end with an efficient twist and drops it into the bag with the hot dogs and rolls. When I first became grown up enough to go to the store by myself, I wondered why there were six rolls but only three hot dogs. Later I came to realize that this was Mama's way of stretching every penny. She would boil the hot dogs and then slice them in half lengthwise, thus providing each of us with two hot dog halves in two separate rolls. Mama knew how to get her money's worth.

The smell of the hot dogs boiling and bubbling sent a wave of desperate hunger through my body. My impatience was hard to control. Mama still was not moving fast enough as she placed a sliver of hot dog in a soft white bun and then generously covered it with mustard, until the juicy meat disappeared from sight. I half-closed my eyes in ecstasy as I raised the soggy hot dog roll to my lips. It couldn't get any better than this. All the chattering and talking in the kitchen came to a complete halt as the three of us kids fell upon this feast. My baby brother, Alec, was soon covered with the mustard oozing out of his roll. That didn't stop him for a minute, even when some of the mustard went up his nose. Himey, who always did everything slowly, was carefully chewing each bite, delicately avoiding the trail of mustard as it dripped out of the roll onto the oilcloth table cover. Mama, always scolding, a wet rag in her hand, was cleaning up after every messy bite. But even that didn't spoil this savory treat. I was the first one finished, for I was keeping an eye on the kitchen clock, fearing we would be late for the one o'clock matinee. I had to be first in line to get a good seat; otherwise there was a chance I would have to sit behind some tall kid or not find a seat at all.

Finally, the meal finished, Mama gave me a handkerchief with a knot in it that held two nickels, the price of admission for Hymie and me. She warned me repeatedly not to let the handkerchief out of my sight, not to open it until I got to the movies, not to let go of my brother's hand, and not to talk to anyone along the way. Before we can get away, however, Mama insists that Himey and I go to the bathroom, adding minutes to our already strained departure time. She also tells me that we are to sit through the double feature twice, as she does not want us back until suppertime. It wasn't until I was much older that I discovered that while we were at the movies, Mama settled down for her own treat of the week, a long undisturbed nap. Bubbe would take care of Alec. Mama would catch up on all the sleep she had lost during the week. Unfortunately, this respite did not have a lasting effect. As soon as we returned, she was as angry as ever.

Mama eventually runs out of rules and warnings. We are on our way to the movies at long last. I hold on to Himey's hand, controlling the urge to run all the way. I know, without turning my head, that Mama is watching me from the window. Himey plods along beside me. His short, fat legs tire quickly. He is oblivious to the importance of getting to the movies on time. As we turn the corner I see a line of children waiting for the doors to open. Every kid in the neighborhood must have gotten there before we did. Now that I am free from Mama's piercing eyes I dare to pull Himey in an effort to speed him up. I ignore his complaints. I am on a mission, and the prize is in sight.

There it looms in front of me. Loew's Pitkin Theater, with its towering sign, the shiny black letters announcing the Tarzan movie, and all the added attractions. Himey is crying as I push him ahead. We find our place in the squirmy double line of hyperactive children. Boys are running in and out of the line playing tag, no longer able to contain themselves. The younger kids are crying and calling the names of their older siblings, who are visiting with their friends. The cries are ignored. The little kids have been instructed not to move out of line and lose their place in the procession that will soon march through the magic portals of the theater. Once we are through the entrance, bedlam breaks loose. Everyone runs to the seats closer to the screen and more than one fight breaks out when two children try to occupy the same seat at the same time. It is almost guaranteed the boys will get into at least one fist fight, which quickly brings two ushers to the scene. Each grabs one of the boys by their arms or ears and drags them out of the theater. The only way the management can exercise any control over the hundreds of excited children, who have escaped from their crowded apartments and the control of their mothers, is not to negotiate or ever give any one a second chance. The boys are thrown out on the street, where they continue their combat.

There are still fifteen long minutes before the picture starts and my worst fear comes true. Himey wants to go to the bathroom. I remind him that he had just gone to the bathroom at home, but it is to no avail. He has to pee again. This presents a difficult problem, for if I escort him to the bathroom, our vacated seats will quickly be occupied by latecomers. There is no honor system here. If I don't take him to the bathroom, Himey might complain to Mama that I did not take care of him, and who knows what punishment would be in store for me. Putting those threatening thoughts out of my mind I remind him that he went by himself last time, and besides, I have to watch our seats. He will just have to go alone. He whimpers for a moment or two but then gives in to nature and timidly heads down the isle, holding on to his crotch in an attempt to control his full bladder. I call after him, giving him directions and tell him to hurry. The picture is about to start.

I try to put him out of my mind, but the minutes pass quickly, and I become concerned that the theater will soon be plunged into darkness and he will be hopelessly lost. My anxiety changes to anger at Himey for placing me in this no-win situation, so I am relieved when he magically appears out of the darkness, stumbling down the aisle, calling my name. I reach out, grabbing him by his shirt before he disappears, and pull him roughly into his seat.

The audience goes wild as the first cartoon bursts upon the screen. Once again I enter the world of make-believe, forgetting about Himey, even about Mama. Maybe this time the magic will never end, and I won't have to go home. I envy the boisterous, happy children who appear to have no trouble expressing themselves. They seem not to worry about any consequences. I am

convinced, however, that Mama's power knows no limits. Even when I am out of her sight, I must be on my
guard. I knew somehow Mama had the power to know
what I was doing and thinking, even when I was away
from her prying eyes. But even that fearful thought begins
to fade as I become lost in the fantasy. I enter the drama
on the screen and join Tarzan in the jungle. I am there,
too, trailing behind him, dressed in leopard skin. My bare
feet are accustomed to the rough terrain, and I have no
trouble keeping up. The best part is when Tarzan lifts me
up on to his back and tells me to hold on tightly as he
swings through the jungle on an endless network of vines.
We are heading for the elephant herd to save them from
the heartless hunters. Every now and then Tarzan emits
his bloodcurdling jungle cry. I can feel it surging through
his body. My muscles vibrate with every sound he
projects into the dense overgrowth. We travel for many
miles, high above the ground.

The journey seems timeless. Only when the film
comes to a triumphant end do I realize I am in my seat in
the darkness of the theater. Himey is next to me, his
mouth open and relaxed. A thin line of saliva escapes
from his lips, testimony to his own deep concentration.
He also has been in his own world. The minutes have
disappeared into hours, but no one leaves the theater
when the first show is over and the lights go on. Pande-
monium sets in again as boys begin to wrestle each other
with new energy. A long pushing and shoving procession
heads for the bathrooms, where blessed relief from full
bladders awaits those who arrive first. The noise and
activity that takes over is more than the ushers can con-

trol. Their flashlights are now held in a threatening manner, like weapons.

The bathroom break must be accomplished before the second show starts. I am able to send Himey on his way in care of a friend of mine. On his return, he guards our seats as I run to the bathroom, hoping to get there before my bladder humiliates me. Making my way back to my seat, I hope Himey has not been distracted and wandered off. My racing heart calms down when I see his curly head leaning against the back of the seat about to drift off into a nap. Himey loves to sleep and can sleep anywhere, no matter how much noise there is or how he has to contort his plump body. As the lights go out I can already hear his deep breathing. Once again I become lost in the drama on the screen, as if I had never seen it before. All my cares and worries are again forgotten. All my fears about returning home have disappeared for now. Mama is at home sleeping and not yet concerned with which rules I have broken. For now, each of us is blissfully in another world. The second show is even better than the first. Himey sleeps quietly and doesn't awaken until it is time to go. As we walk home in the dusk, my head is filled with images of Tarzan and the jungle.

Mama is still asleep when we return. Bubbe and Alec greet us in the kitchen, where Bubbe has reheated both chicken and soup for supper tonight. We take our places at the table. The excitement of the afternoon lingers a little longer as I tell Bubbe about the picture, between mouthfuls of her delicious noodle soup and *matzoh* balls. Encouraged by her laughter I spare no detail. Even Himey forgets to be shy as he gleefully reports the antics of Mickey and Minnie Mouse. Alec in his high chair, with noodles on his chin, claps his hands and calls for more.

The sound of Mama stirring in the bedroom upstairs is a signal to prepare for her arrival. Without a word, Bubbe wipes Alec's chin and quiets us with a finger to her lips and we continue eating in silence. Saturday has come to an end.

The Subway Train Ride

I have been lost more times than I care to remember. I am sure I came honestly by this directionless behavior. My father never owned a car. I was never exposed to the traveler's experience of noticing landmarks. To this day, if I am not facing the setting sun, I do not have a clue where west is. My family seldom traveled anywhere when I was growing up. Every excursion to a park or rare visit to a relative was a major event. I did not really travel on my own until I went to high school and became familiar with public transportation. Being away from home was not encouraged in my family. There was an implied message that the world was dangerous and threatening. There was a time, however, when these fears were put aside, and on my own I embarked on an adventure.

I was about eleven the first time I was allowed to take the subway to meet Papa in Manhattan, where he worked. He instructed me over and over again which train to take and where I was to sit in the very last car so he could be sure to find me. I loved Papa very much and did not want to disappoint him, but this trip had so much anxiety attached that my stomach was upset even more than usual. I didn't sleep very well the night before my maiden voyage. Nevertheless, the thought of meeting

Papa in the city and having him all to myself for a whole afternoon made it possible for me to overcome my fears.

Mama walked me to the subway station, which was only four blocks from our house; she issued enough warnings to almost take the joy out of this holiday. I had to enter the station alone. It would have been extravagant for Mama to pay the five-cent fare for herself to take me to the train platform. While I was relieved to get away from Mama, I felt very small and alone, though there were many other people waiting.

The sound of the approaching train filled the air long before it came into view. It was followed by a rush of dusty, sooty wind that forced you to close your eyes to protect them. When you opened your eyes again there was the train, from out of nowhere, coming to a slow, screeching stop. I could see impatient passengers pressed up against the doors waiting to be released the instant they opened. The noise was deafening. There were many people pushing and shoving and talking very loud. My heart seemed to want to jump up into my throat. Before I had time to think, I was carried along with the boarding crowd and miraculously found a seat in the back of the last car. My joyous excitement had long since disappeared, and panic was well on its way as I sat down. The train was dingy, with hard, metal seats. The soot that blew in through the open windows coated everything, including the passengers. At the first stop a large lady lowered her heavy body into the seat next to me, and I pulled myself into the farthest corner fearing I would be suffocated. I don't think I took a full breath until she exited, about six stops later. I was so relieved that I forgot to be scared for a moment or two as I wondered how many more stops it would be to Thirty-Fourth Street, where Papa would meet me. There was a large subway map right above my seat, but it meant nothing to me. I did not even know which direction the train was headed. Even if I had known, the glass that covered the map was so grimy that it was almost illegible. It wasn't until the unfamiliar names of the stations we passed changed to numbered streets that I became less anxious. Numbers I knew. It was clear we were getting closer to my street.

By some miracle, not only did the train manage to find the street, but I could see Papa, standing at the very end of the platform, waiting for the train to come to a stop. Even then I didn't jump off the seat, remembering Papa's instructions to wait until the train came to a full stop, and he would come and get me. He reached for my hand and held on to it tightly. My hand felt safe in his rough, callused palm and the familiar curl of his fingers guided me out of the train. Only then did he stop to pick me up, and give me a hug and kiss, and tell me what a brave and smart girl I was to have come such a long distance by myself.

The adventure was not over yet. Papa was taking me out to lunch to a cafeteria. My panic forgotten, I was once again preoccupied with the luxury of eating out and having private time with Papa. I ate my hot dog slowly, keeping an eye on the slice of huckleberry pie waiting alongside. Papa kept up a steady monologue, pointing to people he knew who worked in the factories where he repaired sewing machines. Later, Papa took me to one of those factories and introduced me to the owner. This nice man told me to pick out a dress for myself from the rack as a present. I hid behind Papa as he coaxed me to look at the beautiful dresses. Though I was painfully self-conscious, the temptation was too much. I allowed Papa to choose a pretty pink-cotton sunback dress, trimmed with white lace. I blushed when I had to thank the nice man for the gift. Inside, I was very pleased indeed.

The subway ride home was free from earlier concerns. There was no reason to be nervous now. I was an experienced traveler. Besides, I was with Papa. We sat together, and I excitedly recounted all the joys of the day. Again, Papa praised me for being such a big girl. I saw the same look of pride he had had on his face when he saw me waiting for him in the train, all by myself.

When the excitement of this day faded into memory, as all adventures must, I put aside any further thoughts of striking out on my own again for some time. The sensation of being carried at breakneck speed in the noisy train through the dark subway tunnels did not fill me with desire to leave home again too soon. That did not stop me from boasting to my little brothers that I really was a big girl and could take a subway ride alone any time I wanted.

Uncle Harry's Visits

Twice a year our small, crowded tenement apartment in Brooklyn would come alive with preparations for a visit from Uncle Harry and Aunt Bluma from Philadelphia. Uncle Harry was Mama's only sibling and her senior by four years. He was also the black sheep of the family. He had escaped from self-imposed prohibitions of immigrant Jewish beliefs and values and had written his own rules. Life was to be enjoyed and experienced. Old-world superstitions, sacrifices, and self-denial did not dictate his behavior. He was a fun-loving man, known to drink too much, and, rumor had it, he was not indifferent to the ladies. Aunt Bluma was the martyred wife destined to bear her husband's irresponsible behavior. She was a woman of many opinions and judgments with little evidence of intelligence to support them. None of her manipulative skills, however, ever trapped Uncle Harry into changing. He could laugh and joke his way out of any threats or arguments Aunt Bluma aimed at him. In any case, the prospect of a visit from Uncle Harry would immediately brighten my day.

It was difficult for my brothers and me to control our excitement and expectations as the arrival date of our visitors drew near. We were not aware of the sacrifices my parents would have to make to feed two more people for the weekend. Such hospitality could quickly exhaust the family's meager budget and belts would have to be drawn tighter after Uncle Harry and Aunt Bluma returned to Philadelphia.

With today's abundance and bountiful shopping expeditions, it is hard to realize there was a time in this country when most people lacked money to fill their basic needs. For instance, we could not afford to buy toothbrushes, pajamas, or bathrobes. Our hair was washed with the same harsh soap that Mama used on Mondays to do the weekly laundry. Anything but the barest necessities was considered frivolous.

When Uncle Harry and Aunt Bluma would unpack, however, out would come such luxuries as sweet-smelling tubes of toothpaste and not one but two toothbrushes. Aunt Bluma would also bring bright yellow bars of bath soap in the shape of lemons for her private use. She never arrived without her box of cocoa powder, which meant we would be treated to steaming glasses of cocoa in the morning. Aunt Bluma even had jewelry that she wore with propriety. She had more than one pair of shoes as well as bedroom slippers. She proudly displayed her round box of Coty's face powder, rouge, and lipstick as evidence of her economic status. She was never without a stick of spearmint chewing gum in her mouth. I could not imagine spending money on something only to spit it out. It is no wonder that all this represented a bitter pill for my poor but proud Mama to swallow. Mama tolerated it all for Uncle Harry's sake.

In the morning, Bubbe would be the first one up, preparing Uncle Harry's favorite breakfast. She would skin a plump salted herring, slicing it carefully. With it would be served a large, hot boiled potato still in its skin. This delicacy was topped off with a large, whole yellow onion, which Uncle Harry would bite into as if it were a crisp, juicy apple. The sound of his teeth against the onion would bring tears to my eyes as I watched in disbelief. Before Uncle Harry had breakfast, he would go through his morning routine. As soon as he woke, Aunt Bluma would hand him a raw egg. Carefully he would pierce the shell with a pin and with much slurping would aspirate the egg without even cracking the shell. Each time we witnessed this incredible feat, my brothers and I would grimace and try to control a gagging reflex. Recovering quickly we would then stand in the bathroom doorway to watch Uncle Harry shave. First, he whipped up a frothy lather in a cup with his shaving brush, using a bar of soap bought especially for that purpose. Unheard of. Papa used the same laundry soap that answered all hygienic needs for the family. In a matter of minutes, Uncle Harry's face would all but disappear under billowing soap bubbles. He massaged his cheeks, his chin, and his neck with the thick lather. All the time, mind you, he would keep up a steady flow of playful teasing and joking that kept us in stitches.

The hilarity would reach its peak when he would call for Mama or Bubbe, pretending urgency. As soon as one of them appeared in the doorway, his magician's hand would dart into action, delivering a generous blob of shaving foam with his brush across the face of the unsuspecting victim. No matter how many times this scene was replayed, it was done with skill, flare, and perfect timing.

Wonder of wonders, even my stoic Mama and unsuspecting Bubbe helplessly surrendered to the laughter. I would almost trample my brothers in an attempt to escape the next swipe of the brush, squealing with delight. I was not always successful. Uncle Harry would win again. For a moment, life was not quite so grim. Our little apartment could scarcely contain all the slapstick joyfulness. Often our screams and laughter would pour down into the apartment below us, and the neighbors would bang on their ceiling with a broom handle in protest. We would then smother our voices with hands over our mouths, but our eyes would be sparkling with mischief, wondering when the next skit would begin. We knew even Aunt Bluma's scoldings could not dampen Uncle Harry's love of pranks and fun.

One summer visit stands out in my memory. Not only was there no school but my aunt and uncle had arrived that morning in their Chevy. After dinner, Uncle Harry announced he would take us to Coney Island that evening. I felt quite grown-up to be included in this excursion. My brothers were too young and had to stay home with Bubbe. They let out a duet of angry cries as the rest of us piled into the car and pulled away from the curb. We were off.

I sat near Mama, next to the window. The sound of the engine and the rocking motion of the car helped to quiet my racing heart. I heard Papa and Uncle Harry, sitting in the front seat, discussing the directions to Coney Island. What I didn't know was that neither one of them had ever been to Coney Island before. I was oblivious to the many turns and stops we made, the two men frequently consulting a dog-eared map. I was much too preoccupied with the feel of the leather seat, the silver trimming around the handle that raised and lowered the window, and the little crystal flower vase next to the porthole window above my head. Nothing escaped my examination. I leaned back in the seat, my feet not touching the floor, and felt my hair blowing in the breeze from the open window. My mind was full of pictures I had seen of Coney Island, the beach, and the ocean.

We must have been riding for an hour. It had grown dark while I was planning what I would do first when we got to Coney Island. Maybe if I was very good my uncle would buy me a sugarcone heaped high with swirls of soft frozen custard. I had been told about this delicacy, and I could almost taste it now. I was awakened from my daydream when the car came to a halt and Uncle Harry got out. I jumped up with unrestrained joy, assuming we had arrived. I was shocked when Mama pulled me back and told me to sit down and be quiet. Uncle Harry had only gone to ask for directions. We seemed to be lost. Disappointed and dejected, I fought hard to keep back the tears.

Long minutes passed slowly before Uncle Harry reappeared with his usual enthusiasm and we were off again. Papa and Uncle Harry were soon laughing about having made several wrong turns. My aunt took this opportunity to complain loudly to my uncle, attacking him for getting lost. Besides she was tired now and wanted to go home. Mama began to complain, too, because it was past my bedtime. I reminded her there was no school tomorrow and started to say that I was not the least bit sleepy. Her disapproving glare stilled my voice at once. Arguing with Mama only made matters worse. I hoped my uncle would have the last word and overrule the negative statements from the backseat. After all, he was the driver and no one else knew how to run the car. So we continued on into the night. There was nothing Mama or Aunt Bluma could do. Uncle Harry was determined to drive us to Coney Island.

Despite my earlier protest, I began to have a little difficulty keeping my eyes open. We had been driving for over two hours. At every bright light I would sit up straight, suddenly fully awake, ready to see Coney Island. I was also beginning to get a little carsick because Uncle Harry would make sharp turns around corners to demonstrate his expert driving skills. We passed many streets with rows of tenement buildings, their windows opened like gaping mouths gasping for air in the hot summer night. The streets were filled with happy, playful children and grownups sitting on steps or chairs hoping for a stray breeze to delay the time when children would have to be herded off to bed in humid, stifling apartments. No one was in a hurry to go inside.

When we drove by one such scene, Papa leaned out the window as Uncle Harry took another swipe at a sharp corner on two wheels. In disbelief Papa said, "I could swear I just saw my mother-in-law sitting out there in front of that building." Uncle Harry laughed and said, with some authority, "That is impossible. We are on our way to Coney Island. We are not anywhere near your neighborhood. We have been riding for hours." My aunt, quick to side with her husband, assured Papa he didn't know what he was talking about. Papa insisted that Uncle Harry drive around the corner again. He knew he had seen Bubbe. Uncle Harry good-naturedly decided to humor Papa, and laughed as he told him how foolish he would feel when we reached Coney Island in just a few minutes.

Around the corner we went, my uncle laughing and joking all the way. In the meantime an escalating argument was taking place between Mama and Aunt Bluma, each of them defending their husbands. My head filled with the noise, and I was getting upset because everyone was talking so loud. I was also beginning to suspect we might never see Coney Island, but couldn't bring myself to give up hope entirely. Then that last glimmer of hope was shattered. In disbelief I rubbed my eyes hard, but there was the evidence. Bubbe was sitting on the steps of our apartment building, just where we left her, fanning herself with a newspaper, her ample lap covered with the apron she always wore. Tears of disappointment trickled down my face, but I did not make a sound. No one would have heard me anyway, for now the arguing had changed to unrestrained boisterous laughter. The four adults tumbled out of the car, everyone talking at once, eager to give their version of the trip to Coney Island. I was left sitting in the car, unnoticed, crying softly, my hopes shattered.

Uncle Harry noticed me alone in the car. He came and sat down next to me, trying to comfort me, but I was inconsolable. He put me on his lap, reached into his pocket and brought out a crisp one-dollar bill and put it in my hand. My tears stopped in midstream. My eyes and mouth opened wide. I had never been given more than five cents for an ice-cream cone in my whole life. Perhaps life was worth living again after all, but all the excitement began to make me very tired. I did not protest when Papa carried me up the three flights of stairs to our apartment and put me to bed. I fell asleep as soon as my head hit the pillow, dreaming about finding my way to Coney Island and what I could buy there with my one-dollar bill.

Mama Fights with Papa

Mama and Papa's devoted relationship came to a devastating end when Papa suddenly died of a heart attack at the age of forty-two. Theirs was a very old-world, stereotypical yet seemingly idyllic marriage. Papa took care of everything outside the house and supported his family as best he could. Mama was of course relegated to woman's work—childbearing and child rearing, endless household tasks, and the worries that went along with the responsibilities.

Until I was about eleven years old I had never heard my parents quarrel or even disagree. Mama's frustrations were never aimed at Papa. Her worries were usually directed to the heavens as she complained about the overwhelming burdens imposed upon her by the Depression. Her pent-up anger was also often pointed in my direction. Once Papa came home, however, peace would miraculously spread its snow-white wings over the household. Mama's shrill voice would become gentle and genuinely adoring when she greeted Papa—except for one fateful Sunday.

That morning Papa took his weekly hot bath. Since the kitchen washtub doubled as the family bathtub, everyone else had to leave the kitchen. At best, this offered Papa a modicum of privacy. Cleaned and refreshed,

Papa carefully dressed in the only suit he owned. Soon he would be off to visit his friend and landsman Meyer, who lived in the neighborhood. His one day of leisure was off to a good start. When Papa reached for my hand and told Mama he was taking me with him, my heart was filled with joy. Mama was only too happy to have one less child around. She bundled me into layers of clothing, as if to squelch any thoughts of freedom I might have had. Even that did not lessen my excitement. It was a long walk, but we stopped often as Papa would greet the neighbors and catch up on news of the week. I held on to his hand patiently. Soon we were on our way again.

Still several blocks from Meyer's house, our walk was interrupted by the distant cry of kittens. Papa never could ignore the cries of animals. They drew him like a magnet. He seemed compelled to act as savior of such unfortunate creatures. Promises he had made to Mama to never, ever bring home another helpless animal were quickly forgotten when he faced another rescue mission. He was hooked. As a result, a steady parade of such rejects had found their way to our cramped apartment, much to Mama's dismay. So I was not surprised when our walk came to a halt. Papa headed off in the direction of the faint meowing, and I followed him. He spotted a box near some overflowing garbage cans up against a building. In his Sunday suit, which Mama had so carefully pressed, he stepped over the garbage and lifted the box. As soon as it was moved, the cries got louder. We looked into the box. There were five newborn, blind and hungry kittens. They could not have been more than a few days old and were totally helpless. Papa and I knew we had to save these babies. First, we had to protect them from the cold. Papa put four of the kittens in his pockets. I was allowed to put the fifth one inside my jacket. Its squirming quickly came to a halt as it warmed itself against my body. The visit to Meyer was forgotten. On the way home, Papa stopped at the neighborhood drugstore, bought several medicine droppers, some baby nursing bottles, and nipples. Next, we stopped at the grocery store for a quart of milk. By now the sun had disappeared and the weather became brisk and cold. I was grateful now that Mama had insisted I wear an extra sweater under my winter jacket.

Once inside our apartment, Papa freed the kittens from the confinement of his pockets. He placed them in a box that he had been smart enough to save for just this moment. Following suit, I extracted the warm purring bundle from inside my jacket. It opened its pink little mouth into a huge yawn, displaying sharp baby teeth and the rough surface of the smallest tongue I had ever seen. It quickly snuggled against its siblings in the box, which was home for now. Mama was nowhere in sight as Papa began to busy himself. He warmed the milk and poured it into a cup from which he filled the feeding droppers. Papa and I began feeding the kittens. We made small comforting sounds to the starving babies as we squirted warm milk into their mouths. The milk revived them, and they became very active. Their meek little cries changed to healthy sounds of hunger.

Papa and I were so absorbed in keeping up with the kittens' demands for milk that we had completely forgotten about Mama. Suddenly she appeared. I took one look at the fire and fury in her eyes and released the kitten I had been feeding. I stepped behind my Papa, because I knew a storm was coming and it was best to seek shelter. Papa appeared oblivious. Perhaps he was lulled into a false sense of security, remembering the many times he had persuaded Mama to accept one more batch of helpless creatures. This time Mama attacked him with her years of frustration and repressed anger before Papa had a chance to open his mouth. It was a terrible sight. Out came a torrent of complaints and accusations against Papa I had never heard before. "What do you want from my life? It is all I can do to keep up with the needs of three small children and feeding the family on your meager income. I am sick and tired of dodging bill collectors and asking for credit at the butcher and grocery stores. My hands are worn to the bone from cleaning and scrubbing and washing. I am exhausted from having one baby after the other and now you bring me five hungry kittens to take care of. I have enough to do. Why don't you pity me the way you pity the kittens?"

Papa stood there speechless, as if trying to catch his breath. It was as if he had been hit by a tidal wave. He staggered under Mama's surprise attack. He offered to be totally responsible for the kittens. This led only to a fresh assault. Mama was on a roll and started a second stormy offensive. She had been silent for years and now felt her life was over. She wished she were dead. Finally, exhausted by the force of her explosive words, she collapsed in tears. Papa was mute. He was powerless in the face of the unexpected verbal storm. He had never, ever seen Mama in this state.

Afraid I might be caught in the cross fire, I tiptoed out of the room. I hid in the bedroom, under the bed, trying to shut out the angry, venomous sounds. I began to cry. I was convinced Mama and Papa would surely get a divorce, though I scarcely knew what that word meant. Papa would be driven out by Mama's relentless anger. Maybe even Papa was not safe. His presence had always saved me from Mama's attacks. What would become of me? Would I never see Papa again? I was no longer thinking of the kittens as I stifled my sobs under the bed. Finally, with a tear-streaked face, I fell into a troubled sleep.

I awoke with a start, suddenly remembering Mama and Papa fighting. The house was ominously silent. The stillness filled me with dread. Had Mama attacked Papa again? Had Mama left and Papa gone after her? Dire possibilities made my head ache. It was then I heard my brothers' laughter coming from the other room. Maybe it had all been a nightmare. My fears began to subside, and I let myself take a full breath again. Quietly I crept out from underneath the bed and I moved toward the kitchen where the battle had occurred. My ears strained to pick up any angry sounds. Then I heard the meowing of the kittens. At least they were still alive. I pressed against the doorway in case I needed to run for cover.

Nothing prepared me for the scene. I was stunned. There were Mama and Papa sitting very close together at the kitchen table. Each was feeding a kitten from a dropper filled with milk. They were smiling at each other and talking in soft, loving tones again, as if nothing had ever threatened their harmony. Mama was no longer the demon. She was a loving wife. Papa had succeeded in saving the doomed kittens. Nothing had changed after all.

In time all the kittens were raised. Mama actually became their primary, efficient caretaker. Homes were found for four of them. One gray-striped tabby was kept, a reminder of the day my world almost came to an end. So all was well that ended well. Papa had survived Mama's blitzkrieg. Mama and Papa did not get a divorce or ever quarrel again, that I heard. The kittens had survived. For a long time I remained watchful, in case Mama attacked Papa again. But she never did.

Mama the Nurse

I was not quite thirteen in 1935 when a bad cold developed into a persistent cough. Mama became angry at me as she always did when I got sick. There was an old joke about a child who sneezed and the mother said, "God bless you." The child sneezed again and the mother said, "May you grow big and strong." A third sneeze brings the mother's wrath out and she screams, "Go to hell already, you have a cold." But my mother would not have stopped there. She would have continued to scold and attack me. "What do you want from me? I told you not to go out without your sweater. Now you want me to take care of you? What have I done to deserve this? Because of you we will have to call the doctor and tell him again we don't have the $3.00 to pay him. Why do you always disobey me?" It is not that Mama didn't take care of me when I was sick. But it was always with a litany of tragedy and her angry resistance to one more task that I was adding to her already overburdened existence.

One morning I could not get out of bed, and the coughing would not stop. I cowered under the covers as Mama began her verbal attack. She didn't seem to need to stop for breath. Finally she stopped because she noticed how quiet I was. My cheeks were flushed, and perspiration glistened on my forehead. Then the anger changed to a look of fear in her eyes—even more frightening to me. I must really be sick for Mama to look at me that way. My head pounded. Any movement brought a wave of nausea. The rattle in my chest scared me when I gasped for air. Mama and Bubbe could be heard whispering in the hallway. I collapsed on my pillow, weak and terrified.

Mercifully I drifted off to sleep, awakening when Mama came back into the room. This time she was wearing a harried and no-nonsense expression on her face. Before I could sit up, she began to undress me in preparation for one of her alcohol sponge baths. These were a cross between a brisk Swedish massage and an icy, chilling assault, administered with the impersonal efficiency of an army sergeant, her lips tightly clamped together, the muscles of her work-worn hands and arms moving with such purpose and speed that there was no time to protest. I was too weak to do anything but submit to Mama's clinical procedure, and I surrendered. For once I was grateful for her attention because my body cooled off and I was more comfortable by the time Bubbe came in with her Russian cold remedy, which I loved. She held a steaming glass filled with hot, boiled water and milk, a generous pad of butter, and lots of sugar. She sat down next to my bed, propped my head up with pillows, and began to feed me the sweet, hot potion with a large soup spoon. The contrast of this remedy with the briskness of the cold sponge bath made me feel at once clearheaded and relaxed. Bubbe assured me that I was going to be well soon, and maybe we would not have to call the doctor after all. With those comforting words in my ears, I again fell asleep, even though it was only midmorning.

I slept deeply all day. The evening dusk was visible in the window when I opened my heavy-lidded eyes. Before I could lift my head I was overcome with a coughing attack that brought tears to my eyes and took my breath. I gasped for air and began to vomit. Finally the pain in my chest and the weakness receded, only to be followed by anxiety, for the bed was getting covered with smelly mucous that made me even more nauseated. I was sure Mama would punish me severely for this mess.

Mercifully, Papa was the first one to answer my sounds of alarm. He quickly turned the covers back, hiding the malodorous evidence. Immediately I felt safer. Mama was not likely to get angry when Papa was there. Mama and Bubbe then quickly stripped the bed while Papa held me on his lap. Mama rushed the bed linens off to the bathroom. There they would soak in a tub of soapy bleach and water before Mama would get down on her knees and scrub them in the bathtub on a small, metal washboard. After a long time both Mama and the linens emerged from the bathroom, smelling strongly of harsh chemicals. Mama's hands were even more chapped and red than usual. In the meantime Bubbe made up my bed again with sweet-smelling linens, decorated with several of her dainty patches over worn areas, and Papa tucked me in. He told me I was a good girl, that I could not help making a mess because I was sick. Again I drifted off into a deep sleep, happy to escape from the frantic scene.

When next I awoke, the room was dark and the sound of talking from the living room made me feel anxious again because I recognized Dr. Levy's voice, and he sounded concerned. Before I could try to make sense of this, the door opened and the light was turned on, blinding my bloodshot eyes. My head began to pound anew. There was Dr. Levy in the doorway, with Mama and Papa and Bubbe hovering in the background. I was frightened. Dr. Levy had come to our house many times before, but he had never come to see me. He usually came to take care of my brother Himey, who was prone to croup attacks during the night. I heard Bubbe cautioning both my brothers not to come into my room because I was very sick. The words brought a new terror to my heart. I began to cry silently, embarrassed by the tears, but Dr. Levy was very gentle and soon had me calmed down. He took my temperature and listened to my chest with his stethoscope, but I didn't need the stethoscope to feel and hear the gurgling, rasping sounds made every time I breathed. Although I was lying perfectly still I was soon exhausted, because Dr. Levy wanted me to breathe deeply and cough, and that developed into another breathless attack, leaving me exhausted and in tears. He told me I had to be a good girl and stay in bed for a long time, for I was very sick. I saw Mama, Papa, and Bubbe watching silently, huddled together in the doorway waiting for the doctor to complete his examination. After the doctor washed his hands, everybody left the room and I was alone, totally overcome by fear.

It seemed like hours before Papa came back into the room, looking grave behind his smile. He told me I didn't have to go to school and could stay in bed until I felt better. Questioning him, I soon learned, was totally useless. He could not tell me how long that meant; nor would he

tell me what was wrong with me, as if uttering the word
pneumonia would make matters worse. He left to go to
the drugstore, bringing back a sweet-tasting cough syrup
that helped considerably to ease the horrible coughing
spasms. But the fever raged on, interrupted briefly by
Mama's alcohol sponge baths. It was as if her work-worn
hands had long since forgotten a gentle touch, and she
could only attack my fever the way she had attacked the
smelly linens. I realize now, however, that her rough
nursing was effective. She committed herself to this
treatment several times every day as well as during the
night. It is possible that her roughness helped cover up
her fear and anxiety that I might not recover. Those were
the days before antibiotics. Bacterial illness would either
reach a crisis and kill the patient, or the fever would
break and the patient would live.

In spite of all this attention, the coughing and fever
were relentless and Dr. Levy advised Papa to call in a
specialist. The very sound of the word filled the household with dread. The doctor's orders emphasized the
seriousness of the situation. He had done everything he
could, and I was still not getting well. The level of worry
and fear increased considerably when Papa left for the
nearby candy store to call this strange doctor on the public telephone.

The day Dr. Anderson was to arrive, Mama and
Bubbe engaged in a flurry of housekeeping, washing, and
dusting usually reserved for preparing for religious holidays. There was always a flurry of activity when Dr. Levy
was expected, but Mama and Bubbe outdid themselves as
they prepared for Dr. Anderson's arrival. Following the

sound of the doorbell I heard a deep male voice asking Mama for information about my illness. I quivered under the covers at the prospect of being examined by this strange man with the big voice and no Jewish accent. A sudden silence from the other room announced his arrival in my bedroom.

Even his loud, deep voice did not prepare me for his size. He was the largest man I had ever seen and seemed to fill the entire doorway. He barely fit into the one small chair. Although he greeted me kindly, I was overcome with shyness and fear. I was trapped and could not escape. He did not say very much as he listened to my bare chest and thumped it with his large hands, and this with my budding breasts exposed. I tried to disappear into the covers, but there was no place to hide from his touch or his eyes. The whole examination took no more than ten minutes, but I was drenched in perspiration and thoroughly terrified.

Dr. Anderson then called Mama and Bubbe into the bedroom and talked about prognosis and treatment. He told them I was a very sick girl and that the pneumonia was on its way to infecting both lungs. I was to be given liquids frequently, Mama was to continue her alcohol rubs, and above all I was not to get chilled or leave the bed, not even to go to the bathroom. He then outlined a diet for me that immediately filled the room with a foreign threat the likes of which no one in my family had ever experienced. He instructed Mama to feed me bacon and eggs every day. She did not tell him about how impossible that would be because we were Orthodox Jews and bacon was forbidden. It was unclean, not kosher. She didn't mention it at all because, after all, he was the specialist and had impressed her with the fact that I would recover only if she followed his instructions.

Although Dr. Anderson's orders were to be obeyed, the Rabbi would first have to give permission for such unorthodox treatment. It was several days before this could be accomplished, during which time I coughed and slept and perspired until my very bones ached. If bacon and eggs were to cure me, why was it taking so long for Mama and Bubbe to feed me this magic remedy? Much to my parents' relief, the Rabbi gave permission for the *trayf,* or unkosher food, to be prepared in our home because it was prescribed by the doctor. Restriction out of the way, Mama must have sneaked into the *goyisher,* or Gentile, meat market and purchased the vile stuff, hiding it in a double wrapping. Next she purchased a cast-iron skillet. She did this to avoid contaminating our kosher cooking utensils, and she kept it on a hook outside the kitchen window, as far away from the house as possible. The next day she prepared bacon and eggs for me for breakfast. She could barely fry the bacon without gagging. The windows were open wide to free the kitchen from the odor. All the time she begged God to forgive her for her sinful behavior. In addition she was horrified that the neighbors would find out she was not keeping a kosher home. But prepare the bacon she did.

Though I had no appetite, the smell and taste of this strange cuisine did pique my interest in food, and I was able to eat half of the breakfast, more than I had eaten in days. Even that exhausted me and I quickly drifted off into another deep sleep. In time, however, I looked forward to my bacon and eggs and even preferred them to Bubbe's chicken soup. The fact that no one else was allowed to share my remedy breakfast made me feel special. There must surely be magic in bacon, for I was feeling stronger, and the color was coming back into my cheeks. Soon I could sleep through the night without violent coughing attacks.

Days turned into weeks as the miracle of Dr. Anderson's cure did its work and eventually I got well. I knew I was going to recover when I was awakened one morning by the chirping of a little sparrow, sitting on the sill of the open window in my room. Bubbe said it was a good omen, for the bird was a symbol of life. It must have been true, and after six weeks I was allowed out of bed on my weak, shaky legs.

Years later I understood how close to death I had been, the sacrifices Papa had to make to pay the specialist, and what it must have cost Mama to break her religious commitments in order to nurse me. She attacked the pneumonia with the same ferocity and determination with which she scoured and purged the house of any defiant grime or dirt. All of this she tolerated as she cast a pious eye toward heaven, pleading with God to spare me and not to strike her down because she fed me bacon.

Mama and I
Go on Vacation

My recovery from pneumonia was miraculous considering the limited remedies that were available in 1937. The long illness left me pale and weak, my bones covered with a thin layer of flesh. I could see the worried look in Papa's eyes every time he looked at me and stroked my hair. Even Mama used softer words as she tried to entice me to eat the dishes Bubbe had prepared just for me. For once Mama didn't scold me for not cleaning my plate.

Finally after days of anxiety and apprehension, Papa made a most unusual and surprising announcement. Mama was to take me to Lakewood, New Jersey, where the country air would pique my appetite and put color back in my cheeks. I listened in disbelief as Papa laid out the plan for the trip. At thirteen I was painfully aware how poor we were. Such a vacation was most unusual and would have to be paid for with many sacrifices. I knew my illness had already drained the family's resources. How would Papa find the money? What was he thinking of? Many years later I learned Papa had put aside his pride and had arranged a loan from the Workmen's Circle fraternal organization, breaking his own rule about never borrowing money. Even when we had been hungry, Papa had never before broken that rule.

I had mixed feelings of excitement and fear at being alone with Mama for a whole week. Bubbe would not be there to protect me when Mama got angry. I would miss waiting for Papa's return from work in the evening. When he was home the house became peaceful, and Mama spoke softly. While he was home I was safe from her fierce eyes and cursing words. But I had to go away with Mama. There was no way out for me.

Not since I was eight years old, when Uncle Harry and Aunt Bluma took me to Atlantic City for the summer—a trip that ended in disaster—had I ever been away from home. That added to my anxiety as I watched Mama packing the cardboard suitcase purchased from a pushcart for the occasion. Two shopping bags held food and some cooking utensils. Papa had worked another miracle. He had found a boarding house with kitchen privileges in Lakewood where Mama and I would stay. It was well known that Mama was an inexperienced cook; that was Bubbe's domain. No tasty meals would result from Mama's efforts. Nevertheless, she did pack the cast-iron skillet in which she would continue to fry my daily portion of bacon and eggs, just as the doctor had ordered. I must admit I felt special when Mama put me in charge of carrying that package. Of course she wanted to stay as far as possible from that non-kosher contamination.

The bus ride took most of a day. Frequent restroom stops gave me brief respite from the waves of nausea that rolled over me every time the crowded bus lurched or turned. Although it was May, Mama insisted I stay bundled up. I could tell she was worried about me. Actually the small, weary face that looked back at me from dirty bathroom mirrors at rest stops worried me, too.

The room Mama and I shared for a whole week was like a cell. There was no stove or icebox. Food was prepared in a communal kitchen. A small table with two chairs and a metal utility cabinet took up a third of the cramped space. A wardrobe closet was crammed into one corner, partially covering the one window in the room. The rest of the space was occupied by a double bed, which Mama and I would have to share for a whole week, much to my distress. It was difficult to sleep with Mama. Being that close to her, listening to her breathing at night, filled me with apprehension. The possibility of Mama touching me during the night while I slept was threatening, and it wasn't until the end of our vacation that I was able to feel relaxed enough to sleep through the night.

In spite of these concerns, we quickly fell into a daily routine. Fresh air is supposed to heal all ills, so Mama insisted that we take walks, which included going to the local grocery store every day. We would walk also to the candy store in the evening so Mama could call Papa on the pay phone to report my progress and events of the day. When I heard Papa's voice on the phone I experienced a fresh bout of homesickness. Mama was sad, too, after those phone calls—I knew she missed Papa.

After our walks Mama insisted that I rest, reminding me how sick I had been and how frail I still was, giving me something more to worry about. I actually did not mind resting; I had brought books from the library and would lose myself in the fantasy world of King Arthur's court. Soon I would be traveling with Lady Guinevere and Sir Lancelot in a distant land of long ago. Mama would take advantage of this quiet time as well to take a nap during the day, a luxury she seldom could afford at home.

When we had been in Lakewood about three days I got my period—the third period I had ever had. Again I was caught in the grip of cramps that brought my knees up to my chin, and the ache in my back made it impossible for me to find a comfortable position. Mama scolded me and said I had better get used to this, for it was woman's curse. She was angry that she had to go to the drugstore and spend money for sanitary napkins. At least she didn't make me use rags, like she did. Finally she did borrow a hot-water bottle from the landlady, which brought some relief, so I drifted off to sleep.

The next day, perhaps regretting her inability to comfort me, Mama said she had a treat for me. That night we were to go to the movies. The cramps magically disappeared as I began to fantasize what it would be like to go out with Mama at night. I had never been to the movies with her. Usually she went to the matinees alone to get away from her worries and burdens. My brothers and I were sent to the movies Saturday afternoons to give Mama a rest. Going to the movies at night was an adventure. In the excitement, I even cleaned my plate at dinner. Mama was in a good mood.

We walked the few blocks into town and sat in the darkened, almost empty theater to see Robert Montgomery and Rosalind Russell in *Night Must Fall*. This was a murder mystery so full of tension and suspense that we sat on the edge of our seats most of the time. Often I covered my face, peeking out through my fingers, hoping it was safe to open my eyes. Montgomery portrayed a chilling psychotic killer who carried the decapitated head of his victim in a hatbox, which he kept in his closet. Cold, steely, and inhuman in this character portrayal, the actor certainly convinced Mama and me.

We fled from the theater in terror into the dark night, rushing back to our room. Echoes of our footsteps sent chills down my spine as we hastened home, looking over our shoulders as if Montgomery himself was chasing us for his next victims. It was also a delicious moment, however, for this was the only time I can remember seeing Mama like a child, clinging to me as if closeness could protect us from the bogeyman. It was wonderful.

The May days in Lakewood were balmy and there were fields of flowers I had never seen before. One time Mama and I actually stopped to pick some wild flowers and brought them back to the room, filling the cramped space with their sweet scent. I was actually feeling stronger and excited about going home in a couple of days. Mama and I were sitting at the little table eating our dinner. Outside I could see the flowers and hear the birds. I was filled with a rare sense of tranquility. Maybe there was nothing to be afraid of any more. Maybe things will change when we get home and Mama won't be angry at me all the time.

Suddenly this peaceful pastoral scene was shattered by the sound of a horrendous explosion. It shook our little room, rattling the windows as if to suck them right out of their frames.

Mama and I jumped up, terrified. I had never heard such a frightening noise and my heart was racing. I began to cry and ran to Mama, hiding my face in her dress. I was as tall as Mama now and could feel her breath quickening and her heart pounding, making me even more frightened.

In a matter of seconds the air was filled with the sounds of sirens and blasts from a faraway amplified system. In the distance could be seen a blaze of fire filling the sky. I was sure the world was coming to an end. Would I never again see Papa or Bubbe or my brothers? Would Mama and I be able to get home again? The sirens continued to scream until my ears hurt and my head ached.

Just then, a man came running down the street, yelling and waving his hands. The *Hindenburg,* a German dirigible, had just exploded at Lakehurst. The whole airfield was ablaze, and people were falling out of the burning zeppelin. A small crowd gathered around this man as he repeated the details of the disaster. Smaller explosions kept erupting even as he described in detail what he had witnessed.

The sirens kept screaming and screaming. Would it never stop? The local volunteer fire department was no match for such a debacle. Soon fire engines from neighboring towns arrived to assist in quelling the towering flames that reached higher and higher in the sky. I covered my eyes, hoping to make the fire disappear. Maybe it was only a nightmare.

It was very late before I could fall asleep that night, even though Mama tried to assure me that the fire was under control. I was not convinced. Every time I closed my eyes and began to drift off, I would hear the rumbling again and wake up shaking and perspiring.

The next day everyone in town was talking about the tragedy, and some people began to gather to go to Lakehurst to see the damage. The air was still filled with the smell of fire and fumes. The sun was hidden by the dark clouds of smoke that continued to drift upward. Neither Mama nor I had any desire to go to Lakehurst. We were both still shaken. When Mama called Papa she assured him we were both safe. I could hear her making plans for our trip home the next day and I began to feel less frightened. Even the long, uncomfortable bus ride began to appeal to me. I was ready to leave at the crack of dawn. Once we boarded the bus, it seemed to move at a snail's pace as we pulled out of the depot. I kept looking over my shoulder at the still black sky, marking the site of the disaster. I vowed never to leave home again. I sat still, close to Mama, forgetting to be afraid of her.

Papa was there to greet us at the bus depot in Brooklyn. Only when he kissed me and I smelled the sweet scent of his shaving soap did I begin to feel safe again. Papa had a newspaper with him that was covered with pictures of the explosion. On the way home in the streetcar he sat between Mama and me and read us the report of the *Hindenburg* explosion. The next Saturday when I went to the matinee with my brothers I saw the newsreel devoted to this historical event. I told my brothers, with some authority, that I was there when it happened. Little by little the horror of the experience was replaced with a sense of adventure. Mama often told and retold the events of that night while I listened and remembered our vacation. In time the brief closeness Mama and I had shared began to fade. But for a while I would drift off to sleep remembering her as we ran from the scary movie, holding on to each other like children, and how much softer her face looked when we picked wildflowers together.

Brotherly Love, or the 'Pipik' Fight

My only siblings, two younger brothers, were twenty-two months apart and inseparable while growing up. Himey, the older of the two, was shy and sensitive. He was a beautiful, blue-eyed child, with a rosebud mouth and soft curly hair. His feelings were easily hurt, and it didn't take much to intimidate him. My youngest brother, Alec, had large, black, sparkling eyes that spelled mischief. He was stocky, with coarse, wiry hair and a quick wit. He was always ready for any challenge the day had to offer. He could make Mama laugh even when she was angry. My Uncle Harry could do that too, but he was a grownup and Mama's older brother.

My brothers were really bonded and shared an understanding that Alec would protect Himey from the world. Since Himey was easily threatened, Alec had a pretty active role to perform. He never avoided it, and if the truth be known, he thoroughly enjoyed his position as guardian. The antithesis of this relationship was played out at home, where none of the outside rules applied. It was every man for himself once the door was closed. For instance, both boys loved to build model airplanes. These were cheap balsawood kits that came equipped with razor blades and strong-smelling glue. Each would set up his project on the small worktable they shared, keeping up a steady patter of fighter pilot fantasy conversations. Alec, true to his flamboyant personality, was an improviser and was not always careful about following blueprints. He didn't really care about the results anyhow. He was going to have fun, and to him that meant breaking rules. It was not surprising that his models often were lopsided, fell apart, or never flew at all. Himey, on the other hand, was meticulous and had the mind of an engineer. He took pride in making perfect, tight, clean joints, and produced an aerodynamic model that could fly anywhere.

The more focused and exact Himey became, the more playful and prankish was Alec, often teasing Himey. On more than one occasion what had started out as a joint workshop scene would end up like a battlefield. Airplane parts, razor blades, open glue bottles, and furniture would be scattered across the room, while Alec and Himey were on the floor, locked in a wrestling match. Himey would ultimately lose and run crying to Mama. These battles never dampened their relationship for long and once the storm was over, they would huddle together and plan the next event. It was Alec who could be relied upon to create the mischief that kept them in a partnership of infinite games and battles. He took it for granted that he would be in charge. He would attack Himey if Himey didn't follow orders or refused to go along with his plan. The screams and blows always brought Mama to their room. She would add to the commotion with her own shouting threats, slapping whoever was closest as she tried to separate them. Each boy would try to convince her that he was an innocent bystander. The loyalty that was steadfast outside the house was nowhere to be seen during these indoor free-for-alls.

One place in the house that almost guaranteed a hostile engagement was the kitchen table, where all family meals were served. The children were always fed before Papa came home. I never knew either my Mama or Bubbe to sit down at the table and eat with us, which might have produced a quieter meal. Their place was at the stove or the sink, so there were plenty of opportunities for whispered challenges or insults to ignite into full warfare behind their backs. Often it would take no more than a glance or a sneering face to start the action. This would be followed by an appeal to Mama to make the offender stop what he was doing. "Mama, he is looking at me. Make him stop looking at me." If Alec was the accused, and he often was, he would turn a totally innocent face to Mama and, barely able to keep the twinkle out of his dark eyes, insist "I didn't do nothin'. He's lookin' at me. I'm not lookin' at him." Predictably Mama would respond with a litany of threats and curses, upping the ante by promising to tell Papa. Peace would settle in only to be disturbed again as soon as her back was turned. I had disdain for this infantile behavior. I was two years older than Himey and four years older than Alec.

One evening the three of us were seated around the table, and Mama had just served steaming chicken soup with my Bubbe's homemade noodles. Immediately, both my brothers began to beg for the *pipik*. The *pipik* is the chicken gizzard that had been thoroughly cleaned and had been cooking in Bubbe's chicken soup. It was considered a delicacy and since there was only one *pipik*, the one lucky recipient was king of the mountain that night. The boys had devised many scenarios around this organ, the most popular one being Pipik Island. The prize would be placed on top of a mound of noodles and the soup carefully spooned around it. They would maintain this structure as long as possible until Pipik Island would collapse and the morsel would at last be eaten.

This particular evening Alec was awarded the *pipik* amidst Himey's loud protests of "fowl play," insisting that Alec had gotten it last Friday. Mama stood her ground, and the *pipik* landed in Alec's plate. No sooner had she done that and turned toward the stove again than Alec made faces at Himey and with slow, deliberate gestures, began to install Pipik Island in his own soup bowl. Himey did not take kindly to this. He kicked Alec, shaking the table in an effort to topple Pipik Island, and he raised his fist threateningly in Alec's direction. But Alec, smug in his victory, avoided the kicks and threats and rubbed more salt into Himey's wound. Even more slowly and deliberately, he exaggerated his display of Pipik Island, stretching out the glorious moment as long as he could. Himey could take no more. In one desperate moment he pushed the table hard, almost upending it, and Pipik Island slid off its foundation and landed on the table. Alec, furious, forgot that Mama was nearby. He picked up the hot *pipik* and threw it at Himey. It made a loud splat as it hit Himey squarely on the forehead, then bounced off, landing on the floor. It left a hot red tattoo of the *pipik* on Himey's forehead. His face was red. His eyes protruded. If looks could kill, Alec would have dropped dead. Himey was furious. It would not have surprised me to see smoke coming out of his ears. He let out a scream and Mama came running into the room with Bubbe close behind.

Everyone began talking at once. I chipped in as the voice of reason, trying to explain what happened and who was at fault. Himey was holding his throbbing head, accusing Alec of attacking him without provocation, while Alec proclaimed his innocence. Mama screamed at them until the dishes on the table trembled. I became silent, not daring to move for fear I might somehow be accused of having a role in this melee.

Mama was in full battle dress. Her hair was in disarray. She held a dish towel in one hand and a wooden spoon in the other. She was breathing hard, and the expression on her face was menacing. We were in for it now. Bubbe, in her usual peacemaker's role, was close behind, trying to calm Mama down, telling her not to lose her temper, we were only children, it was Shabbas night, and there should be no disharmony in the house. She ended with "Sam [my Papa] will be home any minute. Don't make any trouble." This had no effect on Mama. Once her juices were boiling, the best you could hope for was that you would not be in the way of her wrath.

During all of the commotion, accusations, and counter-accusations, Mama began to piece the story together. This was not an easy task. Everyone was talking and gesturing at once. At one point Mama began to chase Alec around the table. In an attempt to get away from the wooden spoon she was aiming at him, he turned over each of the kitchen chairs, making it difficult to avoid injury. The kitchen was a small, crowded room. Inevitably, Mama came in contact with an upturned chair that jabbed itself into her shin. Now her anger was multiplied by piercing pain, and if she had been able to catch the boys there would have been a heavy consequence. Alec, seeming to lose his senses, did something very stupid. To throw Mama off balance he broke rank and began to run against the flow of traffic. In seconds he ran head on into Mama, who lost no time delivering several blows before he could regain his balance and put some distance between them. His legs were moving so fast they seemed not to touch the floor at all. Himey, glad to have the attack focused away from himself, grinned from ear to ear and even egged Mama on like a cheerleader. "Get him, Mama. Make him sorry for what he did to me. Give him a good smack." Mama, without missing a beat, shouted at him, "You had better hold your tongue. I will get you next. I know you made Alec throw the *pipik* at you." All the time she was chasing Alec like a trained quarterback on a football team. Periodically she would raise her eyes toward the ceiling and scream, "Dear God, what have I ever done to be cursed by such demons? Better I should have died in childbirth than to give birth to such monsters!"

In time her anger was spent, the din died down, and the chasing and cursing stopped. Attacker and prey were equally exhausted. But there was no rest for the weary. Mama suddenly remembered the missing *pipik* and began to search for it on the floor; but it was nowhere in sight. She began another round of interrogations and her eyes became wild again. "Where did you throw the *pipik*? How far did you throw it? Show me where it landed. Find it or I will kill you." Her threats were to no avail, for the *pipik* had indeed disappeared. Bubbe now joined in the search. There was no sense in eating the Shabbas meal tonight. The *pipik* had to be recovered. What would Papa think if he discovered a *pipik* on the floor? Mama's reputation as a scrupulous housewife would be ruined, and she would never be able to lift her head in public again. Bubbe tried to calm her but was just as upset as Mama. There would be no rest until the *pipik* was found.

The boys began to cry that they were hungry, and the soup was getting cold. I was still frozen in silence and couldn't have swallowed anything anyhow. Nothing would get past the lump in my throat. Although I was an innocent bystander, I knew at any moment Mama's scorn could be aimed at me. Nothing else would do but we all had to get down on our hands and knees and search for the illusive *pipik*. It was a scene to behold. Every corner was searched. Every chair was turned over. The table was moved. The dishes and the tablecloth were removed. No *pipik*.

It was getting late. The moment of Papa's arrival was fast approaching. Mama was getting more desperate and more vocal. My brothers, regretting the whole incident now, began to apologize and begged to be allowed to eat their dinner, go to bed, or just leave the room. But no pleadings or promises quieted Mama. Finally Bubbe bent down on the floor with a lit candle in her hand and looked under the China closet one more time and there, thank God, was the illusive *pipik*, where it had landed, out of sight, after it glanced off of Himey's forehead. It was tucked into a far corner behind a leg of the cabinet and never would have been discovered if Bubbe had not lighted a candle. Mama's honor was restored, and she slumped down on the floor, totally exhausted. At this point the kitchen was in complete disarray and fast repairs had to be made in time to present Papa with a peaceful Shabbas scene.

The five of us were greatly relieved that the tumult had finally come to an end and the *pipik* safely deposited in the garbage can. Everyone became very cooperative, and in short order the table was set again, we were served fresh bowls of soup, and we ate the rest of the meal quickly and in silence. No one looked at any one for fear the vendetta would erupt anew.

Utterly drained and well behaved, we must have presented a scene of peace and harmony when Papa arrived for his dinner. Even the mark on Himey's forehead had faded. There was absolutely no evidence of the chaos that had taken place. My brothers were laughing and joking good-naturedly. Pals again. Bubbe was stirring the soup to assure that a healthy portion of noodles would be placed in Papa's bowl, and Mama, like a proper wife, was making him comfortable at the head of the table. The same God who earlier had cursed Mama with demons for children now smiled down on her approvingly. It was Shabbas. Papa was home. Once more peace prevailed.

The Lesson

Aunt Bluma and Uncle Harry were coming for a visit, and once again the household was in a frenzy of preparations. Mama went into frantic housecleaning, muttering and cursing under her breath with each soapy stroke of the floor mop. She was determined to scour the apartment and took her life in her hands, hanging precariously out the window, reaching for a stubborn streak that dared sully the windowpane. Mama bitterly resented the intrusion and inconvenience of the visit, and how in the world was she going to be able to feed two more people? It took all of her ingenuity to make ends meet with Papa's meager income. Her obsessive cleaning fired her bad temper as she remembered old arguments with Aunt Bluma. There were many. Bubbe, on the other hand, was already pickling a herring for Uncle Harry. She told Mama to buy a plump chicken so she could have a good size *heldzle* to stuff for him. Stuffed *heldzle* was always Uncle Harry's favorite dish.

There was an undercurrent of secrecy that suggested this visit was not like other visits. There was much whispering between Mama and Bubbe. They spoke in Russian, language of the grown-ups. I was used to Mama expressing her anger at having to offer a modicum of hospitality to the unwelcome guests, but secrecy was a new element. It began to dampen my excitement a little. I did not understand why Mama was so angry in the first place. I dearly loved to have Uncle Harry and Aunt Bluma visit. It meant gifts and surprises and lots of fun. I know now one of the reasons Mama rejected Aunt Bluma's generosity was her conviction that Aunt Bluma was trying to take her children away from her with bribes of gifts and treats. In spite of that, Mama would ultimately drop her guard and laugh at Uncle Harry's jokes and pranks. It was just too difficult to stay angry when you were around Uncle Harry. You had to laugh, and I loved him.

As the visit drew nearer, I began to overhear conversations about Aunt Bluma wanting to adopt a baby again. Aunt Bluma and Uncle Harry had never been blessed with children of their own. There had in fact been two earlier adoptions—a baby named Abe who died in infancy, followed by my adopted cousin, Shiffra, who caught measles when she was about seven and also died. Since Shiffra's death, there had been no more children. Now Aunt Bluma was once again determined to have a baby.

Once Uncle Harry pulled up in his shiny Chevrolet, it was the beginning of a special holiday. We all ran out to greet our visitors. Much to Mama's horror, Alec and Himey immediately began to beg for gifts. She pinched them, and pulled them away. I hung back, shyly waiting to be noticed, then felt miserably self-conscious when attention was paid to how much I had grown. I was twelve. The fact that my developing breasts did not go unnoticed by Uncle Harry brought a blush to my cheeks.

Once we were in the house, the discomfort vanished as I was pulled down on Uncle Harry's lap, and he gave me a whole dollar to spend for my very own.

Mama and Bubbe were in the kitchen, frantically preparing to serve dinner, and Aunt Bluma was collapsed in a chair. Uncle Harry was already teasing and joking as he carried their suitcase to my room, which I gave up for their visit. I would sleep on a folding bed in the living room, leaving me with no privacy at all.

At the dinner table, conversation filled in the reason for this particular visit. Aunt Bluma had heard of a Catholic home for unwed mothers on Staten Island. Tomorrow they were going to explore the possibility of adopting one of the babies. Mama and Papa protested that this should not be discussed in front of the children. Aunt Bluma overruled them, saying it would be good for me to come along. Again, I felt exposed and self-conscious to the point of misery but was comforted to learn that Mama and Papa would also be making the trip. What did Aunt Bluma's adoption of a baby have to do with me? Why was it important that I visit this home for unwed mothers? Why did Mama and Papa protest?

It must be remembered that in 1935, twelve-year-olds were naïve and innocent. I was raised in a family where even the slightest reference to anything sexual was met with swift and dire punishment. When I was six, I went to see an Eddie Cantor movie and came home singing the song "Making Whoopie." My mother slapped me across the face and told me, "I'll teach you to bring such filth into the house." I was stunned into disbelief, not knowing what rule I had broken this time. Of what was I guilty? Everybody had laughed and clapped when Eddie Cantor sang the song. I knew it was useless to argue or ask for an explanation. I soothed my hot cheek and went to Bubbe for comfort.

Back to the adoption trip: The next morning Mama, Papa, and I took our place in the backseat of the car. Bubbe was having a difficult time keeping my brothers from jumping in also. I could still hear their voices as the car drove off. I sat between Mama and Papa in silence as I waited for the meaning of this journey to be revealed. As if reading my thoughts, Aunt Bluma began to describe the home for unwed mothers, that it was a place for bad girls to have their babies. A blush started up my neck and blazed on my cheeks in seconds.

As archaic as it may sound, I really knew nothing about sex or how babies were made, yet immediately I felt guilty of some unknown transgression, a sin I sensed I carried inside me. When Aunt Bluma began to warn that I could end up in the home for unwed mothers if I were a bad girl, I was totally miserable and confused. Mama scowled at Aunt Bluma. I knew on some level this was forbidden knowledge, yet there I was sitting, squashed between Papa and Mama, and no one was offering me any information or comfort. In silence my body stiffened. I sat mute, wishing I were dead, or at least could suddenly disappear from the trap I was in. But this was a benign experience compared to what awaited me at the Catholic refuge for young girls who had become pregnant and were going to give up their babies for adoption.

A child from an Orthodox Jewish family, I had never been inside a church. The cathedral edifice with its huge gold cross on top of the steeple literally stopped my breath. To make matters worse, two black-clad nuns appeared, and though they were sweet and quiet-spoken, I was terrified at their appearance.

We waited in a cool, tall chamber while Uncle Harry and Aunt Bluma were interviewed by the Mother Superior. Time dragged on and on. When my aunt and uncle appeared again, the same two nuns led us to another building where the "bad girls" lived. This was Aunt Bluma's explanation, not the nuns'. Aunt Bluma never knew how to be discreet, and her loud coarse accent cracked through the formality of the sacred chambers. The scene became bizarre. Everywhere you looked there were young women and girls, some no older than myself, who were very pregnant or holding infants. They seemed perfectly happy and natural out in the open, but I wished the floor would open up so I could sink into oblivion. All the time Aunt Bluma was loudly whispering that this is where I would end up if I were not careful. Again I could feel the heat rushing to my face.

When I had just started getting my period a few months earlier, Mama had been making oblique accusations to express her anxiety that I might one day "bring a package home." When I had asked her what she meant, she became even more vague and angry and warned me I had better not find out. On some subconscious level I felt guilty of a crime and at the time did not know that the crime was that of being female. I was a suspect but didn't have a clue of what I was being suspected. But I felt it was a dirty little secret that I must somehow keep hidden. I puzzled over the riddle of why I had to be careful just because I was now getting my period. The fact that my mother had also told me that I had become a woman was totally ludicrous. I was still the anxious and frightened child I had always been.

My bleak reverie was interrupted when a girl about my age, very pregnant, approached me with what I am sure was a friendly gesture. She asked me whether my family was going to leave me today, and when did I expect my baby. I jumped as if she had touched me with a hot branding iron. My throat tightened and I literally could make no sound. I frantically looked for Mama or Papa and headed for them, putting some protecting distance between me and the girl. Maybe just being in this place would get me into trouble and I would be left here. But I had done nothing, and I wanted to go home now.

After what seemed an eternity filled with fear and heart-pounding anxiety, Aunt Bluma said we were leaving. I measured every step to the parking lot, not daring to look behind me. It was not until we were actually driving away that I felt safe enough to let my breath out. Papa noticed I was very quiet and asked what was wrong, but I had no words to tell him. Just the memory of the girl talking to me brought fear and nausea again. I shook my head and said nothing, wanting to be ignored.

No sooner were we on our way than Aunt Bluma began to talk with loud prejudiced words about the *shiksas* who would go to bed with any man and have a baby. Then she turned directly to me and began to give me my first lesson in sex education. Papa protested mildly, but Mama became infuriated. In a matter of minutes these two mortal enemies were locked in combat again, separated only by the seats of the car. Mama yelled at her, telling her she had no right to use such language in front of me; after all I was just a child. So now I was a child again when just the other day I had been told I was a woman and had to be careful. Aunt Bluma was not one to turn away from a challenge and became even more overbearing and used more explicit language until Uncle Harry threatened to stop the car. Miraculously this did shut her up, but the damage had been done. I felt totally exposed, vulnerable, and powerless. Even when Papa tried to comfort me I felt unsafe not knowing how this woman/child was supposed to behave.

It wasn't until later, when my thoughts quieted that I found some relief and slept the last hour of the ride. When we arrived home I must have looked ill, for even Mama felt I'd had enough and told me I did not have to eat dinner that night if I didn't want to. I was allowed to lie down in Bubbe's bed until everyone went to sleep. Then I moved to the folding bed in the living room. Maybe Mama felt I had learned enough lessons for one day. But how could I know what to expect when I didn't know what crime I had committed? I couldn't help it if I had gotten my period. I would have stopped it if I knew how. How could this mystery change my body in such a frightening way and cause so much trouble?

That night my confusion became worse. I remembered that when I was little, I would comfort myself at night by imagining a beautiful princess who was surrounded by adoring people. In a half-dream state, I began to see the princess again and settled down deeper into the folding bed, watching the princess through half-closed eyes, feeling warm and safe again. Only for a split second, as my eyes closed, did the puzzle about the lesson I had to learn interrupt the visit with the princess. But mercifully I drifted off to sleep. Safe for now, I could be a child a while longer.

Bubbe Gets Married

My Bubbe was my guardian angel and the source of all good things in my childhood. She was the provider of delicious food even when we were very poor. Her thick, work-worn hands could create the most mouth-watering cuisine. From meager scraps, Bubbe could make a "stone soup" that filled your belly and fed your soul. I never stopped marveling at her ability to turn out a whole tabletop full of mouth-watering *knishes,* each one exactly like its neighbor. She was always in the kitchen, her head covered with a white kerchief, her ample body wrapped in an apron that she took off only when she went to bed. I never heard her complain as she stood at her post in the kitchen by the sink or the stove, day after day.

She was no less constant as my protector from Mama's attacks. If I could just get to Bubbe and hide behind her apron, I knew I would be safe. She would protect me. She would appeal to Mama to have pity on me. Should that fail, and it often did, Bubbe would warn Mama not to tempt God. He would punish her for all her evil deeds. That almost always stopped Mama in her tracks, even if she did continue to scold and curse. I could always count on Bubbe being there when I needed her.

It never, ever occurred to me to worry about the possibility that Bubbe might leave. Where would she go?

What would we do without her? Surely Bubbe would always be there. Neither did it ever occur to me that Mama and Papa might wish to have Bubbe out of the house so that finally they could come into their own as adults. All of their married life, Bubbe had lived with them. In fact, Mama had never been separated from Bubbe from the day she was born. When Mama and Papa began to whisper to each other, I suspected something was going to happen.

Though I had not yet figured out what was going on, my heart felt cold when one Sunday a little old man, Max Silverman, appeared at our door. It was unusual for a stranger to be invited into our home. He immediately began to scrutinize Bubbe. Nothing like this had ever happened before. Bubbe was dressed in her one black *Shabbas* dress. She also wore her pearls, which were reserved for holidays and for lighting the *Shabbas* candles on Friday nights. But this was just a Sunday afternoon. Earlier I had noticed Bubbe standing in front of the bathroom mirror, combing in the cheap dye on her graying hair, which she only did on very special occasions. I sensed something ominous might happen.

Mama, Papa, Bubbe, and Max Silverman sat in the kitchen, drinking tea and eating Bubbe's very special strudel. I stood out of sight behind the kitchen doorway and heard this stranger addressing my parents and Bubbe in an authoritarian manner. He gave a brief description of his circumstances, implying that he was financially comfortable. He had been a widower for many years and lived alone in a small apartment nearby. He boasted of having a good reputation and conducting himself with the airs of a man of stature, though there seemed very little physical evidence to support that. His worn tweed suit smelled of perspiration and old tobacco smoke. His bedraggled mustache grew over his mouth and dipped into the tea each time he took a sip. He had an annoying habit of clearing his throat to punctuate his presentation of important information. His small hands were in constant motion, lighting one cigarette after the other, noisily blowing his nose into a less-than-clean handkerchief, or reaching for yet another piece of Bubbe's strudel. He never once commented on this delicacy, though Mama made a point of telling him what a wonderful cook and baker Bubbe was. He seemed to take everything for granted.

I felt sick, watching Mama and Papa fussing over this dirty little man. Bubbe was quiet through all of this, looking down at her hands, while Mama and Papa talked about her to this stranger as if she were not in the room. She just sat there, a silent witness to her own fate. I listened in confusion, choking back my tears. Every now and then Bubbe managed shyly to answer a direct question. In contrast Mama and Papa were very animated as they entertained Mr. Silverman. This was suspicious; Mama was always on guard against anyone who wanted to know our business. She seldom volunteered information about herself or about the family, yet here she was being positively chatty and smiling at Mr. Silverman frequently, offering him more tea and strudel.

After about an hour Mama and Papa left the smoke-filled kitchen. I barely escaped discovery. Max Silverman and Bubbe were alone now, and I waited until I was sure

Mama and Papa were not returning before I resumed my watch from behind the door. Mr. Silverman was now talking about how hard it was for him to live alone. He wanted to have a wife to take care of him and his apartment. He assured Bubbe that he had enough money to take good care of her. I could not believe what I was hearing. Bubbe said nothing, her head bowed. When this dirty little man leaned over at that moment and planted a noisy kiss on her cheek, I put my hands over my mouth to stifle a scream.

Something was terribly wrong here. Mr. Silverman was doing all the talking about how much he needed a wife, but Bubbe said nothing about needing a husband. Even at thirteen I knew that she didn't need a husband and that Mr. Silverman would get the better part of this bargain. Besides, what would Bubbe get from Mr. Silverman that she didn't already have here with us? She had a place to live and a family to take care of. Surely she would not actually consider leaving us to live with smelly Mr. Silverman?

As I watched and listened it became painfully clear that Max Silverman had come to take my Bubbe away from me, from our home. Bubbe continued to just sit there. I felt sick and faint and could listen no more. I fled from the house and ran out into the backyard to hide my tears. I was overwhelmed by the possibility that I would lose Bubbe. I felt betrayed by Bubbe. She was abandoning me without a word of protest. It never occurred to me that Bubbe might not have had any choice.

I did not return to the house until it was close to dinner time. I kept my face down, hiding the evidence of my tears to avoid Mama's questions. Bubbe was back in the kitchen, and Max Silverman was gone. His repulsive presence, however, prevailed in the form of the body odor and cigarette smoke left behind. I wanted to run to Bubbe and plead with her to stay, but that would have exposed the fact that I had eavesdropped. I had to pretend that I knew nothing.

My life began to change. I would tiptoe to the kitchen as soon as I awoke in the morning to make sure Bubbe was still there. Only then did I heave a sigh of relief and run to her to give her a hug before I went back to my room to get dressed. I would rush home from school to check on Bubbe again. I continued to worry silently but never talked to Bubbe about this for fear she would give me the answer I did not want to hear. In time, however, I began to relax my vigilance. Nothing was changing after all. I began to feel more secure. Then one Saturday Max Silverman appeared again. This time he did not talk to Mama or Papa, but took Bubbe out for a walk, just the two of them. Would he bring Bubbe back, or was she actually going to live with Mr. Silverman now? I could not hold back my tears, and there was only Mama to turn to. Pushing aside my fear of her anger, the words all poured out before I could decide whether it was safe. "Mama, Mama, where is Bubbe going? Why does she want to go with Mr. Silverman? Doesn't she love us any more?"

Mama immediately went into facts that were totally unreasonable as far as I was concerned. She told me that Bubbe wanted to have her own home and was getting too old to take care of all of us. Mr. Silverman would be good to Bubbe, and he would take care of her. I didn't believe that for a minute. We already took care of Bubbe, I protested. When she got sick she could lie down. We even called the doctor sometimes. She was a *balaboosta* already, here in our house, and what about us? Who would take care of us while Mama was busy cleaning or shopping? Whom could we count on to be waiting for us when we came home from school? And who would make tasty remedies when we got sick? Bubbe was the only one who knew how to make a mustard plaster that would not burn you or stick to your skin. She was the only one who knew how to wash your hair with kerosene to get rid of the lice without making your eyes sting. And Bubbe had blessed the candles every Friday night of my life. Who would do that if Bubbe left us? And what about the holidays? Who would prepare all of the delicious foods for Passover, and the meal that breaks the fast at Yom Kippur, and the delicacies for Purim? As I continued to question Mama, my heart became heavier. I knew how barren the house would be without Bubbe. My brothers, who had been playing in their room, heard my wailing and joined in when they realized what was at stake. Himey, who was particularly attached to Bubbe, began to cry loudly.

Mama ran out of patience and suddenly became angry. She aimed slaps in our direction and they found their mark before we could get out of her way. I went to my room, threw myself across the bed and cried and cried until I fell asleep. When I awoke it was dusk, and the house was unusually quiet. When I went to the kitchen, however, there was Bubbe, as she had always been, pealing potatoes for the evening meal. I gave up any attempt to control my feelings, relieved that Bubbe had not left yet, but devastated knowing that she would soon be leaving. I let out all my pain and pleaded with Bubbe not to go. I was on my knees, in front of her as she sat on a kitchen chair. I was racked with sobs, but she said nothing. I must finally have run out of tears and lifted my head to look at Bubbe. My heart broke anew, for Bubbe was crying without making a sound.

Now it was my turn to take care of Bubbe, and I hugged her and wiped her face with the dish towel. Only then did Bubbe talk to me. It was time for her to have her own home, she said, and it was time for Mama and Papa to have their own home. In disbelief I asked what would it be like for her to live with Mr. Silverman? Did she like him? She didn't even know him. How could she like him? She smiled sadly and said there were some things that I couldn't understand and that she was making the right decision. She would have to make the best of it.

There were several more visits from Max Silverman, but I didn't like him any more than I had the first time I laid eyes on him. He still smelled as bad, and he still acted as if he owned Bubbe. I hoped that the more Bubbe saw of him, she might yet come to her senses and refuse him. Then one Friday, while I was at school and Papa was at work, the dirty deed was done. Bubbe and Max Silverman had gone to the synagogue, and the Rabbi had married them. There were Bubbe's pitiful packages of her few belongings in the kitchen, ready for her to take with her as she left to live with Max Silverman. We said our tearful good-byes. I controlled myself, not wanting to upset Bubbe. Nor did I want to cry in front of Mr. Silverman. He was now my new grandpa, my Zada, but he didn't fool me. He was stealing my Bubbe and giving her nothing in return.

It took a long time for the wrenching pain in my heart to fade. I would stop at Bubbe's apartment every day on the way home from school. Sometimes Mr. Silverman was there, and that would spoil the visit, but at least I would see Bubbe. He seldom greeted me and continued to sit by the kitchen table, smoking cigarettes and reading the Jewish paper by a dim light bulb. When he was not there Bubbe would make me a glass of hot cocoa and give me a slice of her delicious pure-white *challah*. If I closed my eyes it would almost be as good as having Bubbe home again—but not quite, for she was never going to be home with me again. Her new home was a small, bare three-room apartment, dark and dingy. It was on the ground floor of a tenement, the windows facing the busy street, teeming with people and noisy children. The apartment was cold in the winter and stifling in the summer. Bubbe did her best for Mr. Silverman, but she soon discovered that there was little security for her. He was a miserly little man and wanted an accounting for every penny she spent for their food. He would refuse to turn the lights on until it was quite dark because electricity was too expensive. He did not trust my Bubbe, my angel.

When Passover came Bubbe didn't even get a new dress for the holidays, but she did not complain. No longer did she make Passover wine for us, and no longer did we have a Seder with food prepared by Bubbe's magical hands. Bubbe was living in a small, dark apartment, and I was living in my dark room, which would never be bright again no matter how many lights were turned on. Bubbe was gone.

As I grew older, Bubbe would even confide in me that she had made a mistake, and she was not happy. I would encourage her to leave Mr. Silverman and come back home to us. She didn't have to be a prisoner anymore. She would put her finger up to her lips, cautioning me not to ever mention what she had told me. Then with a sigh of resignation she would say, "This is the way it has to be; it will never change." And it never did. I continued to see Bubbe every day for the eleven years she was married.

By then I had a baby, my son, Michael, and would take him with me to visit Bubbe. The three of us would sit in the dark, dingy living room, while Mr. Silverman sat in the kitchen, alone, smoking. I had Bubbe to myself during those brief visits and we would talk about the past. I would tell and retell the memories we had shared: how she made wine in the cellar, how she and Mama burned the tablecloth to collect the insurance money for the Passover order, how she protected me and my brothers. I would tell her how she filled the kitchen with her radiance when she wore her pearls and her *Shabbas* dress and blessed the candles on Friday nights.

One night Max Silverman came running to our apartment, waking us up in the middle of the night to tell us that Bubbe was dead. The days that followed were a nightmare. I could not bring myself to go to Bubbe's funeral. I excused myself because I had a small baby, but the truth was that I could not accept the fact that Bubbe

was gone forever. I couldn't watch her casket being lowered into the earth. I held on to the illusion that I would
visit her again, pushing the baby carriage up to her front
window. There she would be as she always had been,
waiting for me, her face lighting up when I appeared.
Soon I would be with Bubbe again. Her smile would
brighten the day for me and my baby. I could sit at her
knee once more and put my head in her lap, believing
that she could make everything all right one more time.
She had never been Mrs. Silverman. She was always my
Bubbe.

Epilogue, August 1999

When Bubbe left to marry Mr. Silverman, her personal sacrifice took its toll on all of us. No longer would the family be nurtured by her fine culinary skills. No longer would the home be filled with sweet-smelling rising dough for the *Shabbas challah*. No longer would there be holiday feasts that somehow defied poverty, and no longer would she stand as a silent buffer against Mama's anger and punishment. Always taken for granted at her post in the kitchen, like an invisible spirit, her precious worth was now apparent by her absence.

I will never know with what emotions Mama met her liberation as, for the first time in her thirty-one years, she was separated from her mother. Whatever freedom she may have gained must have been affected by the additional burden of cooking for the family. It was no secret that Mama had never had to cook before. While none of us suffered from malnutrition, neither did we look forward to Mama's experiments in the kitchen. Papa, I am sure, never complained.

My childhood abruptly disappeared in the void left by Bubbe's departure, and I missed her to the point of pain. At thirteen I was beginning an adolescence that was to be filled with anxiety and depression. I would never again wake to the sound of Bubbe in the kitchen or to the warmth of the furnace, which she would have stoked in the cold, dark winter dawn. And never again would her warm, protective arms be there to catch me. Life became more of a daily emotional struggle for me. There were no therapists in the late thirties and forties. Even if there had been, we could not afford their services. Nor were there self-help books or a psychological climate to support investigation of the despair and isolation suffered by a lonely teenage Jewish girl living in a Brooklyn ghetto. While the physical beatings stopped, the psychological abuse did not. I developed into a painfully shy young woman, withdrawn and inhibited to the point of panic and paralysis.

Looking back, I can still remember the fears, emotional pain, and stress of my childhood. Age and distance have made it possible to recognize, however, another journey that was taking place though not apparent to me at the time. The traumas also planted a seed of silent strength that survived—like the lone flowering weed that anchors its roots beneath a layer of impenetrable concrete. Somehow it is determined to find that almost invisible crack, pushing its way up to the light so its blossom can unfold. So it was that in the midst of the stifling tenement life, a Rose grew in Brooklyn.